Internet Memes and Society

This book provides a solid, encompassing definition of Internet memes, exploring both the common features of memes around the globe and their particular regional traits. It identifies and explains the roles that these viral texts play in Internet communication: cultural, social and political implications; significance for self-representation and identity formation; promotion of alternative opinion or trending interpretation; and subversive and resistant power in relation to professional media, propaganda, and traditional and digital political campaigning. It also offers unique comparative case studies of Internet memes in Russia and the US.

Anastasia Denisova is Lecturer in Journalism at the Communication and Media Research Institute at the University of Westminster, UK.

Routledge Advances in Internationalizing Media Studies
Edited by Daya Thussu, University of Westminster

For more information about this series, please visit: https://www.routledge.com

Internet Memes and Society

Social, Cultural, and Political Contexts

Anastasia Denisova

Routledge
Taylor & Francis Group

LONDON AND NEW YORK

First published 2019 by Routledge

2 Park Square, Milton Park, Abingdon, Oxfordshire OX14 4RN

52 Vanderbilt Avenue, New York, NY 10017

Routledge is an imprint of the Taylor & Francis Group, an informa business

First issued in paperback 2020

Library of Congress Cataloging-in-Publication Data
CIP data has been applied for.

ISBN: 978-1-138-60278-6 (hbk)
ISBN: 978-0-367-67117-4 (pbk)

Typeset in Sabon
by codeMantra

MIX
Paper from
responsible sources
FSC
www.fsc.org   FSC™ C013985

Printed in the United Kingdom
by Henry Ling Limited

To my husband Paolo and my parents

Contents

List of Figures

Acknowledgements

This work owes to the support from my friends and colleagues at University of Westminster; I should specifically say thanks to Dr Anastasia Kavada for her deep knowledge and beautiful mind. I am grateful to all people who agreed to do the interviews for this book – it has been a fascinating journey.

Introduction

Before starting my academic career, I had been working as a journalist for over a decade in Russia. One of my favourite workplaces was the newsroom of the leading independent TV channel NTV. I was doing night and day shifts as the international news editor and reporter, but rarely felt tired thanks to the amazing drive of telling balanced news to the people. We were a great team of young professionals – the editor-in-chief was barely in his late 20s. We gave all we had to the job, we would spend 40 minutes brainstorming a single opening line to a report. Creativity, amazing language and cultural references, when appropriate, cinematographic edits and thought-provoking explanations were as important to us as the objectivity of news reporting.

Then something happened. In mid-2000s, the Kremlin has turned an eye at free press. New management flew in, while the previous, liberal-minded administration was forced to leave the TV channel. The creatives were the first ones who fled our newsroom. One of the incredible things I have learned in that experience is that talented, enthusiastic people cannot breathe censorship – when a journalist knows that they are not allowed to pronounce certain names or give air time to certain events, they not only curb the information they provide, but also curb their enthusiasm. And this is the dead end to creative, challenging journalism. I was not the most talented of the group, I was still in my early 20s, but I left soon after all the people I looked up to were no longer in the building. NTV channel is still out there, it looks very different now, and the quality of the news is incomparable to the 'golden era' I was lucky to witness and contribute to.

Frustrated and disillusioned, I was then drawn to the new stems of creativity that came from the place I expected the least – political protest. Creativity cannot be contained for long – it found an outburst in the resistance. In Russia known for the passive, conformist population, something has changed in the early 2010s. Thousands of people went to the streets of major cities to express their rage at the corrupt elections. They organised via social networks, where they published stories and memes to unite the like-minded crowds – they even printed memes on the placards that they took to the squares!

Now, almost ten years later, it has become clear that memes are present, impactful and here to stay, not only in Russia, of course, but all over the world – the examples ranging from Azerbaijan to the US illustrate that these instantly shareable, humorous bits of information and opinion play a significant role in modern, digital politics. This book covers the development of the concept of memes, its role in society and politics, as well as most recent investigations in the impact of memes on society in the Russian Crimean annexation in 2014 and the US presidential election in 2016. It offers an innovative vision of the concept, format and roles of memes. Importantly, this work addresses the gap in the research on memes in both Western and non-Western countries.

The book examines Internet memes as one phenomenon of digital communication. Having derived from the emoticons and geeky jokes from online forums, they have developed into significant means of information, interaction and political deliberation in the 2010s. Nowadays, millions of users communicate information, opinion and emotions through this peculiar vehicle of self-expression. This book builds upon the existing definitions, offers new nuances and finally provides a complete working conceptualisation of memes for media studies.

This book is intended for media, sociology and political studies scholars and students, as well as for general publics who want to see more than meets the eye in their daily dose of moody cats, sarcastic frogs and portraits of the surprised Keanu Reeves.

The first definition of memes was provided in 1976 by the biologist Richard Dawkins who compared memes to genes in their replication, mutation and fecundity characteristics. This book, however, argues that despite its initial theoretical attractiveness, the Darwinian approach does little help in analysing memes of the Internet. The memes that we are studying today, 40 years after Dawkins' idea, are not defined as any unit of cultural production that survives through time and adjustment. Internet memes are intrinsically linked to the logic and rhythms of networks and social media, as well as to the ways a society expresses and thinks of itself.

Chapter 1 reflects on the early definitions, but links them to the folklore and storytelling: it argues that memes as we know them today are part of the common language that Internet users employ to communicate on all possible topics. Moreover, memes are seen as the form and practice of storytelling; digital artefacts that permit users to showcase their creativity and connect with others. This chapter sums up with the forward-thinking conceptualisation of memes that not only encompasses the previous developments, but also adds the discussion on the viral power of memes, their political value and multilayered contextual references.

Chapter 2 looks into the historical practices of alternative media and art (such as Dada and Situationism), tactics of political deliberation and resistant media that have contributed to the formation of memes as vehicles of political resistance on the Internet. It scrutinises theoretical background on tactical media and connective action, culture jamming and the role of satire and humour in political communication online. This chapter also discusses the benefits and limitations of the concept of participatory Internet cultures for meme studies and incorporates the most recent academic studies on digital censorship and surveillance.

Chapter 3 expands to look at memes as more than everyday vocabulary, but symbolic rhetorical arguments. Studying memes as the units of persuasion and locating them within propaganda studies unveil their potential in condensing complex issues to clear-cut judgements. Politically active users employ Internet memes as the discursive weapons of power struggles. A meme does not belong to any specific group or community; it has no inherent political or cultural connotation except for the promise of entertainment. Memes are empty conduits or layouts that anyone can fill with meaning or commentary. This means that neither elites nor opposition own memes; the autonomous and non-aligned character of memes makes them especially worth studying in the political research. Memes can change sides and connotation through their journey in the digital space. Mikhail Bakhtin's theory on the carnival as a form of dissent helps to further connect artful political communication, media activism and Internet memes.

In the global Internet environment, as Chapter 4 uncovers, memes form the type of storytelling that mingles global discourses with local tradition and culture. Owing to their origins in poster culture, cartoons and advertising, memes preserve a number of highly recognisable configurations that may vary by colour, font, composition of elements and vocabulary, but retain trademark features of the original style. This chapter provides the classification of pervasive global meme formats, which include Demotivator, Image Macro, Photoshopped Image, LOLCats, Advice Animals and Comic. It also points to the examples of local formats of memes that reveal a contextually driven variation on their shape and content. The studies on memes in non-Western environments such as China or Azerbaijan are discussed to show how memes can function in repressive media environments; how both aggressors and defenders, propaganda and resistance can exploit memes. This political feature of memes only begins to be addressed in the media scholarship – many governments have acknowledged the power of memes and have started to actively exploit this conduit since the mid-2000s. This new utilisation of memes is discussed in this chapter with examples from various contexts.

Chapter 5 focuses on the main case study of the book, Russian resistance and propaganda through memes in 2014. In the beginning of 2014, Russia intervened in the civil war in the neighbouring Ukraine and facilitated a referendum in one of its parts, the Crimean Peninsula.

This resulted in the withdrawal of Crimea from the Ukrainian territory and inclusion in the Russian land. Western political leaders met the actions of Russia with outrage, while the liberal publics inside the country questioned the tough politics and non-diplomatic approach of the Russian elites. This case has led to the flows of memes circulating on both sides of the argument. Those for and against the annexation of Crimea used the memes to discuss politics, national identity, imperial ambitions and even gender relations that shined through the exchange of memes.

This chapter first explains the media environment of the contemporary Russia; how the limitations on the freedom of speech operate through law, media, decision-making of people and political processes. It looks at the social, economic and cultural developments that paved way to the rise of resistant moods among the Russians in the 2010s. Then, the analysis of hundreds of memes and interviews with the Russian meme makers reveal the motivations and risks, benefits and drawbacks of making and distributing memes. This chapter also shows how Internet, social media and viral cultures are adding alternative dimension to news, opinion and political struggles.

For the first time ever, this book brings to the light the testaments of the Russian resistant and pro-government meme makers. The analysis of their responses demonstrated that, for instance, in Russia meme makers have become the new journalists, civil activists and political protesters at the same time. The vague structure of the Russian political system and lack of established social institutions and platforms of negotiation with the state make the Internet the only vibrant site of the public discussion. Meme making and sharing have many other meanings for the interviewees, which include personal as well as collective gains and motivations.

The last part of the chapter provides a unique experiment of tracing a journey of a meme through mutations. The results show the methodological complexity of meme studies, but illuminate the incredible network and idea-sharing potential of these vehicles of communication.

Chapter 6 explores the recent US presidential campaign between Donald Trump and Hillary Clinton that has featured an unprecedented number of memes. The analysis of the memes that circulated on the Internet around the election day exemplified three important features of memetic communication in the United States of America. They range from persistent curation of memes and the reliance on media agenda to the carnivalisation of political discussion. A sample of exemplary memes from various political perspectives is presented and discussed in this chapter.

The book ends with the conclusion that brings about a critical reflection on the role of memes for society and politics in Western and non-Western contexts.

This book makes three significant contributions. It provides a solid, encompassing definition of the Internet memes as we know them in the end of the 2010s. This book enriches the scholarship with the novel roles of memes as 'fast-food media' and 'political mindbombs'. The author has picked these ideas from the understated academic entries and elaborated and studied them in her own practice, which led to the arresting results. The concept of memes as the alternative media vehicle, 'fast-food media', has been especially visible in the political communication, and deserves further development.

The second major contribution of this book is the argument that memes are beacons of public opinion and the condensed snapshots of the identity debates. Comparable to the tips of the icebergs, memes signify which collective and national identities receive approval, and which remain stumbling points. This is especially important in political communication online when such narratives as gender equality, racism and nationalism, macho politics and patriotism receive incredibly layered discussion through memes. This book classifies global and local formats of memes, and then elaborates on the socially and politically significant uses of those in various contexts.

The third contribution is the timely research of the non-Western context of meme circulation. The Russian case study is the primary practical case that explains the uses of memes during the 2014 Crimean Crisis. The nuanced examination of Russia-related memes enabled to explore the issues of national, individual, gender, social and political identities. This study has also revealed the growing power of memes in the political discourse in social networks and ability to thrive even in the censored media environments. Both Russian and US case studies in this book reveal that the meme-infused communication in social media differs from the mainstream media narrative: many additional themes and conversations arise.

Memes may not change the world, but they nonetheless act as sensitive indicators of public opinion, trending themes and collective identities, they promote and oppose propaganda, they entertain, inform and educate. By doing that, memes act as baits of attention and triggers of controversy. Ignoring memes is impossible – knowing, understanding and exploring them is a way to go.

1   Definition and Evolution of the Concept of Memes

From biology to media studies: how the theory of memes developed

What if culture had the similar mode of replicating itself, as animals and humans do? How do ideas, patterns and habits travel across generations and societies? Is it a 'natural' process or the result of conscious human agency?

Biologist Richard Dawkins is the pioneer of meme studies. His seminal book *The Selfish Gene*, published in 1976, first mentioned memes as a cultural analogue to a gene. Dawkins (1976: 206–209) argued that memes resemble genes in their structure, mechanisms of distribution and survival, productivity and fecundity. A gene is a molecular unit of people's bodies, a biological code holding important information for building and maintaining cells and passing the invaluable hereditary data to offspring (Dawkins, 1976: 211–212). Memes are similar to the genes in the way they pass cultural information and ideas between individuals and generations.

It is important to note, though, that genes are extremely accurate in their algorithms, and a mutation leads to damaging errors (Dawkins, 1976: 30–33). Memes, conversely, survive in the process of constant replication and transformation. Dawkins (1976: 208–209) distinguished three main features of a meme: fidelity, fecundity and longevity. Fidelity refers to the inner trustworthiness that makes a meme appealing; fecundity (or replicability) renders easy and quick imitation; and longevity is the aptitude to survive among other memes for a long time, thus ensuring the meme's continued existence. Dawkins (1999) compares the development of a meme with the childhood game of Chinese Whispers (also known as Telephone): in a line of children, one draws a picture and shows it to the next kid; he memorises what he thinks he saw and draws his own image, and then passes it to the next child. The result obtained at the end of the chain might have little in common with the original drawing, yet preserves recognisable features or elements that would allow linking the final sketch with the initial one.

Despite the acknowledgement of its conceptual novelty, Dawkins' (1976) original theory of memes has received much criticism. Its weakest

tenets were the analogy with genes and vague definition of the characteristics and function of memes. The differences in copying processes
and fidelity rate between genes and memes challenge the legitimacy of
their comparison (see Blackmore, 1999; Sperber, 2000). The mutation of
genes leads to the malfunction and collapse of the system, while for memes the mutation is desirable and often unavoidable. Blackmore (2010)
assumes that memes are counterproductive for genes: genes endeavour
to keep the energy for survival, and memes overwhelm the brain space,
occupying thought with the burden of excessive information to process.
Moreover, Sperber (2000) strengthens the point that memes are not direct genetic counterparts in preserving and distributing culture, but more
complex tools. They are not reliable in delivering accurate information
yet are beneficial for the development of ideas: people can fill them with
additional details and foster new meaning and style of expression.

Furthermore, social scientists and non-academic critics questioned the
necessity of introducing a new term that resembled the already existing
notion of 'patterns'. Brown (2014), for instance, dismissed 'memes' in
the Dawkinsian rendition (1976), arguing that they possessed the same
characteristics as 'ideas', and any transmission of cultural information
involved recreation and modification. Dawkins himself responded to
criticism decades after having devised the original concept. He reviewed
the biologically determined notion and added that the laws of natural
selection do not bind memes. Users create memes to deliberately hijack
the original cultural text; thus, the choices and decisions of people drive
memes forward (Dawkins & Marshmallow Laser Feast, 2013, as cited
in Wiggins & Bowers, 2014; see also Shifman, 2011, for corresponding
assumptions).

Still, the apparent ambiguity of the common definition of a meme remains one of the major drawbacks of the notion for interdisciplinary
studies, and even champions of meme research acknowledge this issue.
Knobel and Lankshear (2007) are generally supportive of studying memes
academically, yet state that memes resemble other designations of cultural
production: 'idea', 'pattern', 'tune', 'structure' and 'set'. They admit that
'pinning down precise criteria for something counting as a meme is close
to impossible' (Ibid.: 205).

However, narrowing the definition down in relation to the specific field
of science helps to overcome the challenge of defining memes. Psycholo-
gists and computer scientists, for instance, attempted to complement the
idea of Dawkins (1976, 1993, 1999) by expanding the meme concept
beyond the cultural unit to an information unit in general. Advocates of
this approach considered memes as 'the building-blocks of your mind'
(Brodie, 1996: 36; see also Plotkin, 1993). From this standpoint, memes
are not only units of cultural production, but they also include broader
modes of human knowledge and comprise names, relationship patterns,
principles of society, choices at a traffic light, information about other

planets and solar systems (Blackmore, 1999). This conceptualisation champions Dawkins' (1999) statement that memes travel through time and transmit ideas in-between generations, but it falls short in establishing clear boundaries of what a meme is.

The issue of identifying the borders of a meme has been another point of criticism to the scholars who study this cultural phenomenon. Does the whole song or the chorus form a meme, is it the tag line or the picture with the tag line that makes an Internet hit, and is it the one-liner from a movie or an actor saying a one-liner to the camera that makes a meme? (see, for example, Gill, 2011). Developing the idea expressed by Dennett (1995), Blackmore (1999) defends the study of memes by limiting a meme to the smallest meaningful element that replicates itself with trustworthiness and fertility. Most researchers share this tendency to decrease the potential meme to the smallest meaningful replicable entity. The first four notes of Beethoven's Fifth Symphony are often referred to as the classic example of a self-sufficient meme unit (Dawkins, 1976; Dennett, 1995; Brodie, 1996; Blackmore, 1999, 2010).

Memes differ from iconic images and from viral texts that do not experience much alteration. They are never fixed symbols, stories or icons, but interactive aesthetic artefacts that provide a snapshot of the immediate tendencies of culture and public discourses (Goriunova, 2013); they can change shape, size and style through mutation. The example of the Che Guevara iconic poster demonstrates that icons function in close relation to the subject (Goriunova, 2013: 3–4). Memes, instead, offer a much weaker representation of the original subject and thus hail individual expressiveness and encourage further reiteration of symbol. Shifman (2011) adds that people share memes not because they want to disseminate the story they found interesting, but because they want to have their input in the retelling and propagation of the story.

Furthermore, media and sociology scholars (Knobel & Lankshear, 2007; Shifman, 2011, 2013) call for the distinction between 'viral texts' and memes. Contradicting Brodie's (1996) suggestion of defining memes as 'viruses of mind', they insist on examining the difference between those texts that spread in their original state and those experiencing alterations (Shifman, 2011: 4). Shifman (2011) advances separating 'viral texts' from 'memes' on the basis of possessing or lacking modifications. Wiggins and Bowers (2014: 12–15) accordingly propose a two-step algorithm to study the ascent of a media text to a meme. They suggest that when a user alters a unit of media production, such as a music video or an expressive photograph (what Gal et al. (2016) call 'a prototype'), he or she coins an 'emergent meme'. This emergent meme escalates to a full 'meme' when other users contribute and share their alterations, thus validating the popularity and interest of the community towards this text.

This book develops the conceptualisation of memes for media studies. I am grounding my conceptualisation in the achievements of sociology and media scholars. One of the most recent definitions, such as the one produced by Esteves and Meikle (2015), contributes an important link between memes and storytelling. Memes are at the same time the form and the practice of storytelling and derive from the centuries-long practice of altering and merging ideas and stories (Esteves & Meikle, 2015: 1–8). Since the emergence of the first forms of communication and interaction, from newspapers to jazz improvisation, people have exchanged ideas. The reproduction of memes relies on the classic ethos of storytelling. As early as in the 1930s, Sir Frederic Bartlett (1932) proved that a story changes every time with its retelling, becoming either decorated with new details or losing components. Memes are not comprehensive stories; they are elements of storytelling. They are the artefacts of remix culture. As Milner (2016: 1) puts it, memes are 'remix, play and commentary'. The concept of a meme is therefore valuable for the social sciences, cultural studies and media and communication research as it explains how ideas accumulate in condensed units and evolve through social interexchange.

Media and communication scholarship (Knobel & Lankshear, 2007; Burgess, 2008; Meikle, 2010, 2014; Lievrouw, 2011; Davison, 2012; Börzsei, 2013; Milner, 2013, 2016; Esteves & Meikle, 2015; Gal et al., 2016) has appropriated the concept of memes to study the viral texts that spread over the Internet. In the most common contemporary rendition, Internet memes are 'multimodal artefacts remixed by countless participants, employing popular culture for public commentary' (Milner, 2013: 2357). Börzsei (2013) contributes that the majority of memes on the Internet these days are manifestations of visual culture: a meme can consist of a still image, an image with a phrase, a GIF (Graphics Interchange Format, an animated image) or a video; it may contain a punchline (aphorism quotes, movie catchphrases or any witty slogans) or make a statement without added text (see also Blank, 2014). This heavy reliance on visual formats links Internet memes with the advertising industry (Lasn, 1999): many memes resemble advertising posters with an expressive image and a compelling laconic slogan.

From a different perspective, the accretion of memes in the digital sphere can be associated with the rise of emoticons (Davison, 2012; Börzsei, 2013). The innovative idea to employ punctuation marks to resemble a sideways smiley face appeared in 1982. An avid user of the text-based social network USENET, Scott E. Fahlman conceived emoticons to combat misunderstanding in virtual communication, where the lack of visual means often leads to misinterpretation of the message. The smiley gained popularity in many other online communities, evolving in a minimalist prototype of what we now know as an Internet meme (Yus, 2011, as cited in Börzsei, 2013). The primary functions of emoticon were to inform (pass the non-verbal, non-textual information) and entertain members of the network. Eventually, the smileys matured in the large variety of coded symbols with the meaning often more complex and contextual than forthright expression of emotion (Börzsei, 2013). These traits of emoticons relate them to memes, which often serve as the in-jokes of digital communities (Milner, 2016).

The burgeoning popularity of memes throughout the 1990s–2000s owes to the increased accessibility of the Internet connectivity and graphics editing software (Börzsei, 2013). By the mid-2000s, memes had grown from subcultural jokes into a mainstream gimmick. Large meme aggregators, such as 9GAG and 4Chan, enjoy popularity compared to the major news outlets and entertainment Web sources (in 2012, over four million users visited 9GAG each month (Börzsei, 2013)). Nonetheless, the exchange of memes is by no means limited to the particular meme-centred platforms. In recent decades, netizens have scattered them in large numbers to blogs, microblogs, forums and interactive social networks, thus emancipating them from the constraints of geek communities to the mainstream. Esteves and Meikle (2015: 565) point to the remarkable aptitude of memes to cross not only the boundaries of digital platforms but also of contexts and narratives. Memes have matured into the elements of commonly understood Web narratives (Burgess, 2008), and their role expanded from entertainment tools to the means of political and social deliberation. In recent years, social media users have been employing this language of the Internet communication to interpret the news, debate on social issues and campaign for various causes (Shifman, 2013; Milner, 2013, 2016; Meikle, 2014; Esteves & Meikle, 2015). Moreover, circulation of memes has a vivid social function – people discuss and form social norms and values through memes (Gal et al., 2016). When users endorse, like or adjust memes, they by doing so agree or disagree with the norms and values that these spreadable texts promote. Memes are a site of contestation of collective identities, the arena where the hegemonic meets the alternative, and the public chooses the winner by clicking 'like' or 'dislike', and, most importantly, 'share'.

Memes are a phenomenon of the Internet culture and a cherished communication artefact of our times. In this book, I propose the all-encompassing definition of memes for the Internet studies as the context-bound viral texts that proliferate on mutation and replication. They are remarkably versatile for meaning-making, emotion-sharing and attention-grabbing in the oversaturated Internet environment. Users exploit them to comment on or discuss all possible issues, from the personal to the societal. A meme is an imitable text that Internet users appropriate, adjust and share in the digital sphere. The initial text may be a hashtag, an expressive image with a tag line, a catchy tweet, an interesting comment, a YouTube video – any digital unit of expression, as long as it conveys certain meaning or emotion and encourages others to either add something to the content or shape, makes a meme prototype.

A remarkable distinguishing feature of a meme is that it is an incomplete, half-baked joke. It demands user participation to 'finish the sentence'. For example, the famous Internet meme format 'One does not simply...' has an emotional tinge in it and the sarcastic undertone. It means that whatever you fill in the phrase would mean the opposite – that it is indeed difficult and not straightforward to do something. As if, 'One does not simply write a book on the Internet memes'. It conveys a message that the task is challenging and a person is aware of it – yet he or she is trying to nail the issue, and is open to irony and criticism. A format of the meme here suggests the frame of perception, yet it is the audience who needs to finish the sentence to complete a joke and interpret its meaning.

Socially influential and discursively adaptable, memes help people to come together to express their ideas and opinions in a short-term, immediate perspective with the close reliance on the context. I argue that memes are intrinsically connected with context – it is the references to the cultural and social issues, popular and alternative culture, general knowledge and media awareness, the Internet and political literacy, and the ability to connect the disconnected that makes memes a media and social phenomenon of our times.

Bibliography

Bartlett, F. C. (1932). *Remembering: A Study in Experimental and Social Psychology*. New York: Cambridge University Press.

Blackmore, S. (1999). *The Meme Machine*. Oxford: Oxford University Press.

Blackmore, S. (2010). Dangerous memes: Or, what the Pandorans let loose. In Dick, S. & Lupisella, M. (eds.) *Cosmos and Culture: Cultural Evolution in a Cosmic Context*. Washington, DC: NASA, 297–318.

Blank, T. J. (2014). Understanding folk culture in the digital age: An interview with Folklorist Trevor J. Blank, Interview by Julia Fernandez, *Digital Preservation blog*, 30 June 2014. Available at: http://blogs.loc.gov/digitalpreservation/2014/06/understanding-folk-culture-in-the-digital-age-an-interview-with-folklorist-trevor-j-blank-pt-1/ (last accessed July 2015).

Börzsei, L. K. (2013). Makes a meme instead: A concise history of internet memes. *New Media Studies Magazine*, 7, 152–183.

Brodie, R. (1996). *Virus of the Mind: The New Science of the Meme*. New York: Integral Press.

Brown, A. (2014). Serious objections to memes. *The Guardian Religion blog*, 8 July 2009. Available at: www.theguardian.com/commentisfree/andrewbrown/2009/jul/08/religion-atheism (last accessed July 2015).

Burgess, J. (2008). All your chocolate rain are belong to us. Viral video, YouTube and the dynamics of participatory culture. In Lovink, G. & Niederer, S. (eds.) *Video Vortex Reader: Responses to YouTube*, Amsterdam: Institute of Network Cultures, 101–109.

Davison, P. (2012). The language of Internet memes. In Mandiberg, M. (ed.) *The Social Media Reader*, 120–134. Available at: https://archive.org/stream/TheSocialMediaReader/Mandiberg-theSocialMediaReader-cc-by-sa-nc_djvu.txt (last accessed July 2015).

Dawkins, R. (1976). *The Selfish Gene*. Oxford: Oxford University Press.

Dawkins, R. (1993). Viruses of the mind. In Dahlbohm, B. (ed.) *Dennett and his Critics: Demystifying Mind*. Oxford: Blackwell, 13–27.

Dawkins, R. (1999). Foreword. In Blackmore, S. (ed.) *The Meme Machine*. Oxford: Oxford University Press, vii–xvii.

Dennett, D. (1995). *Darwin's Dangerous Idea*. London: Penguin.

Esteves, V. & Meikle, G. (2015). "Look @ this fukken doge": Internet memes and remix cultures. In Atton, C. (ed.) *The Routledge Companion to Alternative and Community Media*. New York: Routledge, 561–570.

Gal, N., Shifman, L., & Kampf, Z. (2016). "It Gets Better": Internet memes and the construction of collective identity. *New Media & Society*, *18*(8), 1698–1714.

Gill, J. (2011). Memes and narrative analysis: A potential direction for the development of neo-Darwinian orientated research in organisations. In *Euram 11: Proceedings of the European Academy of Management*. European Academy of Management.

Goriunova, O. (2013). The force of digital aesthetics: On memes, hacking, and individuation. *Zeitschrift fur Medienwissenschaft*, *8*. Draft in English. Available at: www.academia.edu/3065938/The_force_of_digital_aesthetics_on_memes_hacking_and_individuation (last accessed July 2015).

Knobel, M. & Lankshear, C. (2007). Online memes, affinities and cultural production. In Knobel, M. & Lankshear, C. (eds.) *A New Literacies Sampler*. New York: Peter Lang, 199–227.

Lasn, K. (1999). *Culture Jam*. New York: Quill.

Lievrouw, L. A. (2011). *Alternative and Activist New Media*. Cambridge: Polity.

Meikle, G. (2010). Intercreativity: Mapping online activism. In Hunsinger, J., Klastrup, L. & Allen, M. (eds.) *International Handbook of Internet Research*. Springer Netherlands, 363–377.

Meikle, G. (2014). Social media, visibility, and activism: The Kony 2012 campaign. In Ratto, M. & Boler, M. (eds.) *DIY Citizenship: Critical Making and Social Media*. Cambridge: MIT Press.

Milner, R. M. (2013). Media Lingua Franca: Fixity, novelty, and vernacular creativity in Internet memes. *Selected Papers of Internet Research*, *3*.

Milner, R. M. (2016). *The World Made Meme: Public Conversations and Participatory Media*. Cambridge: MIT Press.

Plotkin, H. C. (1993). *Darwin Machines and the Nature of Knowledge*. London: Penguin.

Shifman, L. (2011). An anatomy of a YouTube meme. *New Media & Society*, *14* (2), 187–203. Available at: http://nms.sagepub.com/content/14/2/187.short (last accessed April 2013).

Shifman, L. (2013). Memes in a digital world: Reconciling with a conceptual troublemaker. *Journal of Computer-Mediated Communication*, *18*(3), 362–377.

Sperber, D. (2000). An objection to the memetic approach to culture. In Aunger, R. (ed.) *Darwinizing Culture: The Status of Memetics as a Science*. Oxford: Oxford University Press, 163–173.

Wiggins, B. E. & Bowers, G. B. (2014). Memes as genre: A structurational analysis of the memescape. *New Media & Society,* first published on May 26, 2014.

2　Before Memes

Tactical Media, Humour and Affective Engagement with Politics Online

Historical perspectives on the developments that paved the way to the proliferation of memes. Alternative media and tactical uses of humour

Participatory Cultures and the Internet Divide

Media scholarship has been trying to assess the new possibilities offered by the digital media for the society; distinguish them from the affordances of the traditional media environment. Jenkins (2009) famously coined his classical term 'participatory culture' that implied that any user can now be a co-producer of the media (see also O'Reilly, 2005; Bruns, 2007; Scholz, 2008; Szilvasi, 2011). The liberating digital ecology opened low-cost (if not free) opportunities for people to correct media, adjust media, supplement or substitute media by their own channels, blogs, videos, tweets and other individual digital expressions of all sorts. Consequently, those with the optimistic world view claimed that new media are instrumental in facilitating democratic participation and discussion (Habermas, 1989; Benkler, 2006). Nevertheless, the majority of media academics treat the liberating promise of digital sphere with much caution, if not scepticism.

Papacharissi (2002) was among the first ones who reminded that the online realm is a continuation, a mirror of the offline reality. It has significant interactive and communication potential, yet is limited by the human nature, social and political structures. The existence of opportunities does not mean that people would use them. Citizens exploit social networks and Internet for a variety of reasons and motivations: access to information, entertainment and socialisation are among the primary incentives, while political participation remains on the periphery of interests (Helsper, 2008). The structures of online realm may be able to accommodate large aggregations of people, but they cannot guarantee that people would come to these vast virtual space to listen and talk; that they will attend the same digital platform and engage in a meaningful debate (Sunstein, 2001; Wellman, 2001; Dahlgren, 2006; Cammaerts 2008; Gilbert et al., 2009). Sunstein (2001) particularly points to the risk of fragmentation of the public discussions – it is likely that, as in the offline societies, people would rather adhere to the like-minded individuals, to those of the similar class, race, gender and status, instead of seeking the alternative views and communities outside of their conventional world. 'Echo chambers' are prevalent in social life – and digital extension of the social practice makes little difference (Sunstein, 2001; Gilbert et al., 2009). People spread the ideas among the crowds who endorse similar views, and they reverberate back to them, creating a false perception that these ideas are universally accepted by everyone in the society.

The father of 'participatory cultures' theory Jenkins (2009) recognised the limitations of this promise. The weaknesses of contemporary participatory culture obscure individual engagement: 'participation gap', 'transparency problem' and 'ethics challenge'. The 'participation gap' emerges from 'digital divide' (Norris, 2001; Iosifidis, 2011), which implies that people have different levels of access to new technologies and uneven media literacy to embrace the possibilities that participatory media offer to them. The 'transparency problem' refers to the overwhelming amount of information that the Internet exposes to the users, making it unfeasible for them to process the multiple gigabytes thrown upon them. The 'ethics challenge' mostly concerns individuals with low levels of digital literacy, such as younger or older users who demonstrate limited awareness of the Internet's potential harms to privacy and reputation, and can be abused by others (Jenkins, 2009). Moreover, the owners of social networking platforms can manipulate individual expression through the design and advertising suggestions to the users. Digital communication is not purely user-generated and user-inhabited, but it constitutes a whirlpool of interactions between users, corporations and platform owners.

The majority of social networks are openly accessible and therefore can be used not only by activists, but by the governments – and this is another major criticism to the optimistic vision of political deliberation online. The elites utilise social media to monitor dissent communication (Andrejevic, 2009), gather information on the participants, and identify leaders (Della Porta & Mattoni, 2014: 57) and points of intervention. They use the collected data to disrupt the discourse by the means of direct censorship, blocking access to the digital platforms and contaminating the discussions with pro-government ideas (Li, 2010; Morozov, 2011). Trottier (2012) and Andrejevic (2009) state that the elites implement surveillance technologies to shape the suppression of dissent. The governments may selectively or totally block the use of electronic technology (cutting off the Internet, denying access to the global social networks or local forums of dissent communication (see Li, 2010; Shirky, 2011)), try to hack dissent accounts and communities online (van Niekerk et al., 2011: 1411) or demand the removal of particular texts, videos or stories (Fuchs & Trottier, 2014).

Yet the pressure of hegemonic regimes expands far beyond these acts of censorship. Power holders attempt to diminish the value of social networks as coordinating channels of spreading the awareness among protest publics (van Niekerk et al., 2011). They not only seek to block particular platforms or challenge collective access to the flows of anti-governmental communication, but also persecute citizens individually. Repressive governments such as China, for instance, implement state-of-the-art technology to track any user's unique IP address and true identity (Poell, 2014: 195). The design of many social networks, such as Facebook, limits anonymity of users: they need to provide their name, location and fill the extensive digital profile in order to benefit from the various opportunities of networking, entertainment and civil engagement (Youmans & York, 2012). Twitter is more liberating in this instance as it permits the exploitation of pseudonyms and does not require the disclosure of personal information and real-life relationship ties with other users (Trottier, 2012).

Socio-Technological Affordances for Generating a Political Change

Technology alone cannot change the world – it requires human agency. From the optimistic perspective, digital platforms do provide opportunities for empowerment for those who seek to find unbiased information, share diverse and unorthodox opinions, express their nonconventional views, connect with the like-minded politicised individuals and mobilise for action (Denisova, 2016). Politically active people utilise the technology as one of the tools that helps them to reach their goals (van Niekerk et al., 2011), similar to how they employ posters, petitions, rallies and meetings. The design of social networks allows for a wide range of mediation practices that may not replace, but can definitely supplement the non-digital political activities.

The most contemporary rendition of the equilibrium between online and offline lies in the idea that the lines are already blurred, if not extinct. We live in a digital society (Lindgren, 2017), and the majority of storytelling in the developed countries is either digital or digitally enabled (Papacharissi et al., 2017). Those in favour of media ecology theory (Parikka, 2007) claim that a society evolves through technology; the digital realm is the environment in which we evolve. This argument mostly applies to the developed Western countries, I have to note. Through this lens, political communication online is a part of the social communication, it is a niche topic of interest when compared to other social interests. Yet it occupies a significant deal of the Internet communication – and it consists of several (overlapping) layers.

First, information. Information is a highly precious asset that digital networks preserve and that activists can utilise for their goals. The elites can impose control over traditional media and even regulate free speech, yet they still have not established a sufficient legal and technological apparatus to restrain the online communication (Iosifidis, 2011; Shirky, 2011). Zuckerman (2013) brings forward the concept of 'latent capacity'. It implies that people may not be interested or directly engaged with political information and debates, yet they may see the important political information from the corner of their eye. It may appear in the newsfeeds of their contacts on social networks, pop up as news notifications or hyperlinks on the websites that they browse. Due to this implicit political education, people may obtain certain minimal awareness of the political issues and debates. Then, if at some point the political situation interferes with the personal interests of the users, they will be able to mobilise the latent accumulated political awareness. They will be already equipped with some necessary information and be aware of the groups and individuals online who are politically active and may provide more insights. Political awareness and the networks of useful contacts lay dormant, but they already form the background of the communication ecosystem of networked users.

Second, connections. Drawing on Castells's (2007) network society concept, we know that the world is bonded more than ever due to the fast communication channels. They bypass the constraints of time and space to deliver information and ideas, and relate individuals and communities. Participation opportunities increase exposure of various political ideologies, as well as promote the actions of their supporters. The spread and ubiquity, the normalised habit of digital use and rapidly growing digital literacy amplify the visibility of political deliberation online (Couldry, 2012; Papacharissi, 2015). At the same time, this visibility is multifaceted and smartly organised: on the one hand, it displays ideas and aspirations, and on the other hand, it protects their authors or supporters. In restrictive environments, politicians persecute those who propagate the unfavourable perspectives and interpretations. Digital platforms empower these dissidents with the layer of anonymity or curated digital identity. In many cases, it is up to a user of social media to decide whether to establish a digital profile that would expose much personal data or a limited amount of individual details; one can determine whether to challenge or protect their privacy (Trottier, 2012). This might not be the case for the likes of Facebook, yet Twitter, Instagram and few other social media platforms do not require the details of the real identity of the users.

Third, new formats of communication. The design of many digital networks suggests various options for the users to participate in digital politics, from those requiring little effort to the more time- and energy-consuming ones. A person can change their userpic or attach a symbol to it to express their political position. For example, in order to champion political tolerance and support LGBTQ community, social network users utilise the rainbow flag as the LGBTQ reference on their personal userpics. As another example, crowdfunding campaigns enabled by the platforms that facilitate the information dissemination, collection of money and communication with followers, provide a civil opportunity of participation. Civil crowdfunding campaigns are different from political activism, yet may be one step away from actual political crowdfunding campaigns. The distinction between civil and political is especially blurred in the authoritarian regimes, where people abstain from anything labelled 'political' for the fear of prosecution. They would still take part in other mobilisations that seek to restore human rights – as long as these activities are not termed 'political' (Denisova, 2016). Moreover, in their networked communication, people can employ various forms of expression such as creative allegoric language that can escape censorship: puns, grammar mistakes, metaphors and Internet memes (Li, 2010). The novel communication genres, such as hashtags, tweets, vines, snaps and, of course, memes create new means of expression that had not existed before the digital era (Lindgren, 2017). This makes these creative digital formats especially attractive for the Internet users – it is their vehicle of information, opinion and communication; the brainchild of their world. This is exactly what makes Internet memes a potent tool of political deliberation in a digital society – they are laid-back and accessible, yet remarkably influential.

From Dada and Situationism to Culture Jamming

Political activism online can take inventive forms, which are inspired by the legacy of political mobilisation framing, art and media practices. Lievrouw (2011: 19–27) classifies five main genres of how people employ new media for political purposes. They comprise culture jamming, alternative computing, participatory journalism, mediated mobilisation and commons knowledge. Although these genres can in practice overlap, the classification helps to distinguish among various forms and strategies of the activists.

Alternative new media derive from the media tradition of political commentary and satire, Dada and Situationism (Lievrouw, 2011), advertising and culture jamming (Lasn, 1999), among others. Tactical media refer to the interventionist media practices, where nonconventional ideas are delivered via nonconventional media formats (Atton, 2004; Lievrouw, 2011). In other instances, nonconventional ideas may be deployed to the most conventional media to create disruption. Tactical media activists interrupt the mainstream discourse, borrow elements of mass culture and traditional media and reconstruct them in a new meaningful form to criticise the dominant political and social order (Garcia & Lovink, 1997). Tactical media activists use a wide range of platforms, channels and methods; they broadcast their texts via theatres and squares, cable channels and new media, to name a few. They do not limit their activity to the DIY (do-it-yourself) projects or large commercial media. Tactical media aim to combine many channels to create a personalised media network and guarantee wide media presence of the alternative ideas. Garcia and Lovink (1997) and Raley (2009: 6) emphasise flexibility and interactivity of tactical media, their openness to remix and new ideas. Kireyev (2006) suggests linking tactical media with the Soviet samizdat, the clandestine reproduction of the dissent textual materials that aimed at spreading alternative ideas in the highly censored society. Alternative media practices of our times can fill the gaps left by the hegemonic discourse, and even question its authenticity. Tactical media are very subjective (Garcia & Lovink, 1997): they represent the point of view of the user, hence derive from the personalised use of social networks and individualist political engagement online.

These non-for-profit activities reject hegemonic ideology, merge art and activism, create new forms of expression and contribute new ways of thinking. Tactical media are 'actions in their own right' and do not require offline extension of activism (Atton, 2004; Raley, 2009). This characteristic is particularly important to make distinction between alternative resistant tactical media practices and mobilisation media. The former generate a discourse that accounts as activism on its own, while the latter mostly support and coordinate the offline political activity. For the study on political uses of memes, the first kind (alternative resistant tactical media) is more relevant. It defines an act of communication as activism, with or without offline extension.

Tactical media has its roots in Dada and Situationism. The Dada movement was started around 1915 in Europe by an international coalition of artists and writers who were condemning the cruelty of warfare, the industrialisation of mass production and consumerist culture (Bonnett, 1992). Dada artists were inventive in expression; they combined novel media technologies such as photography, cinema and print, with the classic forms of art such as painting and sculpture. They were among the first political artists to use remix methods, matching random fragments of photographs with newspaper articles, distorted imagery, absurd text and pieces of clothing. With their projects, Dadaists aimed at disrupting the 'normality', inviting the audience to see the reality in a different light (Bonnett, 1992; Plant, 2002).

Situationists continued the work started by the Dada movement and resumed the attacks on consumerist culture and hegemonic politics in the 1950s–1960s (Plant, 2002: 1–3). This cluster of French and international artists led by the French philosopher and film-maker Guy Debord was confronting the ever-present Spectacle, the newly adopted convention of mass culture to reinforce consumerist desires, surrounding the audience with endless images of advertised goods and lifestyles. Situationists encouraged the audience to generate nonconventional situations in their personal experiences; they called for more creativity and urged people to produce their own culture (Plant, 2002).

Situationists followed Dadaists and relied on remix culture and montage to subvert popular cultural texts. However, they insisted on moving from the ironic subversions made by Dadaists to the partisan propaganda tactics that resulted in not only subverting, but also inverting the meaning of borrowed images and texts. The newly created media items were much more rebellious than Dadaist work and could be as harsh as revolutionary demands. Debord and his followers went to the extreme of creating provoking and even violent situations in the streets and public places to evoke the importance of authentic life experiences (Debord, 1967; Lievrouw, 2011).

The creative interventionist practices of Dada and Situationism influenced the emergence of culture jamming and tactical media. Peretti (2006) calls contemporary tactical media 'micromedia', referring to their autonomous nature and limited coverage. However, subversive media activism is not limited to the specifically designed independent media platforms. Recent examples of political uprisings facilitated by global social networks (see, for instance, Aron, 2012) show that political activism can find a way through commercial user-generated networks. Political activists largely use the Internet tools that were designed for the publication of non-political content for their purposes (Shirky, 2011), because general-use digital platforms can escape government censorship and cater to larger audiences (Zuckerman, 2013). This trend is evident in China, for instance, where the popular social network Sina Weibo became more important for political discussion and mobilisation than the purposely crafted US-funded websites such as 'Internet freedom' (Zuckerman, 2013).

Political Opportunities for the Deployment of Tactical Media

The political environment in each particular country determines the modes and limitations of political activism online. In repressive regimes, alternative digital activism may be restricted to remix practices and mediated dissent, while liberal administrations of other countries allow mobilisations and collective action. Gamson's Strategy of Social Protest (1975, 1992) helps to identify the prerequisites that either facilitate or challenge the development of dissent communication; this theory also allows analysing whether digital resistance in each particular

environment has the capacity of transforming in offline action. A social protest involves a group of people who want to mobilise the passive
crowds against an antagonist who lies outside the audience (Gamson,
1975: 16–17). In order to succeed, the protest group needs to strategically define its target, mobilise as many supporters as possible and, if
feasible, gradually mature from the times of stability until the moments
of turbulence (Gamson, 1975).

Political Opportunity theory (Kitschelt, 1986; Tarrow & Tollefson,
1994) highlights three vital components that facilitate the development
of political activism: Insurgent Consciousness, Organisational Strengths
and Political Opportunities. Tactical media and nonconventional, artistic forms of activism such as production of politicised art and distribution of viral texts online, can point to the issues of common grievances
and unite the protest public around these topics (see Shirky, 2011). Political activists utilise tactical media to promote insurgent consciousness,
which refers to the shared feeling of deprivation and injustice in a community; it leads to calls for justice (see Tarrow & Tollefson, 1994: xvii).
However, the acknowledgement of collective grievances and demands
for change is not enough to motivate people to organise for a dissent. Organisational strength is required; it is defined as compelling leadership
and sufficient resources possessed by the protest organisation to recruit
and mobilise members (Kitschelt, 1986).

Furthermore, even with the existence of established dissent organisations and structures and clear identification of goals and methods of protests, another component should be in place – political opportunity. This
concept implies that the political system is vulnerable for a challenge that
social movements can therefore promote. This vulnerability can be a result of political pluralism, decline of repression, division within elites and
increased political enfranchisement (Amenta et al., 2010). Tactical media
assist in championing the diversity of voices and opinions (Raley, 2009;
Lievrouw, 2011: 120–121) and cultivating relationships among like-
minded individuals (Lievrouw, 2011: 151). Therefore, they have a capacity to propagate insurgent consciousness. However, they are limited in
the ability to compete with the hegemonic media and mass propaganda
(Peretti, 2006). Tactical media have a short-term effect and normally affect small audiences. They may employ a too bizarre or unconventional
style of expression that not all the members of the general audience can
equally understand (Garcia & Lovink, 1997; Raley, 2009: 9–12).

Affective Emotions and Self-Expression for Political Engagement

People become engaged in political communication online for various
reasons, informed by their personal beliefs and intentions or group pressure. According to the classic resource mobilisation theory, those who

share common grievances or aims do not necessarily unite for the cause unless they have other motivations (Olson, 1965). An individual needs to see personal gains in his or her contribution to a mobilisation. Although the majority realise that collective action can bring the desired results for the community, this reasoning is not sufficient to motivate one's engagement in politics. However, the contemporary social mobilisation theory has moved beyond the rational approach and further explored the meaning of identity, emotion, culture, social behaviour, irrational behaviour and opportunity structures (Melucci, 1996; Della Porta & Diani, 2006; Karatzogianni, 2012).

Without neglect to the importance of organisations, leadership and brokering differences, they emphasised the influence of emotions and self-expression on one's eagerness to engage in public activism. Media communication is founded on the concept of storytelling: people compress their experiences and sentiments in the accessible form of a story, a narrative. It has protagonists and antagonists, recognisable archetypes and plot lines. Digital storytelling permits average users to not just witness or retell a story, but to participate in it and become a protagonist. Storytelling is performative in a sense that users select the words, poses, styles, images and sounds that help them to tell the stories (Papacharissi et al., 2017). Very often, these choices do not come from the conscious curation of the online presence, but momentary reactions and emotions.

Interestingly, the power of the emotional affect and non-rational drivers of engagement plays a strong part in contemporary dissent practices (Karatzogianni, 2012; Papacharissi, 2015; Theocharis, 2015). Interactive social media allow users to contribute their own stories and narratives about the participation in offline protests (Karatzogianni, 2012; Papacharissi, 2015; Papacharissi et al., 2017). They also facilitate the sentimental experience of letting people feel a part of a movement, an event, a social entity. Digital storytelling "invite(s) people to *feel* their own place in current events, developing news stories, and various forms of civic mobilisation" (Papacharissi, 2015: 4). This new virtuality of political engagement creates the feeling of involvement, even if a movement or political resistance does not have the offline extension. The symbolic branding of a mobilisation, of an ideology or a digital community (e.g., symbols, hashtags, catchphrases, memes) decorate this new affective field. Coded, symbolic expression assists in building the identity of a mobilisation, as well as the collective identity of participants – which, in turn, strongly impacts a personal identity of each member. Participants of the digital political deliberation *feel* a part of something big and social.

Furthermore, engagement in the civil or political communication in social networks bolsters the imagined communion; it bestows the experience of hope, rage, grief, compassion and empathy (Karatzogianni, 2012). The interactive, connective affordances of social networks allow

users to exchange their affective sentiments, relate to each other's stories, amplify subjective interpretations and drive forward the narratives
that people commonly agree with (Papacharissi, 2015). Users mediate
their affective feelings online, and these feelings often become the driving energy of dissent communication. Lindgren (2017) moves the argument further and suggests that affective affordances are incorporated in
the design of digital networks. The triggers are already there:

> It is affect that makes people use social media and pulls them back
> for more. Calls for support, aggressive outbursts, descriptions of
> harm and hurt, of waves of sarcasm and amusement, are the types
> of actions and experiences that knit digital society together.
>
> (Lindgren, 2017: 131)

Noteworthy, the affective feelings that drive people to political discussion online can be positive, negative or circuitously mixed. Yet what
distinguishes an affective emotional trigger for participation is its ability
to induce a fiery, inflamed desire in a user, a desire for them to click the
buttons (like, share, post) or type on their keyboard (comment, tweet).
In other words, affective arousing foments people to not just watch, listen or read, but actively partake in online communication.

The rise of digital social media has boosted one's capacity to express
themselves online and become noticed by the others. The motivation to
articulate oneself creatively and politically is an influential force that
can embolden one's participation in dissent communication (Gauntlett,
2011). Barry Wellman's (2001) concept of 'networked individualism'
explains the new social order where the abundance of 'personalised'
technologies (email, social networks, mobile phones and so forth) encourages the shift from societies built on place-based solidarity to the
solidarity that grows out of the interaction and conviviality in digital
networks (see also Castells, 2007; Diani, 2001). The pleasure of finding
novel ways to communicate adds spark to the creative and emotionally
stimulating digital communication (Papacharissi et al., 2017). From the
Instagram diaries of one's everyday life, tweets and shares that permit
a user to express an emotional reaction to the news, to the memes, gifs,
hashtags, sound bites, snaps that one deploys to the digital whirlpool to
have a say on all topics. All these sentiments fit in and fuel the digital
rage, joy, awe and excitement; they reverberate back to the users, thus
creating a dynamic cycle of vehement deliberation.

Nevertheless, when many individuals with similar interests and political aspirations go digital, it does not guarantee that they will hear each
other – and this is where emotions can let the discussion down even more
(Morozov, 2013). Many people prefer to speak rather than to listen –
this is what Papacharissi et al. (2017: 1071) denounce as 'opinionating',
expressing one's opinion before earning the knowledge and authority to

do so meaningfully. The digital space can feature multiple spheres and conversations, and users that unite for a civil or political cause may not be tied strongly enough to transfer their online enthusiasm in any offline action; they need to find the affectionate frames that would help them to drive the discussion in the desired direction. In the oversaturated digital environment, the activists often need viral, memetic vehicles of persuasion to distribute their ideas and mobilisation calls with catchy conviction.

All in all, social networks that loosely unite various users with bespoke personal accounts and frames can grow into large networks of multiple interrelation and provide a fertile platform for engagement. Interpersonal communication in social networks often becomes more instrumental for the popularisation of movements than shared ideologies and the appeals promoted by conventional organisations. In this contemporary communication environment of networked distribution and interaction, memes find a fruitful soil to propagate, develop and influence minds and affections. Through the recent decades, they have grown into a potent tool of political deliberation online.

The Internet affordances reward the proliferation of various ideas and aggregation of diverse crowds. On the one hand, its open and ubiquitous nature facilitates political deliberation among large groups of people; users can connect to the like-minded individuals and mobilise for political action, bypassing traditional leaders and institutions. On the other hand, people have varying levels of access to the Internet, digital literacy and interest towards politics. From this perspective, the online realm often acts as the mirror of the offline political situation: those citizens who are politically active offline are likely to participate in digital politics, while the more passive ones may still remain disinterested either online or offline. Politically engaged users utilise many nonconventional practices of spreading the awareness of alternative ideas: tactical media, culture jamming and production of the Internet memes. By doing so, they appeal to the large masses of the Internet public who may appreciate the amusing text, get aroused by the emotional component and acknowledge the political content of a meme. This can lead to more interest in politicised communication and challenge the opinions on the political agenda.

Bibliography

Amenta, E., Caren, N., Chiarello, E. & Su, Y. (2010). The political consequences of social movements. *Annual Review of Sociology*, 36, 287–307.

Andrejevic, M. (2009). *iSpy: Surveillance and Power in the Interactive Era.* Topeka: University of Kansas.

Aron, L. (2012). *Russia's Protesters: The People, Ideals, and Prospects.* American Enterprise Institute for Public Policy Research, Report, 9 August 2012. Available at: www.aei.org/publication/russias-protesters-the-people-ideals-and-prospects/ (accessed April 2016).

Atton, C. (2004). *An Alternative Internet*. Edinburgh: Edinburgh University Press.

Benkler, Y. (2006). *The Wealth of Networks: How Social Production Transforms Markets and Freedom*. New Haven: Yale University Press.

Bonnett, A. (1992). Art, ideology, and everyday space: subversive tendencies from Dada to postmodernism. *Environment and Planning D: Society and Space, 10*(1), 69–86.

Bruns, A. (2007). Produsage: Towards a broader framework for user-led content creation. *Creativity and Cognition: Proceedings of the 6th ACM SIGCHI Conference on Creativity & Cognition*. ACM, Washington, DC.

Cammaerts, B. (2008). Critiques on the participatory potentials of Web 2.0. *Communication, Culture & Critique, 1*(4), 358–377.

Castells, M. (2007). Communication, power and counter-power in the network society. *International journal of communication, 1*(1), 29.

Couldry, N. (2012). *Media, Society, World: Social Theory and Digital Media Practice*. Cambridge: Polity.

Dahlgren, P. (2006). Doing citizenship: The cultural origins of civic agency in the public sphere. *European Journal of Cultural Studies, 9*(3), 267–286.

Debord, G. (1967). *The Society of the Spectacle*. Donald Nicholson-Smith, trans. New York: Zone Books.

Della Porta, D. & Diani, M. (2006). *Social Movements: An Introduction*. 2nd Ed. Oxford: Blackwell.

Della Porta, D. & Mattoni, A. (2014). Social networking sites in pro-democracy and anti-austerity protests: Some thoughts from a social movement perspective. In Fuchs, C. & Trottier, D. (eds.) *Social Media, Politics and the State: Protests, Revolutions, Riots, Crime and Policing in the Age of Facebook, Twitter and YouTube* (Vol. 16). London: Routledge, 39–67.

Denisova, A. (2017). Democracy, protest and public sphere in Russia after the 2011–2012 anti-government protests: Digital media at stake. *Media, Culture & Society, 39*(7) 976–994.

Diani, M. (2001). Social movement networks. Virtual and real. In Webster, F. (ed.) *Culture and Politics in the Information Age. A New Politics?* London: Routledge, 117–128.

Fuchs, C. & Trottier, D. (2014). Theorising social media, politics and the state: An introduction. In Fuchs, C. & Trottier, D. (eds.) *Social Media, Politics and the State: Protests, Revolutions, Riots, Crime and Policing in the Age of Facebook, Twitter and YouTube* (Vol. 16). London: Routledge, 3–39.

Gamson, W. (1975). *Strategy of Social Protest*. Belmont: Wadsworth Publishing Company.

Gamson, W. (1992). *Talking Politics*. New York: Cambridge University Press.

Garcia, D. & Lovink, G. (1997). *The ABC of Tactical Media*. Available at: http://preview.sarai.net/events/tml/tml_pdf/abc_tactical.PDF (last accessed September 2014).

Gauntlett, D. (2011). *Making is Connecting: The Social Meaning of Creativity, from DIY and Knitting to YouTube and Web 2.0*. London: Polity Press.

Gilbert, E., Bergstrom, T. & Karahalios, K. (2009). Blogs are echo chambers: Blogs are echo chambers. In *Proceedings of the 42nd Annual Hawaii International Conference on System Sciences, HICSS, August 2009*, 1–10.

Habermas, J. (1989). *The Structural Transformation of the Public Sphere: An Inquiry into a Category of Bourgeois Society.* Cambridge: Polity Press.

Helsper, E. J. (2008). *Digital Inclusion: An Analysis of Social Disadvantage and the Information Society.* Oxford Internet Institute. Available at: www.communities.gov.uk/documents/.../pdf/digitalinclusionanalysis (accessed December 2011).

Iosifidis, P. (2011). *Global Media and Communication Policy.* London: Palgrave Macmillan, 23–44.

Jenkins, H. (2009). *Confronting the Challenges of Participatory Culture for the 21st Century.* Cambridge: MIT Press.

Karatzogianni, A. (2012). Epilogue: The politics of the affective digital. In Karatzogianni, A. & Kuntsman, A. (eds.) *Digital Cultures and the Politics of Emotion: Feelings, Affect and Technological Change.* Basingstoke: Palgrave Macmillan, 245–249.

Kireyev, O. (2006). *Povarennaya Kniga Media-Aktivista.* Moscow: Ultra. Kultura.

Kitschelt, H. P. (1986). Political opportunity structures and political protest: Anti-nuclear movements in four democracies. *British Journal of Political Science,* 16(01), 57–85.

Lasn, K. (1999). *Culture Jam.* New York: Quill.

Li, S. (2010). The online public space and popular ethos in China. *Media, Culture & Society,* 32(1), 63–83.

Lievrouw, L. A. (2011). *Alternative and Activist New Media.* Cambridge: Polity.

Lindgren, S. (2017). *Digital Media and Society.* London: Sage.

Melucci, A. (1996). *Challenging Codes: Collective Action in the Information Age.* Cambridge: University Press.

Morozov, E. (2011). *The Net Delusion: How Not to Liberate the World.* London: Allen Lane.

Morozov, E. (2013). *To Save Everything, Click Here: Technology, Solutionism, and the Urge to Fix Problems That Don't Exist.* London: Penguin.

Norris, P. (2001). *Digital Divide. Civic Engagement, Information Poverty, and the Internet Worldwide.* Cambridge: Cambridge University Press.

Olson, M. (1965). *The Theory of Collective Action: Public Goods and the Theory of Groups.* Cambridge: Harvard University Press.

O'Reilly, T. (2005). *What Is Web 2.0: Design Patterns and Business Models for the Next Generation of Software.* Available at: http://oreilly.com/web2/archive/what-is-web-20.html (last accessed July, 2014).

Papacharissi, Z. (2002). The virtual sphere: The Internet as a public sphere. *New Media & Society,* 4(1), 9–27.

Papacharissi, Z. (2015). *Affective Publics: Sentiment, Technology, and Politics.* New York: Oxford University Press.

Papacharissi, Z., Lashley, M. C. & Creech, B. (2017). Voices for a new vernacular: A forum on digital storytelling interview with Zizi Papacharissi. *International Journal of Communication 11,* Forum, 1069–1073.

Parikka, J. (2007). *Digital Contagions: A Media Archaeology of Computer Viruses* (Vol. 44). New York: Peter Lang.

Peretti, J. (2006). *Culture Jamming, Memes, Social Networks, and the Emerging Media Ecology.* Available online at: http://depts.washington.edu/ccce/polcommcampaigns/peretti.html (last accessed July, 2014).

Plant, S. (2002). *The Most Radical Gesture: The Situationist International in a Postmodern Age*. London: Routledge.

Poell, T. (2014). Social media activism and state censorship. In Fuchs, C. & Trottier, D. (eds.) *Social Media, Politics and the State: Protests, Revolutions, Riots, Crime and Policing in the Age of Facebook, Twitter and YouTube* (Vol. 16). London: Routledge, 189–209.

Raley, R. (2009). *Tactical Media* (Vol. 28). Minneapolis: University of Minnesota Press.

Scholz, T. (2008). Market ideology and the myths of Web 2.0. *First Monday*, *13*(3). Available at: http://journals.uic.edu/fm/article/view/2138/1945 (last accessed June, 2014).

Shirky, C. (2011). Political power of social media technology, the public sphere, and political change. *Foreign Affairs*, *90*(1), 28–41.

Sunstein, C. R. (2001). *Republic.com 2.0*. Princeton: Princeton University Press.

Tarrow, S. & Tollefson, J. (1994). *Power in Movement: Social Movements, Collective Action and Politics*. Cambridge: Cambridge University Press, 41–61.

Theocharis, Y. (2015). The conceptualization of digitally networked participation. *Social Media+ Society*, *1*(2), 1–14.

Trottier, D. (2012). *Social Media as Surveillance: Rethinking Visibility in a Converging World*. Surrey: Ashgate Publishing, Ltd.

van Niekerk, B., Pillay, K. & Maharaj, M. (2011). The Arab Spring| Analyzing the role of ICTs in the Tunisian and Egyptian unrest from an information warfare perspective. *International Journal of Communication*, *5*, 1406–1416.

Wellman, B. (2001). Physical place and cyberplace: The rise of personalized networking. *International Journal of Urban and Regional Research*, *28*(2), 227–252.

Youmans, W. L. & York, J. C. (2012). Social media and the activist toolkit: User agreements, corporate interests, and the information infrastructure of modern social movements. *Journal of Communication*, *62*(2), 315–329.

Zuckerman, E. (2013). Cute cats to the rescue? Participatory media and political expression. In Allen, D. & Light, J. (eds.) *Youth, New Media and Political Participation*. Boston: MIT Press.

3 Many Uses of Memes

From Fast-Food Media to Political Mindbombs

How memes become political and spark a carnival of resistance

In 2006, a frog named Pepe went to the bathroom to pee and put his pants down. A door opened, and another animal entered the room, catching the frog in an intimate moment. Later on, he told the frog that he saw him, "hey pepe – I heard you pull yer pants all the way to go pee…." The frog named Pepe responded, "feels good man".

This was the episode from the "Boy's Town" comic created by the artist Matt Furie. The San Francisco-based cartoonist uploaded this work to his MySpace account. Little could he predict that Pepe the Frog would become a global meme and a political symbol in the years to come.

Sometime later, an unknown user posted a scan of Furie's cartoon on the niche Internet platform 4chan, known for the distribution of memes. Digital crowds appropriated the charming nonchalant frog to express their good feelings. This became known as the Feels Good Man meme (KnowYourMeme, 2017). Yet, with the years passing, the frog reappeared in many other alterations, finally landing on the social network feeds of 2016, becoming visible in the politicised exchanges of the users during the US Presidential Elections. This is when the sound and fury kicked off.

Many memes of Pepe the Frog by the mid-2010s were spared of the feel-good vibe of the original cartoon. Instead, they were often featuring a rather smug green beast who was bursting out nationalist and hate-infused sentiments.

Users were pushing the innocent Pepe to act as a Nazi, bark racist billingsgate against the Blacks, the Jews, LGBTQ community and various minorities. Many supporters of candidate Donald Trump exploited the memes to endorse the nationalist agenda, propagate the so-called White Supremacism (also known as Nazism) and condemn the non-White communities of the US. The office of candidate Hillary Clinton took the issue with unprecedented severity – they issued an official statement. This is worth stressing. A runner for the US president issued a statement about *the Internet meme*.

Figure 3.1 The meme joins the figures of Pepe the Frog and Donald Trump to present them as a squad "The Deplorables".

HillaryClinton.com published an explainer on 12 September 2016, which denounced Pepe the Frog as the symbol of White Supremacists. The publication compared the meme with the Nazi propaganda and blamed Donald Trump's camp for promoting this symbol of hatred on social networks (Figure 3.1).

Why is the case of Pepe the Frog groundbreaking for meme studies?

1   The high-level politicians not only acknowledged that memes exist and they matter, but they basically engaged with the meme wars in their official communication.
2   They referred to the Internet memes to attract the Internet crowds to their campaigning. Memes are an attention-grabber; they are good for political branding.
3   They approached the online meme logics with the predigital mentality. It was a miscomprehension. This chapter explains why.

Language of the Internet Crowds: When Mundane Chatter Becomes Important

A meme does not belong to any specific group or community; it has no inherent political or cultural affiliation except for the promise of entertainment. Memes are empty conduits or layouts that anyone can fill with meaning or commentary (see Meikle & Young, 2012; Metahaven, 2013). The autonomous and non-aligned character of memes nurtures the idea of their independence from elites and power holders. Memes are a brainchild of the new democratising media ecology (Meikle & Young, 2012), one of the "emerging patterns in public conversations" (Milner, 2016: 1) that permits users to share their opinion with a large community. The reliance on collective creativity fortifies the analogy of memes with folklore and vernacular manifestation (see Burgess, 2008; Davison, 2012; Milner, 2013; Blank, 2014; Howard, 2014). Memes are the common Internet vocabulary.

However, as any language, memetic expression is embedded in the society where it is used. Following the legendary Austrian philosopher of the last century Ludwig Wittgenstein, I argue that the meaning of memes derives from their exploitation in context. As Wittgenstein (1961) stressed about language, words do not have fixed meaning – we derive them from the circumstances, background knowledge and immediate conditions of the act of communication. Similarly, memes as a format do not express any point. It is the users who fill them with sense. From the sociological perspective, memes function as "performative acts": each person decides whether to ratify or oppose a specific way of interpreting the situation – and he or she adjusts a meme accordingly. By doing this, a user agrees with or redefies the social norms that a meme propagates (Butler, 1997, as cited in Gal et al., 2016: 1700). Not all memes are explicitly connected with the negotiation of social norms and values – yet even in the cases that seem purely entertaining, the political and social underlining may be pinpointed.

The case of Pepe the Frog is particularly illustrative of this communication logic. What emerged as a format, was appropriated and infused with meaning through *years* of use. The format of Pepe the Frog has a pre-established emotion: a feel-good, nonchalant and relaxed vibe. There are no rules on when and why to use this meme. No content is implied. Later on, various users were adjusting the emotional, affective component of Pepe the Frog and turned it from the laid-back tranquillity to smugness and arrogance. This reformulation of the format occurred through Internet negotiation and made the format one step closer to the abuse by the nationalist users. Still, no meaning is encoded, only the emotion. When Hillary Clinton and later on many journalists rushed to write about Pepe the Frog as a symbol of White Supremacists, they made a crucial mistake of the offline world: they attempted to fix the meaning that was not fixed. Memes belong to no one, they are the collective product of Internet interactivity and sites of collective negotiation of values, meanings and norms. Unlike icons, as mentioned in Chapter 1, memes are constantly evolving; they are fluid and ambiguous. If tomorrow hundreds of users start exploiting Pepe the Frog in a new context, say, as an emblem of healthy lifestyle or vegan philosophy, it would lose its negative political meaning as soon as it gained it. Memes resonate from the use in context, they absorb and tire concepts and trends. They signal trending ways of thinking in a short-term perspective. In a long-term perspective, the picture can change completely.

A meme does not belong to any author. This is why, when the original comics creator Matt Furie tried to claim his character back, this was a call from the offline mentality. Furie (2016) wrote a column in *Times* where he stressed that 'A chill frog-dude named Pepe' was never about hate, but expressed the feeling of sadness or serenity, 'Pepe is *love*'. The artist tried to symbolically kill his creation – to the amusement of many media outlets and sceptical reception by the Internet users. This symbolic act of one artist neither changed attitude to Pepe the Frog (the digital publics still love it) nor diminished the circulation of the meme (there is no evidence that less memes with Pepe the Frog are produced after Furie's statement). Pepe the Frog belongs to the collective creativity, to the decisions and benevolence of the Internet crowds. Like it or not, this is the memetic logic of our days.

The case of Pepe the Frog proves the idea that memes can overcome the boundaries of closed communities and social groups. Previously, there was a belief that successful meme distribution is limited to homogenous communities: 'the majority of currently famous Internet memes spreads through homogenous communities and social networks rather than through the Internet at large' (Bauckhage, 2011: 49). However, Knobel and Lankshear (2007) and Esteves and Meikle (2015) later contradicted this standpoint, noting that Internet memes can travel beyond the boundaries of digital platforms, discourses and languages they initially flourished in. This capacity of memes to overcome confines of communities and personal accounts makes them instrumental in shaping collective identities (Gal et al., 2016). Moreover, memes can assist in identifying compatible individuals among digital crowds, those who literally 'speak the same language' (Börzsei, 2013; Milner, 2013).

American anthropologist Patricia Lange introduced the concept of affinity videos as channels of socialisation. Lange (2009, cited in Shifman, 2011) identifies amateur YouTube videos as means of growing kinship; users comment on them and on each other's remarks thus creating a tenuous yet visible community within the network. This imagined virtual community has a remarkably low threshold, members do not need to expose their identity or status, but may freely enter or leave and commit to different levels of involvement. The concept of 'affinity spaces' suggested by the sociolinguist James Paul Gee (2004) adds more grounds to this perspective. 'Affinity spaces' refer to the shared areas, often online, where people gather according to their interests, cultural or ideological similarities. Memes are coded viral texts that travel through minds and platforms and form an important connecting element of affinity spaces

(Knobel & Lankshear, 2007). These platforms feed on memes, and memes feed on these platforms.

In previous decades, public figures, institutions and media outlets were setting the agenda and acted as information gatekeepers. In the present Internet media, gatekeeping is more fluid. There is a net hierarchy, and people with more followers, audience, access to networks of people with a high number of followers, may be more visible when they spread memes (Nahon & Hemsley, 2013). At the same time, gatekeeping is not limited to the big players. Average users with a low number of followers and connections can still spread a meme that becomes an Internet sensation – provided that it gets picked by other people with higher network capital, and thus it results in a snowball effect. They share it with their networks, the networks share it with further networks and further down the line. Institutional forces and more popular users do serve as primary gatekeepers (Nahon & Hemsley, 2013), yet the network gatekeeping permits even smaller players to act as gatekeepers and suppliers of creative contributions (Milner, 2016). This is the open public space, the welcoming media environment of networks that facilitates better representation of various minds and voices.

The emerging narratives are particularly valuable to the social groups that are excluded from mainstream communication for various reasons (Langellier, 1999, as cited in Gal et al., 2016: 1699). Political opposition, minorities and youth cultures, for example, can find the sphere of visibility and identity negotiation in the realm of meme making and sharing. The publics have an inclination towards convention, and this proves valid even in the digital realm. Most people would indeed be likely to reproduce the content and shape of a meme with minor alterations (Gal et al., 2016). At the same time, when deviations occur, they are the most intriguing and signify a shift in public thinking.

It would be reductionist to think of the online crowds as a uniform community. As in real life, the online realm has big squares, wide streets, narrow lines and hidden corners; there are platforms of mass aggregation (Juris, 2012) and micro-communities of the more focused, but less populated discourses (Papacharissi et al., 2017). The moral frames, cultural references and political messages in memes need to resonate with the existing frames, cultural knowledge and political awareness of users to be noticed and understood (Dauvergne & Neville, 2011).

Memes are the Internet vernacular (Milner, 2016) – yet, it does not make *all of them* universally understood, even among the digitally savvy users. This also limits their benefits for the discussion about and among the under-represented social categories. The prominent feature of memes is their coded nature – in order to unpack them, one has to be aware of the cultural, social, political and Internet-specific references. The most niche memes can be obscure to the majority, if they don't follow a particular television show or a slang of a particular community, as an example.

From this critical viewpoint, memes incorporate a sophisticated inter-play of common sense and originality (Milner, 2013; Esteves & Meikle, 2015). Users appropriate memes to benefit from *inclusivity* in the cir-culation of an in-joke, and adjust it for the sake of *exclusivity*, attempt-ing to draw an innovative rendition of a common pattern (Esteves & Meikle, 2015). The necessity to conform to the existing unwritten rules of conduct that shape online interaction (Milner, 2013, 2016) preserves the recognizable features of the memetic format.

A recent study of the Belarusian youth and their uses of memes (Lysenka, 2017) revealed that young people tend to see memes as 'in-jokes' of their group of friends and would be embarrassed to share it with parents or older generation. This non-Western research proved the findings of the Western colleagues and suggested that youngsters have 'local' memes for in-group sharing and 'common' memes that they toler-ate in the common space – the Internet at large.

The niche character of memetic communication as a slang of a group brings us to the first drawback of its exclusivity. Meme sharers are very sensitive to the changing trends and appropriation of memes by other groups and elites. When a meme appears in advertisement, for instance, the meme-sharing community ostracises it as something outdated and untrendy (Lysenka, 2017).

The second shortcoming of the reputation of memes as "in-jokes" of the online community is the highly coded, postmodern and sophisticated message of a meme (Lysenka, 2017). Drawing parallels with the issue of digital divide, especially digital literacy, I am following Zuckerman's (2015) point that memes are coded messages and therefore can be con-fusing for various people: members of the audience may have varying abilities and skills to read the 'code'. Those who are unfamiliar with the rules of digital discussion and styles of the Internet slang, or possess lim-ited awareness of the broader sociopolitical context may consider memes meaningless. In order to be able to read a meme, one has to be *digitally* savvy or at least have basic familiarity with this format of communi-cation (Zuckerman, 2015). In some instances, memes can impede the inclusivity of communication – the issue of 'meme divide' questions the legacy of memes as the mutually understood lingua franca.

Fast-Food Media: Tempting for Your Taste Buds, But Low in Nutritional Value

One of the unique ways the users exploit memes is commenting on the immediate news and political agenda. Digital publics appropriate im-ages from the television programmes and quote traditional press and the speeches of politicians and opinion-leaders in the memes. Very of-ten, these shareable texts shed a new light on the event or a political statement and thus recontextualise it, revealing the social and political implications. Those memes that comment on the traditional media agenda may as well confront it and expose the propagandist content or style. In these instances, Internet memes act as 'fast-food media'[1] (Denisova, 2016, 2017b) – they are flashy, tempting and grab your attention. The nutritional value – if we keep the allegory with junk meals saturated with fat and sugar – is very low, yet you get the flavour and taste. Similarly, the memes convey the essence of the idea, or an event, or a sarcastic comment a user may mark it with – and deliver those in the easily digestible form of an image with a sassy tag line. When commenting on or reinforcing messages from the media, publics employ memes to discuss the news and express their comment and opinion on the important events and speeches.

This approach of investing meme power in the negotiation of media agenda turns memes in the quick buzzers of public awareness. One of the Russian opposition leaders Alexey Navalny, for instance, actively uses memes in his social media communication with the followers. The disturbing, informative, or simply funny and sarcastic memes act as beacons to the larger blogposts by the politician. Fast-food media in this case become a 'teaser', a promise of an informational or political 'meal' with a more substantial nutritional value.

Political Mindbombs and Their Persuasive Qualities

Memes are not just the casual vocabulary or the flavoured extracts of media agenda; users exploit them as symbolic rhetoric arguments in conversations and debates. Social network inhabitants interact, co-create and collaborate by the means of memes (Gauntlett, 2011; Meikle, 2010, 2014), which opens new perspectives for the deliberation of politics online. Memes serve as the artful format of sharing ideas and drawing public attention to specific issues. From this perspective, the utilisation of memes for activism relates to the recent media strategy of 'mindbombing' developed by the late Bob Hunter of Greenpeace (Greenpeace, 2005), and in broader historical outlook – to propaganda.

The Greenpeace founding member Bob Hunter (Greenpeace, 2005) championed the distribution of the posters so striking that they would encourage urgent action from the public. This idea of 'mindbombing' fits into the logic of tactical media and illustrates how one can use memes for introduction of the alternative discourse and disruption of the hegemony. For Greenpeace, dissemination of the disturbing and expressive visuals pursued the goal of shifting the paradigm and changing conventional ideas of the public. Hunter drew his media strategy on the ideas of Marshall McLuhan whom he praised for the phrase "we live and think mythically". The mindbomb concept means coining a symbolic message of visual strength, something that would express an idea in a nutshell and have an emotional impact. A mindbomb may not incite an immediate reaction in the recipient, but may lay dormant until the time other triggers make it detonate – and inspire the recipient to act for the cause. Emotion and images are two strong tenets of mindbombs, which makes them visible in the oversaturated Internet discourse full of visuals and texts. It is not guaranteed that the audience would interpret the mindbombs as the authors intended – yet it is proven that they are at least potent in attracting attention of the modern crowds to the burning issues (Dauvergne & Neville, 2011).

The idea of visually striking persuasive symbols is not entirely new. It descends from the centuries-old methods of propaganda as the type of communication aimed at manipulating the recipient's opinions and achieving 'a response that furthers the desired intent of the persuader' (Jowett & O'Donnell, 2014: 1–2). Studying memes as the units of persuasion and locating them within propaganda studies unveil their potential in condensing complex issues to clear-cut judgements (see also Karatzogianni et al., 2017). The circulation of politicised memes online increasingly serves as symbolic ideological negotiation; it may not sustain a coherent public debate online, but can precede the formation of communities or substantial discussions (Peters, 2013). The crowds are propagating the emotionally charged meaningful campaigning units among their networks – and the message spreads.

Symbols and codes are bread and butter of propaganda. Bernays (1928: 9) refers to propaganda as 'the conscious and intelligent manipulation of the organised habits and opinions of the masses', while Bryant (1953, as cited in Jowett & O'Donnell, 2014: 49) defines propaganda more generally as an abuse of rhetoric. The speaker misrepresents the truth and offers biased views as facts. Power holders install a system of symbols and representations, suggesting meaning-making practices and associations for the members of a society. People have been persuading each other since the early days of civilisation, employing verbal and non-verbal means, from the monuments and public performances of the preliterate ancient ages (which signified superiority and wealth of the governors) to the press, literature, music and movie industry of the later centuries (Jowett & O'Donnell, 2014: 58–59). Propaganda utilises simple imagery, omissions and misrepresentations; appeals to feelings; and often exploits conventional stereotypes (Pratkanis & Turner, 1996, as cited in Jowett & O'Donnell, 2014: 7). From this viewpoint, memes can qualify as a genre of propaganda, as users utilise them to present a reduced depiction of reality.

The idea that politically active users employ Internet memes as the discursive weapons belongs to the Dutch research-focused design studio Metahaven. These visionaries published a book that identified memes as the ammunition of power struggles (Metahaven, 2013). I expand their concept in my study by identifying meme making and sharing as the principle, practice and product of narrative intervention in hegemonic agenda. Memes allow publics to initiate 'a strike at the level of discourse' (Peters, 2013: para 3). Users generate memes to share an opinion and often to persuade other users; in many cases the mobilisation of Internet memes empowers people to draw attention to the themes that normally stay out of the dominant public sphere (Lessig, 2004: 70–71; Metahaven, 2013; Peters, 2013). Gal et al. (2016) go as far as suggesting that often Internet memes become the norm, and then the imitated versions of memes can either follow the suggested patterns or deviate from them. In this choice of either reaffirming or confronting the ideology of a prototype (the initial text that triggered memes), users engage in 'performative acts' (Gal et al., 2016: 1710). These acts seek to convince or raise awareness. They are means of discursive interventions.

Contemporary meme activists are similar to journalists who negotiate normality and opposition in their everyday practices. As Gasher (2005) duly noted in his research on the news coverage of Iraq war, journalists had to decide what to portray as conventional and right in their reporting; it was up to them to code and find symbols for the progressive and for the socially harmful. They reflected on the public discourse and generated this discourse at the same time. Similarly, the makers and sharers of memes can disrupt the convention and bring a new angle to it. Otherwise, they can equally propagate the mainstream. Through political memes, citizens make aesthetic, cultural and ideological choices; the decisions they make attribute to the development of the liberated expression in cyberspace – and in the society at large.

All in all, these distinct features of Internet memes make them a viable tenet of political persuasion. They can be extremely biased in the way they depict reality and refer to various concepts and people, yet they help individuals to articulate their views and drop a highly visible sparking mindbomb of a doubt, sarcasm, intervention in the mainstream interpretation that can aid to change minds.

Memes as Carnivalesque Resistance

Mikhail Bakhtin's theory on the carnival as a form of dissent helps to further connect artful political communication, media activism and Internet memes. A prominent Russian scholar, philosopher and semiotician, Bakhtin (1984) founded his concept of carnival on the studies of the medieval times and Francois Rabelais, when laughter and the comical were prohibited in order to protect the hegemonic ideology. Bakhtin (1984: 5–8) identifies medieval carnival as a form of dissent, a legal activity that allows for the promotion of alternative discourse, multiplicity of styles and an intentional polyphony ('heteroglossia'). This idea of multiple voices coming together through humour, political and social commentary, links with what Ryan Milner (2013) calls 'polyvocality' of memes. It means that memes can express varied ideological viewpoints, various voices can be heard, and each alteration of a memetic text can unveil various layers of discourse. Carnival is unregulated in its content and people with various grievances or complaints, joys and revels, ideological aspirations or political allegiances may unite in the marketplace of fun, screams and shouts, parody and billingsgate.

Carnival was a forceful mass manifestation of opposition to the official tone of the medieval ecclesiastical and feudal culture. It was distinctive by the extensive use of humour in all forms: ritual spectacles (carnival pageants, shows of the marketplace), comic verbal compositions (parodies, in the Latin and in the vernacular) and various genres of vulgarity (curses, expletives and popular blazons). Parody is an important component of the carnival's 'inside out' rationality: there should be a continuous drift from top to bottom, from front to rear, numerous spoofs and travesties. The utilisation of various forms of humour for political criticism links carnivalesque resistance with the distribution of resistant memes in contemporary digital environments.

Bakhtin (1984) called carnival a utopian realm of community, freedom and egalitarianism. The state in the medieval times responded to these outbursts of free speech and spirit by organising its own spectacles. These shows were praising and reproducing the existing ideology. The officially sponsored feasts (since the performances of the medieval times to mediated spectacles of our days) are always based on the past and reinforce the existing hierarchy, the conventional political and moral values. Not by chance, the notions of heroic past and patriotism often shine in dominant discourses of contemporary oppressive governments (Livshin & Orlov, 2007; Ryzhkov, 2015); they celebrate the current power relations as eternal, embedded in tradition hence indisputable.

Parody is not free from the pressure of hegemony: a peculiar form of resistant commentary as it is, it reinforces convention while opposing it (Denisova, 2017a). Through centuries, parody has been a paradox (Hutcheon, 1994; Dentith, 2000): it establishes the elites in their status of power holder in order to mock them. The digital reiteration of parody preserves many distinct features. It is intertextual and context-sensitive – parody makers need to draw clear links to the political and social environment to make criticism sound and timely (Denisova, 2017a).

Political meme as a joyful vehicle with meaningful content enhances the logic of satire: it is intertextual, disobedient and multi-linked with layers of political and cultural knowledge. The circulation of memes in the digital space creates the carnivalesque vibe and lighthearted resistance: people exchange jokes and share a laugh, comment on society, culture and politics and make arguments on the heated issues. Bakhtin's (1984) carnival theory allows merging two conceptualisations of memes: products of the mundane Internet's folklore, they nonetheless obtain political connotation and rhetoric strength when deployed against political targets. Promoting a discussion of political abuses is challenging in the countries with repressive regimes, and taking part in a street protest can become dangerous (Iosifidis, 2011). In these circumstances, social networks provide a relatively free space for constructing personalised accounts and sharing identities, grievances and messages of resistance (Wellman, 2001; Bennett & Segerberg, 2012).

In restrictive regimes, digital networks often function as the parallel media reality for the dissent public: the discussions in these spaces differ dramatically from the ones of hegemonic media. Those individuals who come to social media to discuss politics utilise memes as personal action frames. By 'frames' here I mean 'interpretive packages' (Gamson & Modigliani, 1989, as cited in Shifman, 2016: 5647). Frames refer to the way individuals see the conditions and events of reality, by the way they highlight and assign meaning to certain aspects and draw definitive connections between things. In the online realm, even the choice of the username and userpic can signify the choice of a personal frame. When a user engages in political deliberation online, he or she employs memes as frames of meaning-making: they present idea in a particular light and encourage particular interpretation.

It is important that online space facilitates anonymity. Participants of the carnival can wear masks, and users of social networks can hide their personal identities behind usernames and carefully constructed online persona. The exchange of memes between members of the online interaction becomes a political practice with low hazards to personal safety and with high capacity to escape censorship. Yet all this liberating communication and communion may remain invisible for the broader publics.

What makes digital carnival different from the original medieval carnival is that it operates under the *implicit* permission of the elites. The medieval carnival was clearly sanctioned by the governors, while digital carnival seems to happen in the free space of open-access social networks. White (1987) and Gluckman (1965) famously confronted the idealistic progressive vision of the carnivalesque resistance: they argued that it serves as the safety valve for the elites. They allow the population to let off steam and then return to the status quo. Digital carnival falls in the same risk.

The other feature that distinguishes a digital carnival of our days is the peril of falling off the observable pubic space. Bakhtin's (1984: 9) medieval carnival was confined to a specific time of the year and was bounded by the limits of time and space; people knew when to expect the feast and where to participate in mass gatherings; they respected the location and closing dates. The contemporary e-carnival (Boje, 2001) is the virtual reincarnation of the carnival in the realm of electronic media. It is not constrained by time, but by the boundaries of cyberspace. Social networks permit resistant users to exchange ideas and opinions, but may have little impact on the offline discourse. Restrictive governments often permit the resilient crowds to linger in the miniature digital spheres, but prevent any attempts for them to enter the political and media mainstream (Denisova, 2016).

Preservation of the digital political carnival in social networks is therefore expedient for the government, as members of the carnivalesque resistance do not normally seek to mobilise for a political protest or overthrow the elites. Carnival is the meaningful activity per se (Bakhtin, 1984; Boje, 2001). It falls short in expanding the joyful critical discussion into further resistant action – similarly, political deliberation via Internet memes has a low mobilisation impact. Nonetheless, the non-obtrusive language of the carnivalesque mockery and prank can serve as mindbombs, if they escape from the 'information ghettoes' and make it to the large media and offline spaces. There were instances when people printed memes on posters and carried them around during street manifestations. This is one of the ways how mindbombs overcome the boundaries of carnivalesque resistance. Yet, without the carnivalesque simmering of ideas and creative frames, the successful mindbombs would not have been born. Despite the shortcomings, even the carnivalesque outbursts of dissent in the digital realm are expedient in preserving the flow of alternative political deliberation among resistant publics.

Capitalist, Artificial, Unethical: Criticism to Memes

Memes are anonymous and highly popular. Commercial companies, politicians and crowdfunding groups don't pass by such an attractive vehicle of promotion. Big corporate players abuse the copyright-free ethos of meme making by appropriating the texts from the Internet for their campaigning (Esteves & Meikle, 2015). Drawing on these cases of capitalist adaptation of memes, critics denounce their role as the colloquial language of Internet users and call them artificial constructs and progenies of advertising deployed to the cyberspace (see, for instance, Morozov, 2013). This aspect limits the capacity of memes to act as mindbombs. On the one hand, one cannot trace the meme's provenance, and this allows memes to escape censorship; but on the other hand, we're not sure how trustworthy the memes are since we don't know who generated them. Morozov (2013) further challenges the authenticity of the popularity of memes by pointing at the platform-based predisposition in their dissemination. Facebook and Twitter, for instance, have the algorithms that pursue and endorse the popular. Many editors of online media shape their texts and news so that they resemble memes (Morozov, 2013). By doing so they try to ride the wave of the Internet virality and promote commercial services and goods.

The distinction between authentic and artificially engineered memes is tremendously blurred indeed (Godwin, 1990; Knobel & Lankshear, 2007). For instance, if a public relations officer deploys a text online and it goes viral with many alterations, one could admit that the meme is born. Regardless of the aims of a meme producer, digital crowds genuinely enjoy the text and propagate it, attributing their own values and meanings to it; from this moment, the text does not belong to the individual, but to the collective discourse. Do we define the meme as authentic or manufactured in this case? Burgess (2008) defends the immunity of memes to manipulation by stating that one cannot predict what textual hooks or signifiers make a meme popular. From her view, any meme that the digital crowds endorse, adjust and distribute in large numbers can be deemed authentic.

Another drawback of the Internet memes is the ethical aspect. Zittrain (2012, as cited in Orcutt, 2012) raises concerns about the ethical side of meme-engineering: a person can be often 'meme'd' without consent, hence he or she is deprived of the basic right to privacy and control over her image and public representation. The example of the Star Wars Kid meme is the yardstick of the ethical debate. A 14-year-old high school student Ghyslain Raza made a video of himself playing with the imaginary lightsaber, the replica of the sword from the *Star Wars* saga. Ghyslain's classmates secretly posted the video online and attracted millions of views. The teenager received plenty of unwanted comments and bullying, had to drop out of school and receive counselling for depression, while the Star Wars Kid video sparked myriads of parodies and remixes (Pfeiffer, 2013). Zittrain (2012, as cited in Orcutt, 2012) argues for devising a digital tool to tag the individuals who occasionally become heroes of the memes, so that they can either endorse or withdraw insulting memes from the public space. In fact, in 2016, the Russian government implemented a ban on memes that insult real identities of individuals. The communication watchdog in Moscow released a 'recommendation' (which literally means a legal reason for a court hearing), which prohibits "using a photo of a public figure to embody a popular internet meme which has nothing to do with the celebrity's personality" (Sampat & Bugorkova, 2015: para 2). Although the measure may help to tackle the issue of unethical memes, it can also significantly curb the flow of memes that critically portray Russian politicians. While the anti-meme initiative targets defamation, the elites can employ it to repress criticism of the government in the shape of parody, as political actors clearly classify as public figures (Brown, 2015).

There are yet so many ways of how users exploit memes. Publics turn to memes for self-expression, entertainment, as well as contribution to the political debates and persuasion of others. People utilise the condensed format of a meme to construct a convincing argument based on simple expressive means. Conclusively, the distinction between understanding memes as the Internet's vernacular, fast-food media, or discursive weapons is considerably vague. From one perspective, memes are an activity and genre of discourse at the same time. Those who champion memes as the common language of the Internet perceive them as the product of participatory culture and the means of polyphonic public discourse; vehicle of commentary and socialisation; and viral unit of culture that people transmit to each other to attain visibility, promote connectedness and spread ideas. From the other perspective, those who distinguish memes as 'discursive weapons' and deliberate mindbombs of persuasion declare that they provide new possibilities for alternative political activism, as users create memorable visual symbols of resistance. In the first case, users utilise memes as the slang of the trivial babble online; in the second, they exploit memes deliberately to influence the discussion.

Memes as an anonymous artful practice can escape surveillance and censorship. Yet, the elites also exploit the Internet and social networks for propaganda and maintenance of hegemony. Therefore, digital space remains a site of struggle between dominant and alternative discourses; it facilitates many instances of political deliberation, yet has many limitations that obscure its promise as the independent information hub and platform for political debate. Memes do not belong to any political party or institution: they are an empty versatile vehicle that people fill with their ideas and agenda; an attractive conduit that helps to affect discourses and minds.

Note

1   I attribute the establishment of this term to the inspiration gained from the brilliant works by Aaron Peters, Metahaven and Ethan Zuckerman.

Bibliography

Bakhtin, M. (1984). *Rabelais and his World* (Vol. 341). Bloomington: Indiana University Press.

Bauckhage, C. (2011). Insights into Internet Memes, *Proceedings of the Fifth International AAAI Conference on Weblogs and Social Media,* 17–21 July, 2011, Barcelona (Spain).

Bennett, W. L. & Segerberg, A. (2012). The logic of connective action. *Information, Communication & Society, 15*(5), 739–768.

Bernays, E. L. (1928). *Propaganda.* Brooklyn: Ig Publishing.

Blank, T. J. (2014). Understanding Folk Culture in the Digital Age: An interview with Folklorist Trevor J. Blank, Interview by Julia Fernandez. *Digital Preservation blog,* 30 June 2014. Available at: http://blogs.loc.gov/digitalpreservation/2014/06/understanding-folk-culture-in-the-digital-age-an-interview-with-folklorist-trevor-j-blank-pt-1/ (last accessed July 2015).

Boje, D. M. (2001). Carnivalesque resistance to global spectacle: A critical postmodern theory of public administration. *Administrative Theory & Praxis, 23*(3), 431–458.

Börzsei, L. K. (2013). Makes a meme instead: A concise history of internet memes. *New Media Studies Magazine, 7.*

Brown, A. (2015). Internet memes mocking Vladimir Putin are now ILLEGAL in Russia, *Express*, 14 April 2015. Available at: www.express.co.uk/life-style/science-technology/570122/Russia-Vladimir-Putin-Memes-Banned-Ban-Remove-Sadimir (last accessed July 2015).

Burgess, J. (2008). All your chocolate rain are belong to us. Viral Video, YouTube and the dynamics of participatory culture. In Lovink, G. & Niederer, S. (eds.) *Video Vortex Reader: Responses to YouTube*. Amsterdam: Institute of Network Cultures, 101–109.

Dauvergne, P. & Neville, K. J. (2011). Mindbombs of right and wrong: Cycles of contention in the activist campaign to stop Canada's seal hunt. *Environmental Politics, 20*(2), 192–209.

Davison, P. (2012). The language of internet memes. In Mandiberg, M. (ed.) *The Social Media Reader*, 120–134. Available at: https://archive.org/stream/TheSocialMediaReader/Mandiberg-theSocialMediaReader-cc-by-sa-nc_djvu.txt (last accessed July 2015).

Denisova, A. (2016). Memes, not her health, could cost Hillary Clinton the US presidential race, *Independent*, 12 September. Available online at: www.independent.co.uk/voices/hillary-clinton-health-pneumonia-political-memes-a7238581.html (last accessed August 2017).

Denisova, A. (2017a). Parody microbloggers as chroniclers and commentators on Russian political reality. *Demokratizatsiya: The Journal of Post-Soviet Democratization, 25*(1), 23–41.

Denisova, A. (2017b). People Don't Want Politics, They Want 'Covfefe', *HuffPost*, 1 June. Available online at: www.huffingtonpost.co.uk/anastasia-denisova/covfefe_b_16909400.html (last accessed August 2017).

Dentith, S. (2000). *Parody*. New York: Taylor & Francis.

Esteves, V. & Meikle, G. (2015). "Look @ this fukken doge": Internet memes and remix cultures. In *The Routledge Companion to Alternative and Community Media*. New York: Routledge, 561–570.

Furie, M. (2016). Pepe the Frog's creator: I'm reclaiming him. He was never about hate. *Time*, 13 October. Available at: http://time.com/4530128/pepe-the-frog-creator-hate-symbol/ (last accessed August 2017).

Gal, N., Shifman, L. & Kampf, Z. (2016). "It gets better": Internet memes and the construction of collective identity. *New Media & Society, 18*(8), 1698–1714.

Gasher, M. (2005). Might makes right: News reportage as discursive weapon in the war in Iraq. In Artz, L. & Kamalipour, Y. R. (eds.) *Bring 'Em On: Media and Politics in the Iraq War*. Lanham: Rowman & Littlefield Publishers, 209–225.

Gauntlett, D. (2011). *Making is Connecting: The Social Meaning of Creativity, from DIY and Knitting to YouTube and Web 2.0*. London: Polity Press.

Gee, J. (2004). *Situated Language and Learning: A Critique of Traditional Schooling*. New York: Routledge.

Gluckman, M. (1965). *Custom and Conflict in Africa*. Oxford: Blackwell.

Godwin, M. (1990). Meme, Counter-Meme, *The Wired*. Available at: http://archive.wired.com/wired/archive/2.10/godwin.if_pr.html (last accessed March 2015).

Greenpeace. (2005). *Bob Hunter 1941–2005. Greenpeace Founding Member Dead at 63*. 2 May 2005. Available at: www.greenpeace.org/international/en/news/features/bob-hunter (last accessed August 2016).

Howard, R. G. (2014). Born Digital Folklore and the Vernacular Web: An Interview with Robert Glenn Howard, Interview by Trevor Owens, *Digital Preservation blog*, 22 February 2013. Available at: http://blogs.loc.gov/digitalpreservation/2013/02/born-digital-folklore-and-the-vernacular-web-an-interview-with-robert-glenn-howard/?loclr=blogsig (last accessed July 2015).

Hutcheon, L. (1994). *Irony's Edge: The Theory and Politics of Irony*. London: Routledge, 3–4; 28–34.

Iosifidis, P. (2011). *Global Media and Communication Policy*. London: Palgrave Macmillan, 23–44.

Jowett, G. S. & O'Donnell, V. (2014). *Propaganda & Persuasion*. Newbury Park: Sage Publications.

Juris, J. S. (2012). Reflections on #Occupy everywhere: Social media, public space, and emerging logics of aggregation. *American Ethnologist, 39*(2), 259–279.

Karatzogianni, A., Miazhevich, G. & Denisova, A. (2017). A comparative cyberconflict analysis of digital activism across Post-Soviet Countries. *Comparative Sociology, 16*(1), 102–126.

Knobel, M. & Lankshear, C. (2007). Online memes, affinities and cultural production. In Knobel., M. & Lankshear, C. (eds.) *A New Literacies Sampler*. New York: Peter Lang, 199–227.

KnowYourMeme. (2017). *Feels Good Man*. Original post by Tony Dapena, updated by SabrinaTibbets. Available at: http://knowyourmeme.com/memes/feels-good-man (last accessed August 2017).

Lessig, L. (2004). *Free Culture: How Big Media Uses Technology and the Law to Lock Down Culture and Control Creativity*. New York: Penguin.

Livshin, A. & Orlov, I. (2007). *Sovetskaya Propaganda v Gody VOV: Kommunikatsii Ubezhdeniya i Mobilizatsionnyie Mekhanismy*. Moscow: Moscow State University.

Lysenka L. N. (2017). Internet memes in youth communication. *Vestnik SPbSU. Sociology, 10*(4), 410–424.

Meikle, G. (2010). Intercreativity: Mapping online activism. In Hunsinger, J., Klastrup, L. & Allen, M. M. (eds.) *International Handbook of Internet Research*. Dordrecht: Springer Netherlands, 363–377.

Meikle, G. (2014). Social media, visibility, and activism: The Kony 2012 Campaign. In Ratto, M. & Boler, M. (eds.) *DIY Citizenship: Critical Making and Social Media*. Cambridge: MIT Press, 373–384.

Meikle, G. & Young, S. (2012). *Media Convergence – Networked Digital Media in Everyday Life*. Basingstoke: Palgrave Macmillan.

Metahaven. (2013). *Can jokes bring down governments? memes, design, politics*. Moscow: Strelka Press.

Milner, R. M. (2013). Media Lingua Franca: Fixity, Novelty, and Vernacular Creativity in Internet Memes. *Selected Papers of Internet Research*, 3.

Milner, R. M. (2016). *The World Made Meme: Public Conversations and Participatory Media*. Cambridge: MIT Press.

Morozov, E. (2013). The Meme Hustler, *The Baffler*, 22. Available at: www.thebaffler.com/salvos/the-meme-hustler (last accessed July 2015).

Nahon, K. & Hemsley, J. (2013). *Going Viral*. Cambridge: Polity.

Orcutt, M. (2012). Could Technology Tame the Internet Meme? *MIT Technology Review*, 4 May 2012. Available at: www.technologyreview.com/

view/427850/could-technology-tame-the-internet-meme/ (last accessed July 2015).

Papacharissi, Z., Lashley, M. C. & Creech, B. (2017). Voices for a new vernacular: A forum on digital storytelling Interview with Zizi Papacharissi. *International Journal of Communication, 11*, Forum, 1069–1073.

Peters, A. J. (2013). Criticize the Old World in Content and Advocate a New One in Form. Metahaven in Conversation with Aaron Peters, Interview by Metahaven, *Metahaven Tumblr*, 14 April 2013. Available at: http://mthvn. tumblr.com/post/47975414145/aaronpetersmetahaven (last accessed June 2015).

Pfeiffer, E. (2013). 10 Years Later, 'Star Wars Kid' Speaks, *Yahoo! News The Slideshow*, 10 May 2013. Available at: http://news.yahoo.com/blogs/ sideshow/10-years-later-star-wars-kid-speaks-231310357.html (last accessed July 2015).

Ryzhkov, V. (2015). Kremlin doesn't have monopoly on patriotism, *The Moscow Times*, 9 April 2015. Available at: www.themoscowtimes.com/opinion/article/ kremlin-doesnt-have-monopoly-on-patriotism/518902.html (last accessed August 2015).

Sampat, R. & Bugorkova, O. (2015). Russia's (non) war on memes? *BBC Trending*, 16 April 2015. Available at: www.bbc.co.uk/news/blogs-trending-32302645 (last accessed July 2015).

Shifman, L. (2011). An anatomy of a YouTube meme, *New Media & Society, 14*(2), 187–203. Available at: http://nms.sagepub.com/content/14/2/187.short (last accessed April 2013).

Shifman, L. (2016). Cross-cultural comparisons of user-generated content: An analytical framework. *International Journal of Communication, 10*, 5644–5663.

Wellman, B. (2001). Physical place and cyberplace: The rise of personalized networking. *International Journal of Urban and Regional Research, 28*(2), 227–252.

White, A. (1987). The Struggle Over Bakhtin: Fraternal Reply to Robert Young. *Cultural Critique, 8*, 217–241.

Wittgenstein, L. (1961). *Tractatus Logico-Philosophicus* (trans. Pears and McGuinness).

Zuckerman, E. (2015). Cute cats to the rescue? Participatory media and political expression. In: Allen, D. & Light, J. S. (eds.) *From Voice to Influence: Understanding Citizenship in a Digital Age*. Chicago: The University of Chicago Press, 131–154.

4   Globalisation and Memes

Dependence of memes on the local context: when ideology and culture set the tone

Memes are not new – they clearly borrow from the tradition of political cartoon, satirical communication, poster art and advertisement, among other influences. The sources and strength of the provenance vary between countries. Laineste and Voolaid (2017) found that the humour in memes creates intertextual references that rely on both cultural heritage of the local society and on the global cultural references. This twofold nature proves that, despite being a global phenomenon of communication, memes nonetheless bear a special local value that depends on regional culture and tradition.

Who Does Your Country Hate? Why Domestic Culture and Political Tradition Have Much Influence on the Appeal of Memes

As an example, the Russian use of memes lays in close relation to the century-long tradition of elaborate satire. As the country was living under authoritarian regime as the Soviet Union for the length of over seven decades, population got used to the life in intense propaganda and, therefore, flourishing clandestine alt-communication. Tongue-in-cheek ironic messages prevailed in the Soviet non-hegemonic discourse for the whole 20th century. During the Communist governance, allegory and metaphorical humour filled the void for liberal media. It could be argued, for the fairness, that even before the Communist times, in the tsar Russia, opposition had often found itself in information ghettoes and relied on satire and pamphlets – yet only in the USSR, the ironic political resistance reached its swoosh shape.

In the Russian case, the employment of catchphrases, sharp images and satirical texts in public rhetoric is rooted not only in advertising and culture jamming but also in the more local tradition of Soviet modernism (Livshin & Orlov, 2007). After the First World War and the fall of the Russian empire, the new Soviet government promoted the use of laconic, sharp and expressive language in the public media. It borrowed the elements of artistic expression of modernism and relied on the sharp poetry of the likes of Vladimir Mayakovsky, visual laconism of Alexander Rodchenko's photography and newly emerging advertising (Livshin & Orlov, 2007). The government hired poets and artists to create posters, cartoons, newspapers and bulletins for the masses (for instance, the renowned poet Vladimir Mayakovsky was responsible for the propaganda bulletin Okna Rosta (Livshin & Orlov, 2007)).

Satirical magazines were among the very few outlets that permitted criticism of the state, although in a very shallow and lighthearted manner. Such publications as Krokodil (The Crocodile) were approved by the state propaganda – they released cartoons that mocked social vices, low-level bureaucracy and occasionally criticised the West as the embodiment of moral decline and exploitative capitalism (Nelson, 1949; Gamson & Stuart, 1992). Government would approve of the professional cartoonists who worked in the satirical magazines. Their – relatively loyal – cartoons became the official aesthetic culture of the USSR (Nelson, 1949).

Nonetheless, sometimes these state-permitted bits of criticism featured more liberal commentary than was intended by propaganda. Critical Soviet citizens appreciated cartoons for the occasional bursts of free comment on politics and corruption, even on a very superficial and seemingly toothless level of disagreement (Gamson & Stuart, 1992). The visual language of magazine cartoons bears much resemblance to many formats of the present-day Internet memes: it offers a condensed and often simplified representation of a complex situation or event and demands the contextual awareness of the audience (Gamson & Stuart, 1992). In order to interpret a cartoon (similar to interpreting a meme), one has to decode the hints and allusions that the author is making. Besides, cartoons are biased and, similar to memes, advocate a specific viewpoint; they often invite the audience to ridicule a person, a trait or an event.

The important feature of the satire of the old days was the emotional reaction it would trigger: a bit of angst, or laugh, or a shiver of despair. The Soviet government was also aware of the power of emotions in spreading the message. It exploited the visual language of posters and ridiculed figures; bristly slogans and claims.

Here, we need to introduce a short description of the jump in propaganda science of the Soviets in the beginning of the last century, and the role of the Bolsheviks in it. It will inform our understanding of the reasons and psychological triggers that make condensed, meme-like emotional communication powerful in politics.

Russian propaganda of the first decades of the 20th century was a losing enterprise. The First World War was destroying the country, and the

Tsar struggled to boost the morale of the exhausted troops. The government released lengthy and verbose leaflets with the appeal to patriotic feelings of the army. The problem was that most of the mobilised soldiers were coming from uneducated peasants and could not read, never mind digging the meaning from the convoluted expressions of the aristocratic spin doctors. The other issue with the failure of Tsar propaganda was the lack of strong emotion in the message.

Only by the time of the Second World War, the Communist government that overthrew the Tsar, realised the importance of hatred towards the enemy as the mobilising force (see also Lasswell, 1995, on the power of hatred mobilisation). The Soviet propaganda acknowledged the need to target narrative against a certain actor, nation or vice. The dichotomy of good and evil, aggressors and defenders became crucial to conceal the national wrongdoings. It directed public rage at the external targets (Astashov, 2012).

The Soviet Post-Second World War indoctrination appealed to many emotions, and yet hatred was still the strongest and most proliferate one in the narratives on resistance and opposition (Astashov, 2012).

Contemporary pro-government memes in the Russian political discourse online borrow many traits of the aggressive Soviet propaganda: they aim to denigrate opposition and direct the rage of the mainstream public against critics of the state (Volchek & Sindelar, 2015).

Global Meme Formats

Memes form the type of storytelling that entangles recognisable traditional patterns and motifs, but also accepts variation and adaptive modification (Blank, 2014). Despite local peculiarities and language differences, memes employ roughly the same range of main formats worldwide. Some other formats may be popular regionally, but never enter the pantheon of global meme formats. In this section, I talk about the most popular meme types of the international English-speaking social media and add the exclusive classification of the emerging formats from the Russian-speaking Internet.

Memes preserve a number of highly recognisable configurations that may vary by colour, font, composition of elements, vocabulary, but retain trademark features of the original style. According to meme analysts (Davison, 2012; Börzsei, 2013; Milner, 2013), the pervasively used global outlines are Demotivator, Image Macro, Photoshopped Image, LOLCats, Advice Animals and Comic. Local formats that I spotted in the Russian-language research on memes also include Twisted Map and Reworked Cartoon.

Demotivator consists of a black frame exposing an image and text in white capitals. It originates from the satirical posters produced by Despair, Inc. since 1998: the company ridiculed inspirational posters

Figure 4.1 Example of a Demotivator meme.

of the 1990s and manufactured parody versions where the sceptical, mocking text contradicted the solemnity of the image and title. Once these posters had spread over the Internet and penetrated meme aggregating platforms such as 4chan, the meme format was born (Knowyourmeme, 2009). Nowadays, Internet users have almost forgotten the initial composition of a Demotivator; currently, they utilise the layout of a familiar black frame to comment on any subject. Normally, the text is in bigger white capitals and second-line text is in smaller white capitals. Together with the image, they create a comic effect by their conflict (Figure 4.1).

Image Macro is the image with text superimposed; normally, it is formatted in white capitals with black borders and in Impact font (Börzsei, 2013), although any captioned image can broadly qualify for Image Macro. Sometimes Image Macro is used instead of emoticons to express the emotions and reactions of users (Knowyourmeme, 2015) (Figure 4.2).

Photoshopped Image is vaguely any image that has been doctored to create a statement without added text (Milner, 2013). It often appears in close connection with Image Macro, as Photoshopped Images are likely to become elements of Image Macro memes (Figure 4.3).

Figure 4.2 Example of an Image Macro meme.

Figure 4.3 Example of a Photoshopped Image meme.

Advice Animals is the family of memes that originated from the pop-ular Advice Dog meme. They depict a cutout of the animal or its head placed over the generic, colour-wheel or rainbow-coloured background, with text in white pasted above and below the animal. The original

Figure 4.4 Example of an Advice Animals meme.

Advice Dog meme was posted on the fan site of the video game Mario the Mushroom Kingdom. One of the users asked for advice on having his first kiss, and among the replies was the image of the dog's head over the colour-wheel background and a comment "Just do it, man" (Börzsei, 2013). The humorous effect with the Advice Animals series is expected due to the absurd conjunction of the advice with an animal giving it (Davison, 2012). However, lately users have almost abandoned the original textual structure of an advice. They now superimpose all kinds of jokes around the animals' faces. The colour-wheel background is therefore simply used to demarcate a meme and attract attention (Figure 4.4).

LOLCats owe their popularity to the meme aggregator 4Chan that dedicated a specific thread to cat pictures and named it Caturday in 2006 (Börzsei, 2013). The most popular LOLCats site *I Can Haz Cheezburger?*, launched in 2007, was sold for two million dollars and its owner Ben Huh established the Cheezburger network consisting of 75 employees who sustain meme-focused aggregators and forums (knowyourmeme, memefactory, thememebase). The LOLCats meme is normally an Image Macro with an entertaining or charming photo of a cat with the caption written in Internet slang (Figure 4.5).

Comics is the closest genre to the traditional drawn stories in the magazines – cartoons – and bears many features of storytelling: we can see subjects, sequence of events and their outcomes. Despite this seeming completeness of the narrative, actions are not as important in these memes as characters (Börzsei, 2013). Many principal heroes of comic memes have turned iconic: the reproduction of their signature reactions, deeds and catchphrases make the core of the meme's virality. In other cases, comics place famous people in unusual circumstances and depict

Figure 4.5 Example of a LOLCat meme.

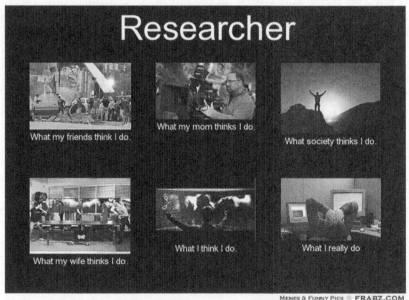

Figure 4.6 Example of a Comics meme.

their imagined reactions or actions. Comics may also include juxtaposition of expectations and reality: the popular meme 'How my parents see me' is based on these rules (Figure 4.6).

Reworked Cartoon is similar to Comics, yet has a closer connection to the tradition of political cartoon in newspapers. This format has been quite present in the Russian political memes. It is not, though, limited to the Russian memetic landscape and can also be seen in abundance in the English-language Internet. It normally builds on the drawing by – most likely – a professional artist, often a cartoonist of an established media outlet. Meme makers draw tiny adjustments atop of the picture or change the text in the cartoon; they may also add a sarcastic tag line to emphasise the meaning or tweak it. Interestingly, the amateur-drawn elements are clearly seen as addition on the body of the well-executed cartoon. This feature, however, only points to the cooperative reworking of the image and further links to the collective nature of the digital meme making. Cartoon authors may not be happy with their cartoons being hijacked, however, users keep appropriating professional cartoons on a large scale. People create or borrow texts and then rework them to their preference, while losing any link with the authorship. Reworked Cartoon blurs the boundaries between the professional and amateur creation. If you like poetic metaphors (like I do), you may see this meme genre as the vivacious and impudent graffiti on the established city wall (Figure 4.7).

Twisted Map is the genre that emerged in the geopolitical debates of the Internet users. In the Russian case, meme makers mobilise this

Figure 4.7 Example of a Reworked Cartoon meme.

format when they need to boast of the vast territory of Russia or claim the right for the lands that used to belong to this country (or could potentially be conquered to expand the territory). Users normally turn to the classic map – like the one you would find in a geographic atlas – and add colour highlights to discuss specific regions or lands. People sometimes place a map in the Demotivator frame to add a satirical commentary. In the Russian case, this format is often used to remind of the imperial ambition of Russia or invoke nostalgic feelings about the Soviet Union (Figure 4.8).

A global Internet darling, memes spread across platforms and borders. Digitally savvy publics are enjoying memes as sights of satirical resistance, vehicles of creative commentary and quick reactions to the immediate agenda. Memes borrow inspiration from a multitude of cultural codes and contexts, which span from popular culture to the ideological and cultural tradition of each particular country.

There can be many more emerging genres and subgenres. The total classification is beyond the scope of this chapter and beyond the scope of any fixed research. As an emerging, ever-changing format of viral communication as memes are, they keep mutating with the flows of ideas and popular visual formats of advertisement and popular culture. The minds

Figure 4.8 Example of a Twisted Map meme.

behind the website KnowYourMeme.com (est. 2008) do a commendable job in trying to collect, archive and classify the trending memes of the Internet sphere.

Whilst the research on global and local features of memes is still in its infancy, this book can confidently claim that memes have this capacity of connecting global discourses with the local agenda. The proliferation of a particular top list of main formats and modes of references that are being used across the planet proves this inherent interconnection.

Bibliography

Astashov, A. (2012). *Propaganda na Russkom Fronte v Gody Pervoy Mirovoy Voyny [Propaganda at the Russian Front in the Years of the First World War]*. Moscow: Spetskniga.

Blank, T. J. (2014). Understanding Folk Culture in the Digital Age: An Interview with Folklorist Trevor J. Blank, Interview by Julia Fernandez, *Digital Preservation blog*, 30 June 2014. Available at: http://blogs.loc.gov/digitalpreservation/2014/06/understanding-folk-culture-in-the-digital-age-an-interview-with-folklorist-trevor-j-blank-pt-1/ (last accessed July 2015).

Börzsei, L. K. (2013). Makes a meme instead: A concise history of internet memes. *New Media Studies Magazine*, 7.

Davison, P. (2012). The language of internet memes. In Mandiberg, M. (ed.) *The Social Media Reader*, 120–134. Available at: https://archive.org/stream/TheSocialMediaReader/Mandiberg-theSocialMediaReader-cc-by-sa-nc_djvu.txt (last accessed July 2015).

Gamson, W. A. & Stuart, D. (1992, March). Media discourse as a symbolic contest: The bomb in political cartoons. *Sociological Forum*, 7(1), 55–86.

Knowyourmeme. (2009). *Demotivational Posters*. Available at: http://knowyourmeme.com/memes/demotivational-posters (last accessed August 2018).

Laineste, L. & Voolaid, P. (2017). Laughing across borders: Intertextuality of internet memes. *The European Journal of Humour Research*, 4(4), 26–49.

Lasswell, H. D. (1995). *Propaganda (Main Trends of the Modern World)*. Houndmills, Basingstoke: Macmillans.

Livshin, A. & Orlov, I. (2007). *Sovetskaya Propaganda v Gody VOV: Kommunikatsii Ubezhdeniya i Mobilizatsionnyie Mekhanismy*. Moscow: Moscow State University.

Milner, R. M. (2013). Media Lingua Franca: Fixity, Novelty, and Vernacular Creativity in Internet Memes. *Selected Papers of Internet Research*, 3.

Nelson, W. (Ed.). (1949). *Out of the Crocodile's Mouth: Russian Cartoons about the United States from "Krokodil," Moscow's Humor Magazine*. Washington: Public Affairs Press.

Volchek, D. & Sindelar, D. (2015). One Professional Russian Troll Tells All, *Radio Free Europe/ Radio Liberty*, 25 March 2015. Available online at: www.rferl.org/content/how-to-guide-russian-trolling-trolls/26919999.html (last accessed April 2015).

5 Russian Resistance and Propaganda through Memes in the 2010s

Russian society and media: context of the 2010s. Main tenets of national identity. History of activism and media development. Limitations on free speech over a decade. The usage of social media for political persuasion.

Memes as Tools of Propaganda, Dissent and Alternative Digital Activism in the Russian-language Twitter. Results of the analysis of memes and interviews with meme makers.

Meme metamorphosis. How memes mutate and 'change sides' while they travel.

Russian Society and Media: Context of the 2010s

The Russian media environment of the 2010s has become a turbulent space for the deliberation of alternative political discourses. By the beginning of the decade, the state had successfully shut down or curbed the influence of leading independent media that used to hold the elites to account. Liberal publics have largely relocated to social networks and various Internet media as the nonconventional sources of information, opinion and political ideas.

This section looks at the historical context to understand the formation of the Russian national and media identity, the country's complex cultural codes and relationship with its immediate geographical members; the rise of control over free speech since the 1990s until the present day. The chapter also looks at the important themes of the Russian resistant Twitter users and asks whether they were able to create their own sustainable discourse or had to counteract to the themes of the media mainstream.

Russia's Liberal Resistant Public 1990–2010s. From Backyard Anarchists to the iPhone Romantics

The civil society of modern Russia has been forming in turbulence since the fall of the USSR. The 1990s were a time of political, cultural and social shift. Citizens experienced a number of immensely chaotic, highly criminalised and uncontrolled structural, power and organizational changes (Robertson, 2012). Soviet structures were collapsing, and new systems were still to be built, hence most of the protest activism of that time was not directed at high-scale changes, but rather concerned specific local issues. The post-Soviet government witnessed hunger strikes and blockades of roads and railways in campaigns on unpaid wages (Robertson, 2012).

Gradual development of social institutions throughout the 1990s along with the economic prosperity of the early days of the millennium secured high approval rating for the government in the 2000s. It also facilitated the rise of Vladimir Putin to power; first as a prime minister, then president of the country (Oliker et al., 2009; Robertson, 2012). The administration of Vladimir Putin has notably promoted a very specific negative labelling of the 1990s in the popular media discourse. The elites have continuously referred to the early years of young Russia as 'the wild 1990s' ('лихие 1990-е') (Parfenov, 2010). This widely used idiom was coined in the early 2000s and is often opposed to 'the fat 2000s' (or 'the gorged 2000s'). This is particularly interesting as the stigmatisation of 'the lawless 1990s' largely contributed to the praise of political and economic stability of Putin's Russia in the 2000s (Parfenov, 2010; Eggert, 2015).

The 2000s brought a remarkable yet barely visible advancement in the formation of politically active, liberally minded public (see Lipman & McFaul, 2010). The protest activity in Russia of that period largely qualifies as 'NIMBY' ('Not In My Back Yard') rallies: people were more likely to participate in activism protecting their essential needs or immediate environment rather than advance abstract political notions and ideologies (Clement, 2012). Among the most notable cases of civil uprising in between the mid-2000s and mid-2010s are the mobilisation against the construction of an ugly oil company office tower that would have ruined the skyline of St Petersburg, the delays of payments for factory workers in Rubtsovsk, the destruction of a forest for a highway in the satellite town of Moscow, the corruption of the administration of the northern town of Arkhangelsk and so forth.

By the early 2010s, Russian protest activities had considerably changed in their tone and range of claims: from local issue-based, direct action protests, they evolved to major political 'democratic' style marches and gatherings with demands to curb corruption (Clement, 2012; Robertson, 2012). Several studies (Gladarev, 2012: 24;

Robertson, 2012) point to the increasing level of theatricality in recent mobilisations, when participants exploited mockery, parody and street theatre to support their claims. Gladarev (2012: 24) refers to the rise of artful dissent practices as glorious 'celebration' of the emerging civil society. Many participants of recent Russian liberal mobilisations were not encouraging hatred, but irony towards their political targets. They spread humorous texts and posters; the inclination of the protesters towards more humour and performative practices fits in the globally experienced 'need for alternative repertoires for political expression and mobilisation' (Norris, 2007: 641). At the local level, it may have also signified the end of fear of the government among the Russian public (Asmolov, 2012).

Self-organisation has become another prominent feature of the Russian protest mobilisations between the mid-2000s and early 2010s. The wide spread of ubiquitous Internet technology enabled citizens to distribute information online and coordinate in social networks, bypassing traditional media and established political and civil institutions (Clement, 2012). Dmitriev (2012) draws an example of a local mayoral election in the small Russian town of Chernogolovka, where citizens employed digital space to form 'networked structures'. Local entrepreneurs largely participated in the online discussions and supported civil activity – as a result, an independent candidate won the elections, largely due to this digital support.

The development of the Russian civil society corresponds to Dahlgren's (2006: 273) concept of citizenship being 'a question of learning by doing'. The steady transformation of the local civic activists into national opposition figures has become a notable pattern of the Russian political activism (Clement, 2012).

The biggest protest mobilisation of the decade erupted in December 2011 and followed the Parliament elections. Excited (though rather freezing) Russians called it 'snow revolution'. Dozens of thousands of people joined rallies in Moscow, St Petersburg and other big cities to voice their criticism of the corrupt government and demand fair elections. As Robertson (2012) points out, the name 'snow revolution' was coined as a bitter metaphor: snow is known to come unexpectedly and melt with the spring. The same was said about the first attempt of politicised Russia to express itself – the massive protests were called 'unexpected' by the press and decreased when the spring came. Since the first widely attended manifestations in February and March 2012, protest activity has declined. By May 2012, the hopes of the protesters faded as the extensively criticised Vladimir Putin was elected President for yet another term. Nonetheless, the rise of civil activism in the 2010s signified a milestone of a decade-long historical development. By 2011, 'the organizational and cultural apparatus for large-scale protests was already in place' (Robertson, 2012: 2).

There are still debates on the social class of the protesters. Several bloggers and later pro-government media rushed to call the protests of 2011–2012 'Mink Revolution' (Sobchak, 2012) due to the high involvement of middle and upper-middle class citizens. Robertson (2012: 4) utilised the term 'urban intelligentsia' to describe the politically aware educated Muscovites and Petersburgers, while Kiriya (2012) refers to this newly distinguished stratum as 'angry urbanites' or 'angry townspeople'. Despite the claims of the hegemonic media, the protests were mostly fuelled by middle-class professionals, students and people in early managerial positions (Levada-Centre, 2011). To support this, Leon Aron (2012) suggests that traditionally and historically, one's belonging to the middle class in Russia is defined not as much by income, but education and occupation. In accordance with these localised criteria, the 2011 protest rallies in Moscow mostly attracted middle-class participants: 70% had a college degree or higher, and 13% were more than halfway through college.

Many researchers link the rise of social protest with the era of economic prosperity in Russia. The classic paradigm of political development in post-industrial society (Lipset, 1960; Huntington, 1968; Bell, 1976; Fukuyama, 2006) enlightens the globally recognised patterns in the local Russian case. After the period of economic prosperity, the middle class expands rapidly and demands not only personal freedom and rights, but also liberty and voice in governing their countries. Aron (2012) points to Spain, Portugal and Greece of the 1970s, South Korea and Taiwan of the 1980s as the examples of the protests that the middle class drives against the authoritarian government.

Economic opulence as a paradoxical trigger of social unrest was thoroughly analysed over a century ago by the French political thinker Alexis De Tocqueville (1856, see 2001 English translation, as cited in Aron, 2012: 3). He utilised the example of the 1700s in France, when stable increase of wealth did not prevent the revolution, but promoted the spirit of rebellion. The 'De Tocquevillian paradox' has recently been seen in the Arab Spring, when the quickly developing economy of Tunisia did not avert the country's revolution (see Aron, 2012). The De Tocquevillian paradox means that **revolutions can grow not only out of despair, but also out of hope**: 'the mere fact that certain abuses have been remedied draws attention to the others and they appear more galling; people may suffer less, but their sensibility is exacerbated' (De Tocqueville, 2001, as cited in Aron, 2012: 3).

Defining Russian resistant publics in Western political terms is a challenging task. Kullberg and Zimmerman (1999) explain that the politically active Russian citizens tend to define their political identity in 'post-communist' terms, which means that they oppose themselves to the governments they do not support, as well as to the political regimes of the past. By doing so, they explicitly demonstrate disapproval of certain identities, but fail to clearly outline the political identity that they can relate to. Many educated Russians who took part in civil activism praise the freedom of speech, free market economy, resistance to the state oppression and manipulation (Robertson, 2012). At the same time, they are sceptical about the existing oppositional parties and express doubts about the affiliation with any established political identity. For the purposes of this book, I have used 'resistant publics', 'opposition', 'anti-Kremlin' and 'anti-government publics' as interchangeable terms that define those citizens who oppose the government or criticise corruption or propaganda. Although I acknowledge that 'resistance' and 'opposition' bear varying connotations, I nonetheless use them as synonyms for the Russian case.

The other issue that challenges the self-identification of the Russian resistant publics is the low number of popular oppositional parties in the political landscape of the 2010s (Robertson, 2012). As people are unable to associate their views with those of any prominent political figures, the resistant publics in Russia can therefore be distinguished as ambiguously 'anti-Kremlin' or 'anti-government' crowds. This classification is limited as it obscures the inner political differences between various parts of the resistant audience (Clement, 2012). Nonetheless, in this book, I have classified those resistant users who have been vocally opposing the elites as 'oppositional crowds' or 'resistant publics'. There can be many more people who silently disagree with the leader's policies and would vote for an alternative candidate. However, only those who visibly criticise the elites in the public realm (street protests, social networks or traditional media) were included in this research.

Post-Soviet Politics, the Crimean Crisis and the 'Polite People' Meme

While the resistant public was still developing its own way of expressing political criticism and participating in politics, the Crimean crisis of 2014 brought major challenges to the self-actualisation of this cluster of the society.

The Crimean crisis of 2014 refers to the annexation of the Ukrainian peninsula of Crimea and its subsequent inclusion in the Russian territory. This event was propelled by the domestic struggles in Ukraine and international confrontation over the influence in this country among Russia and the European Union (EU). In the autumn of 2013, Ukraine was in the middle of negotiations with the EU, which were seen as a spin from the cooperation with Russia (BBC, 2014b). Yet, at the last moment the Ukrainian government led by President Viktor Yanukovich suddenly dropped the agreement on closer trade ties with the EU (BBC, 2013) and thus voted allegiance to Moscow. Massive public protests were sparked, with 100,000 people gathering in the middle of the Ukrainian capital. Protesters occupied the main square called Maidan Nezalezhnosti, and 'Maidan' soon became a globally recognised brand name for the anti-government rallies in Ukraine (Heintz, 2013). By February 2014, the situation on Maidan got out of control, 88 people died over 48 hours in clashes between protesters and police, and president Yanukovich was forced to sign a compromise deal with opposition leaders. The parliament vowed to remove him, and Yanukovich fled to Russia (BBC, 2014b).

The Russian government accused the US and EU of orchestrating a coup in Ukraine (Reuters, 2014). By the end of February 2014, unidentified gunmen arrived at the Ukrainian peninsula of Crimea, the region known for its highest numbers of the ethnic Russian majority. Russian media reported numerous cases of neo-Nazi unrests and threats to the ethnic Russians in Ukraine (Harding, 2014). On the 1st of March 2014, the Russian parliament approved Vladimir Putin's request to use power to protect Russian interests in Ukraine (BBC, 2014b). Meanwhile, Russia kept denying any connection with the armed uniformed forces in Crimea. Russian television was assuring the audience that Crimean people organised the self-defence groups to resist the European and American pressure, preserve independence of the peninsula and keep ties with Russia (Shevchenko, 2014). Nonetheless, these alleged 'self-defence troops' appeared in combat uniform and held professional guns, which cast doubt on the spontaneous and independent character of this mobilisation. The Russian government denied having sent any professional troops to Crimea and argued that if local people wanted to gather in the name of Russia, it was solely their own will. Pro-Kremlin media and social media users utilised many euphemisms in their coverage of the uniformed gunmen, including 'volunteers' and 'self-defence forces' (Ria, 2015); there were bloggers who joked that these troops were 'tourists', others referred to them as 'little green men' (Shevchenko, 2014).

The public debate about the unidentified pro-Russian gunmen in Crimea became a watershed in the communication between loyal and resistant publics. Liberal social media users questioned the government's claims and suggested that these troops belonged to the Russian army (Meduza, 2015). At the same time, the pro-Kremlin bloggers advanced the idea that the gunmen served Russian interests voluntarily; they brought in the nickname 'polite people' as the catchy yet ambiguous title for the troops in question (Shevchenko, 2014).

Supported by the presence of the 'polite' gunmen, the pro-Russian leadership of Crimea voted to abandon Ukraine and announced the referendum on the 16th of March. Despite objections from the West, the referendum took place and resulted in a 97% vote in favour of joining

Russia. The EU and the US imposed a number of sanctions against a list of Russian officials. Russia officially accepted Crimea into its territory on the 18th of March (BBC, 2014b).

Starting from April 2014, new waves of anti-government protests shattered Ukraine, this time against the new administration. The most violent clashes took place in the historically loyal to Russia Eastern Ukraine. The evolving conflict among pro-Russian separatists and government forces advanced in a war with the mass exploitation of armoury and military machinery. Throughout 2014, Russia kept denying its military presence in various parts of Ukraine, claiming that armed forces were independent pro-Russian rebels. Tension with the West increased, as the EU and the US expanded their sanctions on trade with Russia. Russia replied with its own sanctions and banned almost all agricultural products from Europe and other countries that supported restrictions against Russia. As a result, Russian citizens were left without their Finnish yoghurts, Polish apples, French camembert and Italian prosciutto. This is how the confrontation in the high echelons impacted people's fridges. Less visible, but yet as significant, was the effect on their Internet.

The heated political confrontation with the West kindled a remarkable increase of indoctrination in the traditional Russian media (Kachkaeva, 2015). State-controlled television intensified propaganda and labelled Ukraine as the land of neo-Nazi hostility towards ethnic Russians. The news presented pro-Russian separatists as liberators and Western politicians as enemies and threats to Russian sovereignty, society and moral values (Kendall, 2014a, 2014b; Kachkaeva, 2015). The consolidation of propaganda efforts in the state-controlled broadcasting, radio, press and the Internet media (Yuhas, 2014) required cleansing of the digital sphere, including liberal media outlets and user-generated networks.

Kendall (2014a, 2014b) and Kachkaeva (2015) used the term 'hybrid war' to identify Russian military and media activity in the Crimean case. 'Hybrid war' refers to a type of warfare where all significant activity happens below the radar; propaganda and provocation occupy a central stage (Kendall, 2014b). Unlike the Cold War, when the exchange of rhetoric, misleading information and name-calling between the USSR and the US and their allies was the main substance of the conflict, hybrid warfare comprises both rhetoric and military action. It can be argued that any war or conflict in the 20th century comes with the justification in the media. From another perspective, political analysts use the term 'hybrid war' to name a conflict with the blurred distinction between war and peace (Ries, 2014, cited in Kendall, 2014a). The Economist (2015) applied this concept to the Crimean events and referred to Russia as a country that denied its military involvement in Ukraine, but later on took part in negotiations with the West as one of the participants of the conflict.

Three Pillars of Russian National Identity

The escalating Russian propaganda of 2014 thrived on three popular national rhetorical paradigms: nationalism and the idea of the Russian superiority; cult of the leader; and the largely propagated campaign for patriarchal values and revulsion against any deviation from the 'norm', be it religion, sexual preferences or alternative political views (Harding, 2014; Kates, 2014; Laruelle, 2014; Nechepurenko, 2014; Yaffa, 2014). The state media and pro-government Internet users have notably increased their attacks on the liberal public, accusing them of lack of patriotism in the Crimean debate (Kates, 2014; Yaffa, 2014). Before 2014, critically minded citizens were focusing their crusade on corruption. Now, they had to bring the attention of the others to other social and political vices – the manipulation of propaganda, dangers of nationalist narratives and also to defend themselves from being called the state traitors (Sampat & Bugorkova, 2015).

The appropriation of the nationalist rhetoric by the Russian state of the mid-2010s fits in with the long tradition of the Russian nationalist propaganda of the previous times. Post-Soviet culture fuelled the continuous anxiety of the society over national prestige and fear of the foreign influence (Borenstein, 2004), search for the new collective and national identity for social cohesion (Rantanen, 2002; Laruelle, 2014) and framing of Russian nationalism as patriotism (Laruelle, 2014: 7; Ryzhkov, 2015).

Russian nationalism became a staple of young Russia's propaganda in the 1990s. After the fall of the USSR, the country was suffering from an economic meltdown, low level of patriotism and rising discontent of the population with the government (Petersson, 2009). The elites notably enhanced the pressure on a variety of liberal outlets flourishing in the 1990s. Such clichés as 'law and order', 'state' and 'national interest' eventually replaced the notions of 'freedom', 'free speech' and 'democracy' in the public discourse (Zassoursky, 2000).

The appeal to the 'American threat' flourishes in contemporary Russian nationalism (Riabova & Riabov, 2013). The US have been blamed for their influence in global conflicts, invasions of other countries and orchestration of the Ukrainian protests (Kuzio, 2015). The rhetoric of antagonism with America derives from the days of the Cold War in the second half of the last century, when the Soviet Union and the US frequently defined national values and morals in opposition to the assumed amorality of the other country. American presidents depicted the USSR as the wicked, powerful, savage, atheist, totalitarian state in pursuit of global domination (Edwards, 2008). The USSR promoted the similar description of the US to its citizens (Medhurst, 2012). The Cold War was remarkable for consisting first and foremost of rhetoric (Medhurst, 2012). The sharp exchange of witticisms, judgements and bravado was the war in itself, and words replaced deadly weapons (Brockriede, 1968). Although it was mainly constructed on the opposition to the US, the Soviet Cold War rhetoric also appropriated the discourse on Nazism. The country that suffered a lot from the Nazi invasion and finally defeated the beast, Russia/USSR started to call their enemies 'Nazis'. The elites appropriated Nazi labelling broadly to stigmatise the bourgeoisie, liberal dissidents, far-right nationalists and national communists (Kuzio, 2015: 162).

The contemporary Russian propaganda around Crimea inherits many components and rhetoric tactics of the Cold War instruction (Kachkaeva, 2015). For instance, it flexibly manipulates the notions of nationhood, Nazi threat (Harding, 2014), liberal traitors (Kates, 2014; Yaffa, 2014) and interprets the discourse on gender and sexuality in a political light. Russian state indoctrination explicitly labels the LGBT community as 'impure' and critically refers to America and Europe as the prominent advocates of homosexuality. There is a special catchy term 'Gayropa', which is a portmanteau of 'gay' and 'Europe'. Try searching the word 'Gayropa' in the main Russian search engine Yandex, and you will get 406,000 webpages (figures for the 20th of January 2015).

Riabova and Riabov (2013) link the rise of anti-gay propaganda with the tradition of anti-bourgeois rhetoric in the USSR and distinguish this tactic as the emerging trend in negative labelling in Russia. The stigmatisation of Europe as 'Gayropa' allows the elites to undermine the liberal achievements of democratic countries (Riabova & Riabov, 2013). Moreover, the enforcement of anti-gay rhetoric in Russian media correlates with the increased masculinisation of politics.

Furthermore, the contemporary Russian nationalism relies on the centuries-long tradition of the 'Russian idea' as the superiority of Russia over other countries in terms of high morality and spirituality, philosophy and culture (Kantor, 2004). This discourse has become particularly strong in the debates on Crimea. The Kremlin mobilised it to justify Moscow's involvement in the neighbouring country's politics (Kuzio, 2015; Teper, 2016). The concept of Russia's special place among the Slavic countries was prominent over a century ago in the tsarist Russia; it was overshadowed by the Soviet Communist ideology during the USSR and was revived in the post-Soviet times. Russian politics and culture have long promoted two main paradigms to map Russia on the global political arena: siege mentality and messianism (Kantor, 2004).

'Siege mentality' refers to the enduring expectation of the threat from abroad. It forms in the peoples and nations that suffer in numerous wars, invasions and occupations. A range of devastating attacks and conquests marks Russia's turbulent history since the early days. Vast territory and lack of natural geographical barriers to invasion left the population at the forefront of the battle, and entire cities and villages often served as 'defence fortresses' (Kantor, 2004). Personal interests counted for little; the interests of the state dominated. Confino (2013) enhances this argument by highlighting that citizens had to develop an obedient civic mentality to be able to consent to the power and pressure provided by the authoritarian rulers; they received safety and stable distribution of resources in return for their conformity.

The messianism of Russia is another influential national idea that has infiltrated Russian philosophy and political mindset for ages. Since the 14th and 15th centuries, Russian elites have been upholding the idea of Russia as the guardian of true faith, humanity and civilisation. Two historical events predisposed the formation of this concept: two and a half centuries of occupation by the Tatar Mongol yoke in the 13th to 15th centuries, and the fall of the Byzantine empire in 1453 (Kantor, 2004; Confino, 2013). Russians struggled to preserve their unity and identity under the violent Tatar siege and turned to the church for comfort and solace. After the liberation from the foreign occupation, Moscow princes united multiple regions around Moscow and affirmed their leadership by proclaiming the city as 'the Third Rome'. This high title established Moscow as the ancestor of the Orthodoxy from Rome and Constantinople (Il'in, 2004; Tsygankov & Tsygankov, 2010; Confino, 2013). By that time both capitals had lost their statuses as the bearers of Orthodoxy, and Moscow elites claimed to have inherited the duty to champion Orthodox faith in the world. After the Tatar Mongol oppression, this new national idea of Russia appealed to the recently liberated population and flattered the national self-esteem (Kantor, 2004).

The messianic underlining of Russian culture appears in the works of Dostoyevsky, Tyutchev, Nekrasov, Belyi and in the Bolshevik propaganda. Current ruling elites mobilised the 'Russian soul' argument to validate unconventional strategies in international and domestic politics (Helleman, 2004; Kantor, 2004). Confino (2013) suggests that Russian state rhetoric employs the Russian idea to explain or excuse the lack of a market economy, democracy, or a civil society. Helleman (2004) and Il'in (2004) express similar concerns and assess the Russian idea in Platonic terms, as a perfect model for an imperfect world. Any politician or regime can fill it with its own doctrines and projections: 'The Russian idea itself has to be rationalised in order to bring down idealistic and utopian aspirations of mass thinking' (Il'in, 2004: 55).

In addition to the proclaimed right to protect the morals in the pan-Slavic space, Russian propaganda included references to the centuries of a special relationship between Russian and Ukraine. Hegemonic media reminded the audience of the shared historical and cultural background with Ukraine, and referred to it as a 'brother' or satellite in need of protection and guidance (Kuzio, 2015). In a supplementary discourse, Russian media talked about Crimea as the ex-Russian territory and reminded the audience that it used to belong to the Russia from 1783 until 1991. The peninsula formally constituted a part of the Ukrainian Soviet Socialistic Republic, part of the USSR, but achieved independence in 1991 with the fall of the Soviet Union. Reflecting on these historical links, contemporary Russian propaganda suggested that in 2014 'Crimea was returning home' (Khudikova, 2014), thus reinforcing the idea that the Russian/Soviet empire was retrieving its historical borders and might.

Russian elites have been referring to Ukraine in patronising terms for hundreds of years. Moscow's influence over the neighbour country started in the 17th century when the region was under Polish rule. Pro-Russian Christian Orthodox clerics looked for the opportunities to establish Russian influence in the area and promoted the idea of Orthodox unity among the Slavs (Hillis, 2013). They relied on the postulate that the ancient Russia was born in Kiev, the capital of Ukraine. By this time, pro-Russian forces first referred to the Ukrainian southern lands as 'Little Russia'. Russian media of the 2010s have further promoted this well-known nickname for Ukraine (Kappeler, 2003; Hillis, 2013).

In the 18th century, Russia obtained more control over southern Ukraine. The Little Russia nationalist identity was used to counterbalance the strong Polish and Jewish nationalism in the region (Kappeler, 2003; Hillis, 2013). By the mid-19th century, Ukraine had become part of Russia (Hillis, 2013). Moscow fought to preserve the Russian empire by banning the Ukrainian language in schools and book publishing, thus ignoring and suppressing the nationhood of the Ukrainians (Petrovsky-Shtern, 2009). People met the legislation with resistance that lingered until the 1905 revolution. Then Ukraine became a gruesome battlefield in the First World War. In 1917, when the revolutionary forces overthrew the Tsar regime and established the Temporary Government in Russia, Ukraine declared independence. Joseph Stalin allowed nationalities and national identities to flourish in the USSR, advocating Lenin's idea of the supranational state. He expedited the delivery of education and print in the national languages of the Soviet republics as the means of social contract (Szporluk, 2000: 7–16).

Vladimir Putin embraced the rhetoric of brotherhood with Ukraine and employed it in two propagandist narratives. He continuously referred to the Ukrainians as vulnerable brothers and emphasised Moscow's responsibility to intervene in their politics (Kuzio, 2015). In the brotherhood rhetoric, Putin identified the citizens of Russia and Ukraine as constituting 'one nation' (Bateson, 2014).

The growing discourse on Russia's superiority over other countries, nationalist underlining of collective identity and enhancement of the messianic notes in propaganda have boosted the narrative of Russia's imperial ambition. In contemporary political and media studies, the term 'imperial ambition' mostly appears in the works on the USSR and US: during the times of the Cold War, Western scholars coined the term 'Soviet imperialism' (see Galeotti & Bowen, 2014), then Chomsky referred to America's foreign policy of constructing an enemy as 'the doctrine of imperial domination' (Chomsky & Barsamian, 2010). In the Crimean case, the Russian imperial ambition implies the exhaustion of the imperial rhetoric to bolster patriotism at the domestic level, and explain to the population the legitimacy of military involvement in Ukraine (Kassianova, 2001). Sociologists deem the promotion of this rhetorical construction as the compensatory concept that masks the existing socio-economic issues and encourages the population to assess life in a broader perspective (Dubin, 2014).

The intensification of state rhetoric on Russia's exclusive political and cultural path further complicated the efforts of the liberal public in generating resistance to the government. The propaganda on Crimea labelled the critics of the annexation as the traitors of their country (Kachkaeva, 2015) and defined 'patriotism' as full loyalty to the government's politics (Kates, 2014; Yaffa, 2014). The scapegoating of resistant publics coincided with the unprecedented level of public support for the leader (over 80% throughout 2014 – Kates, 2014) and a high level of trust in traditional media (Kachkaeva, 2015). The 2010s turned into a highly challenging setting for alternative political communication.

Cult of a Leader: Putin and the Personalisation of Politics

The appeals to the importance of a strong leader in Russia derive from the historical tradition of having an authoritative head of state. They also largely build on the Soviet notion of 'cult of personality' (Travin, 2015). In the Russian empire, the Tsar was believed to be the highest authority who would be liable to account only to God; then in the Soviet era, the leader was portrayed as the father of the nation (Bjelica, 2014). 'Cult of personality' refers to the political phenomenon when an individual (in most cases, a prominent political leader) exploits the means of mass communication to propagate an idealised and worshipful image of himself in order to seek the adoration of the masses. The term has been widely used in relation to the Soviet leader Joseph Stalin who had established himself as an all-powerful head of state and caring father of the Soviet people in the 1920s–1950s (Rees, 2004; Goscilo, 2012; Bjelica, 2014).

Vladimir Putin has been constantly reminding the nation of how important a strong leader is for keeping together such a large and ethnically diverse country as Russia. Media repeatedly reinforced the idea that a decisive man in power was essential to protect the state from multiple external and internal enemies (Rees, 2004; Cassiday & Johnson, 2010; Walker, 2014a). The need to promote his public persona of a decisive strong leader not only relied upon the tradition but also responded to the drawbacks of Boris Yeltsin's public image. Russia's first president Yeltsin (who had preceded Putin in the Kremlin) was notable for his illogical temperamental decisions, bad health and drinking problems. Putin carefully composed his public identity to embody 'hyper-masculinity' in Russian politics, in opposition to Yeltsin and other feeble politicians of the 1990s (Goscilo, 2012). From the late 2000s until the present day, Putin has orchestrated multiple public appearances in various adventurous settings that allowed him to flash his skills at 'masculine' activities. He flew with cranes, rode a horse with a bare chest, found time-worn pottery shards on the seabed, fired a sleeping drug into a Siberian tiger and plunged to the bottom of the ocean in a submarine. The Daily Mail granted him a comparison with the Bond villain (Williams, 2013), ironically reflecting on Putin's allusion to being a president-action hero.

The series of mannish escapades reproduced popular stereotypes and visual icons from action movies, fostering Putin's public image as a potent man in charge. Travin (2015) accordingly believes that in the times of economic turbulence, Putin's administration has been trying to promulgate Putin's cult as a separate discourse. They split the leader from the rest of the country's management, presented him as a solitary hero and thus disconnected him from the criticism about the struggling economy and corrupt management. Retailers reproduced Putin's iconic activities on T-shirts, mugs and other souvenirs.

Putin's administration has benefitted from the nebulous personal life of the president and shielded grey areas with constructed narratives. Putin's office promoted at least five main public identities of Vladimir Putin in his first presidential term (2000–2004) (Gorham, 2012). The public profiles that made him popular included technocrat, 'doer' (energetic and determinate), 'silovik' (strong man with influence), 'muzhik' ('a real man' in the archetypal sense) and patriot. Gorham's (2012) classification helps us to understand the public expectations of the 2000s.

By the 2010s, the division of roles had changed. Putin's public representation became more sexual (Foxall, 2013: 134, cited in Bjelica, 2014) and ensued an all-encompassing 'macho' identity that incorporated 'silovik', 'doer' and 'muzhik'. Sperling (2012) links the rise of machismo in Putin's political discourse with the need to justify the singe-handed rule of the country. Unlike Stalin who promoted himself as the Father of the nation, Putin prefers to act as a brutal Prince Charming (Bjelica, 2014). Ashwin further explains that in 'the post-communist era the state no longer aspires to be the father to its citizens' (Ashwin, 2000: 85, cited in Bjelica, 2014: 3). This alleged shift in the collective perception of the leader (from a father to a lover) also correlates with the development of the market economy in the country. The state refuses to provide everything for people and expects them to take individual responsibility (see Snegovaya, 2015).

Having passed the age of 60 a few years ago, Putin now faces a challenge about whether to fully embrace his paternal role or insist on remaining the sexually appealing Prince Charming (Travin, 2015); by the end of 2018, he was still balancing on the edge between the two. Russian president recurrently links traditional sexuality with health, power and stability (Riabova & Riabov, 2013). He constructs national identity on the basis of conformity to patriarchal gender roles and portrays the LGBTQ community as a threat to public order and morals. The Russian leader's cult of the 2010s exhibits a highly conservative 'gender regime', where 'gender regime' refers to 'the state of play in gender relations in a given institution' (Connell, 1987: 120, as cited in Sperling, 2012). Elites manipulate gender discourse as 'the scaffolding of regime power – perhaps especially when the government has not allowed much room for political debate over issues' (Sperling, 2012: 254).

The Media Environment: Censorship, Alternative Media and the Internet

Researchers believe that it was Putin who first understood the importance of state control over the media in the young Russian state. After the decade of freedom of speech under Yeltsin in the 1990s, Putin reversed the privatisation and commercialisation of the media (Lipman & McFaul, 2010; Chernikova, 2014). Since 1999 until the present day, the state media policy has become increasingly restrictive over alternative spheres and discourses. Putin has gradually reinstalled many traits of the Soviet media system.

In the 1920s–1950s, maintaining an effective propagandist media machine was crucial for the Soviet leaders. Soon after revolution, the government had to control the large country, promote and preserve the Soviet identity (Kiriya, 2012). The centralised flow of mass communication was accessible to all; television and radio broadcasting reached people free of charge and had no advertising. Newspapers were sold at a fixed price; however, one free copy of every issue was sent to workplaces to indemnify that all citizens have access to the state press (Kiriya, 2012).

From 'Samizdat' to the Internet Memes

Nonetheless, counterflows soon emerged as individuals were seeking a wider understanding and reflection on political, social and economic issues. The shadow production of alternative media and marginal culture in the USSR resulted in 'samizdat'. 'Sam' translates from Russian as 'self-' and 'izdat' is the short form of 'izdatelstvo', which is 'publishing'. The term 'samizdat' refers to the dissident activity of copying prohibited books by hand and secretly distributing them among close circles of trusted individuals (Saunders, 1974). The phenomenon of 'samizdat' emerged in the 1950s and lasted until the late 1970s. One of the active Soviet political dissidents Sergei Kovalev once defined it as 'the Internet-for-the-poor' (Kovalev, cited in Oushakine, 2001: 194), as samizdat permitted access to the never-published texts that were excluded from the dominant discourse.

Furthermore, Oushakine (2001: 195) advocates looking at samizdat texts as not merely political, but inherently artistic: the supporters of this practice opposed not only the state, but the rigid language of Soviet bureaucracy and limited stylistic range of expression for artists. Samizdat, in this perspective, was influential in creating a 'close circle of like-minded people who spoke their own language, inconceivable to others' (Krivulin, 1997, as cited in Oushakine, 2001: 195). These manually reproduced artefacts of culture with alternative ideas can be considered the predecessors of the Internet memes in the ways they united politics and marginal culture. Similar to memes, those hand-written books were scarce, often many of them remained incomplete and rewritten in spontaneity and rush.

The contemporary Russian media environment resembles the Soviet media system as the state dominates media and culture either financially (through ownership and grants to loyal opinion makers) or legally (via restricting laws and censorship). For instance, it is reported that since the 2000s, managers and top editors of national broadcasting companies were informally required to attend Friday meetings in the Kremlin where the instructions on media agenda were distributed (Baker & Glasser, 2007). As a result of media consolidation under the state control, the majority of large broadcasting and print media in Russia of the 2010s are subjected to unceasing filtering of their content.

Passive and Loyal Media Audience. Phenomenon of
'Information Ghettos'

Another trait that relates the contemporary Russian social contract over media with the Soviet tradition is the wide availability of high-quality entertainment on television and prevalence of this programming over serious content. Since the beginning of Putin's rule in the 2000s, the state has invested much money in the development of high and low entertainment shows (Pervyi and Rossiya channels) and criminal news and series (NTV). This approach guaranteed that the audience would stay in front of their television screens and consume not only entertainment but also the government-approved news and analysis (Etling et al., 2010; Lipman, 2010). The majority of Russians are accustomed to using the media as the interpreter of reality (Kachkaeva & Kiriya, 2007). Only a minor part of the audience exercises a more practical approach to the media as a source of information, but seeks varying viewpoints for comprehension (Klimov, 2007). The state caters to these members of the audience by preserving a limited selection of liberal media, which are often evaluated as an institutionalised alternative media sphere (Kiriya, 2007) or 'information ghettos' (Kiriya & Degtereva, 2010). The state tolerates the remaining critical mouthpieces to monitor the alternative political and social discourse (Etling et al., 2010).

The elites have developed a range of strategies to control offline media, yet have not equally succeeded in dominating the Internet (Kiriya, 2012). The economic crisis of 1998 became a first important point in the growth of the Russian Internet – citizens were looking for additional sources of information, primarily on economic issues. The next big advancement for the RuNet (Russian-language Internet) was the year 2008, as the five-day war between Russia and Georgia triggered a wave of publications in independent online media and blogs (Chernikova, 2014). Many of those blog posts gained significant popularity and were featured in the rating of top blogs provided by the biggest Russian search engine Yandex and the mailing system Mail.ru.

Opposition voices suddenly became visible for the general audience, and the Kremlin was considering creating a parallel state search engine, but later cancelled the project (Chernikova, 2014). The government then reportedly pressed Yandex to shut down the rating system (Chernikova, 2014). This move caused a backlash from the blogging community as users blamed the company for restricting the freedom of speech. In 2008, the Kremlin-related oligarch Alisher Usmanov and owner of the largest mailing platform Mail.ru expanded his media empire and seized control over the popular social network VKontakte. Usmanov also attempted to acquire Yandex, but did not succeed despite serious efforts and his loyalty to the Kremlin (Chernikova, 2014). Over the years, many popular liberal media were established on the Internet, such as the e-versions of the popular liberal newspapers Kommersant and Vedomosti, news outlets Lenta.ru, Gazeta.ru and Slon.ru, and news and analytics portal Colta.ru. They were successful in attracting a large number of readers, with the leader Lenta.ru reaching the audience of 20 million readers per month by 2014 (Suleimanov, 2014b).

By 2018, over a 100 million Russians had access to the Internet, which accounted for 70% of the population (InternetLiveStats, 2018). Russian users have unequal access to the Internet, depending on their location and quality of the Internet provider. Big cities and urban areas are, unsurprisingly, better covered. More importantly for the politics and news, Russian Internet users go online in large numbers, but they go to different places. This division is apparent when it comes to the choice of a social network (see Kiriya, 2012). Global and local networking platforms share the social media market, with local companies prevailing. The Russian analogue of Facebook, VKontakte, remained the most popular social networking site in the country: 42% of Russian Internet users access it every day (Russian Search Marketing, 2017), the second most popular is the Russian network Odnoklassniki.ru (27%), while Facebook has the audience of only 7% of all Internet users in the country, and only 3% engage with Twitter.

However, the recent changes in the Russian legislation cast doubts on the future of international social media on the Russian soil. Quite literally, global social media owners have been obliged to keep their servers on the Russian territory. All the companies that operate on foreign servers became illegal from September 2016 (Newsru, 2014). All emails, social networking conversations, personal data from shopping websites and lists of networked connections have to be located in Russia, thus becoming an easy target for the communication watchdog and intelligence services. According to the Russian legislation, this data should be presented to the government officials at the first notice (Newsru, 2014).

The law was passed in 2014, but its first victim appeared in 2018. LinkedIn was the first social network to be banned by the Russian state due to their refusal to keep personal data of users on Russia-based servers (Seddon, 2017).

Russian Politicised Twitter, or 'Hamster Shrugged'

Twitter, the microblogging platform that allows the creation of interest-based, rather than affinity-based networks, became a prominent platform for political communication during the December 2011 Parliament election, as people were reporting violations and their own primary results from the local polling stations (Kelly et al., 2012). Then they utilised microblogs, Facebook and VKontakte to spread information and mobilise their networks of contacts for the offline rallies. One of the major protest activists, anti-corruption blogger turned politician Alexei Navalny, was constantly tweeting texts and photos from the march until the moment he was arrested. Many users kept following him through his journey, and thousands of people were signing each hour to receive his updates (Kelly et al., 2012).

Another popular opposition account on Twitter, @KermlinRussia, is followed by over a million people. During the 2011–2012 protests, it was providing a constant flow of mocking commentaries to the official politics. @KermlinRussia have established themselves among the intellectual elites of Moscow and promoted one of the popular memes that reflected on the self-identification of the protest public. One of the @KermlinRussia founders, the public relations specialist Ekaterina Romanovskaya, kept the 2011 protest meme as her personal Facebook page timeline image for several years. This meme showed a colour block poster with two words on it 'Hamster shrugged'. It cleverly refers to the widely spread discourse of the pro-government journalists who called the 2011–2012 protesters 'Net Hamsters'. This was a derogative way to accuse anti-government users of being couch potatoes who get involved in politics only through leaving Internet comments. This term also referred to the modern way of mobilising for the protest – the 2011–2012 marches were largely coordinated via social networks (Vechernyaya Moskva, 2012; Varlamov, 2014). However, the liberal cyberspace replied to the offence by jokingly accepting the name. They further produced a creative idiom 'Hamster shrugged' ('хомяк расправил плечи') borrowing from the title of Ayn Rand's novel 'Atlas Shrugged'. They stressed that any ordinary user has the right to be heard and demand change. Call us hamsters, they said, but we will not drop our political and civil rights.

The other reason why Twitter became the network for oppositional voices was its resilience to government disruption. Pro-government hacker attacks took down many liberal websites, including LiveJournal and independent media, during the 2011 Parliament election (Roberts & Etling, 2011). Yet, Twitter remained safe, so the oppositional media outlets turned to Twitter to address their audience.

The success of Alexei Navalny and @KermlinRussia in reaching hundreds of thousands through their microblogging has exemplified the efficiency of digital storytelling for grassroots activism, raising political awareness and mobilisation (Gambarato & Medvedev, 2015). In the meantime, the power of digital platforms became evident to the government. Since the first interruptive campaigns on the digital liberal discourse in 2011, the Kremlin has fortified its digital media presence and reportedly established a specific department for social media communication. The Russian government reportedly maintains an Internet department – often referred to as 'troll factory' in the media – with at least 400 employees who generously post comments online (Toler, 2015). These 'trolls' are state-sponsored labourers who redirect the discourse from meaningful deliberation into quarrels and noise (Volchek & Sindelar, 2015). Supervisors brief them on the pre-packaged points and keywords to disseminate, and trolls sandwich them on various websites, from media outlets and forums of local administrations (Volchek & Sindelar, 2015) to trivial social media discussions on any topic, from politics and lifestyle to fashion and sports (Toler, 2015).

Russian Internet expert Anton Nossik (cited in Toler, 2015) reasons that not all pro-Kremlin users work for the Kremlin, and those who do are easily identifiable by the artifice of their speech. He believes that they do not hold much influence over the views of real people on politics. Conversely, other experts (see Bugorkova, 2015; Toler, 2015) note that trolls do not pursue the goal of convincing the audience, but aim at confusing it. Pomerantsev (cited in Bugorkova, 2015) terms this digital tactic as 'reverse censorship': the government cannot censor interactive digital media, but can pollute it with aggressive comments, hate speech, praise of the government, meaningless links, conspiracy theories and gossip.

Restrictive Laws on the Media, Internet and Memes in the 2010s

Besides the indirect pressure on the liberal discourse in social networks, the Kremlin has also introduced a number of constraining laws that imposed legal limitations on the self-expression of digital publics. In 2016, Russia's state Internet regulator issued a 'recommendation or warning' against 'using a photo of a public figure to embody a popular Internet meme which has nothing to do with the celebrity's personality' (Sampat & Bugorkova, 2015: para 2). This suggestive measure followed a scandal with the picture of the pop singer Valery Syutkin that the Internet crowds exploited to illustrate a meme 'Smack the Bitch in the Face'. The obscene phrase that glorifies violence against women was juxtaposed with the portrait of smiling Syutkin who is known for romantic songs and has no relation to the phrase. The artist appealed to the court demanding the removal of the meme from a popular amateur website Lurkmore that publishes information about memes and Internet culture. The court ruled in Syutkin's favour and subsequently prompted the more general recommendation from Russia's communication watchdog. In addition to the existing ban on parody microblogs that exploit the names of real people (Sampat & Bugorkova, 2015), this new initiative against memes with the pictures of public figures can significantly curb the flow of memes that portray Russian politicians. While the new measure targets defamation, the elites can employ it to repress criticism of the government in the shape of parody, as political actors clearly classify as public figures (Brown, 2015).

Other legislative projects that followed the 2011–2012 social unrest installed severe restrictions on freedom of assembly and freedom of speech. The amendments to the Law on the Freedom of Assembly were passed in June 2012, soon after the large protest against corrupt Presidential elections took place in Moscow. Human Rights Watch (2012) called these amendments 'draconian' as they virtually prohibited any public gathering exceeding six participants. In order to organise a march, one was required to apply for official authorisation, and the violation of this procedure was entitled to a high fine – up to 300,000 roubles (50,000 pounds) for individuals and up to 600,000 roubles (100,000 pounds) for organisers.[1] Repeat offenders could face a prison sentence of up to five years (Dobrokhotov, 2012; Human Rights Watch, 2012). This legislative measure, for instance, led to the much-debated court decision to sentence eight participants of the May 2012 anti-Putin rally in Moscow. Although deemed as a 'deeply flawed case' with 'inappropriate charges' by the Human Rights Watch Russia (2014), in February 2014 the judge handed down sentences varying from two and a half to four years of prison to all the defendants on the grounds of alleged violent behaviour during the march.

The elites accompanied the attack on freedom of assembly with a series of laws restricting freedom of speech. In July 2007, the odious Law on Extremism was passed that set the criteria for the state prosecution of those promoting 'extremism' in the public space. The Law became especially notable for its vague definition of extremism ('inciting hate or enmity, or, similarly insulting the dignity of a person or a group on the basis of sex, race, nationality, language, heritage, religious affilia-tion...').[2] The Law on Extremism was immediately dubbed as 'casting a wide net' (Eckel, 2007) with reports that many prominent human rights activists, politicians and political analysts were called to appear in court for their writings (Oliker et al., 2009).

By 2014, the government had updated the law by imposing an un-precedented penalty (up to five years in jail) on those posting 'extremist' pledges in the electronic media, including 'liking' or 'reposting' extrem-ist information (Kremlin, 2014b). The law labelled offences to the hu-man dignity and spreading non-Russian values as possible grounds for sanctions, making the directive vulnerable to misinterpretation and ma-nipulation. Additionally, in 2012 the Russian government passed a law allowing officials to shut down any website without a court order – the measure was explained as a means to protect children from inappropri-ate content, such as drugs or suicide promotion and child pornography (BBC, 2012). Liberal media condemned the new decree arguing that it is open to abuse and leads to further censorship of the Internet.

The Crimean crisis has brought about more laws against the freedom of self-expression and debate online. From the 1st of August 2014, all popular blogs (with more than 3,000 visits per day) were required to reg-ister with the communication watchdog and qualify as a media outlet. This measure granted the watchdog permission to silence any popular blog without a court order. Besides, it set the end to online anonymity, as the blog owners were obliged to pass their personal details to the state agency. The ambiguity of terms in the Blogger Law opened room for speculation. As the commentator Andrey Malgin (2014) explains, the law does not clarify whether the owner of a personal Twitter ac-count or Twitter as a whole should register; or clarify what exactly a 'user-generated platform' definition comprises (e.g., blogs, microblogs or the likes of Amazon.com). The Blogger Law established grounds for the potential trial of those posting 'false information presented as truthful'; suppressing or concealing the publicly important information (Malgin, 2014). The broad scope of offences and obscurity of the Law implies that executors can interpret it using their own discretion.

In 2014, the newly imposed constraints on social media users were par-alleled with the pressure on independent media and alternative discourse platforms. The government attacked the biggest online news outlet, a ma-jor social network and an independent television channel. Galina Tim-chenko, the respected editor-in-chief of Lenta.ru, the largest independent news website, was ousted for political reasons. The dismissal of Tim-chenko urged the resignation of dozens of journalists working in Lenta.ru, and the complete change of content of the website (BBC, 2014a). The statement released by the editorial staff in response to Timchenko's sack-ing produced a now famous summary of the decline of free journalism in Russia: 'The problem is not that there is nowhere left for us to work.

The problem is that there is nothing left, it seems, for you to read' (BBC, 2014a: para 12). The largest independent online television channel Dozhd (TV Rain) also experienced pressure for its unbiased investigation on corrupt officials when leading cable and satellite operators suddenly dropped it, causing significant profit loss. Pavel Durov, the founder and general director of the most popular Russian social network, VKontakte, refused to provide user data to the security services; he was fired at the company board meeting and had to flee to the country (The Moscow Times, 2014).

Lastly, in 2014 the Russian government officially banned four main Russian curse words from use in the media, theatre, literature, music and blogs (Omidi, 2014). The law on profanity was presented as a measure to protect the beauty of the Russian language; yet, media professionals (see, for instance, Klishin, 2014) regarded it as an attack on the freedom of expression. Profanity played a serious role in resistance communication during the Soviet era. Soviet dissent literature engaged with foul expressions and slang as the linguistic opposition to the loquacious clumsiness of the bureaucratic vocabulary (Klishin, 2014). Noteworthy, in China the similar ban on vulgarity led to a rise in euphemisms online (Omidi, 2014), suggesting that Russian Internet users also have to resist the ban by coining euphemisms and savvy puns that further distinguish the resistant publics from the conformists (Klishin, 2014).

Memes as Tools of Propaganda, Dissent and Alternative Digital Activism in the Russian-Language Twitter

Results of the analysis of memes and interviews with meme makers and sharers. The role of memes for free speech and persuasion; how the themes of national identity, polarisation of views and cult of personality shine through memes. Motivations, experiences and risks of meme makers.

Russian political deliberation through memes in the mid-2010s is the main case study of this book. In the beginning of 2014, Russia intervened in the civil war in the neighbouring Ukraine and facilitated a referendum in one of its parts, the Crimean Peninsula. It was once a part of the Soviet Union and is still populated by the majority of ethnic Russian citizens. Pro-Russian armed forces arrived to the peninsula to help the local government to organise a referendum of independence. This resulted in the withdrawal of Crimea from the Ukrainian territory. The peninsula appealed to be included in the Russian territory soon after. Western political leaders met the actions of Russia with outrage, while the liberal publics inside the country questioned the tough politics and non-diplomatic approach of the Russian elites. This case has led to the flows of memes circulating on both sides of the argument. Those for and against the annexation of Crimea used the memes to discuss politics, national identity, imperial ambitions, even gender roles that emerged as an important topic through the exchange of memes.

The analysis of over 600 memes collected throughout 2014 on the Russian Twitter as well as 15 interviews with the Russian meme makers reveal the motivations and risks, benefits and drawbacks of making and distributing memes. My study also shows how Internet, social media and viral cultures are now adding alternative dimension to news and opinion. Russian government has severely restricted the freedom of speech and assembly over the last two decades. The majority of traditional media are directly and indirectly controlled by the state. The laws on public information cast a wide net for the prosecution of popular bloggers and microbloggers. In this challenging media landscape, the ambiguous, anonymous, humorous means of communication such as memes obtain a specific value.

It was extremely difficult to find, contact and build trust with the meme makers in Russia. Living under constant threat of prosecution for opposing the government, many of them prefer to hide behind pseudonyms and rarely talk to the press or academics. My personal networks of journalistic contacts permitted me to access quite a few meme makers and have an honest conversation with them. The same research would be impossible now, as more and more restrictions on public communication are coming in place in Russia, and people are even more frightened to speak with the Western scholars.

It is for the first time that the testaments of the Russian opposition and citizen meme makers will see the light. The analysis of their responses demonstrated that, for instance, in Russia meme makers have become the new journalists, civil activists and political protesters at the same time. The vague structure of the Russian political system and lack of established platforms of negotiation with the state makes the Internet the only vibrant site of the public discussion. The format of a meme has evolved to become instrumental in these circumstances.

Furthermore, the Russian government clearly attributes much influence to memes, as the recent legislative measures and pursuit of meme makers illustrate. Memes remarkably irritate the elites that struggle to control spontaneous mockery and counterbalance it with fabricated texts. The authorities have deployed significant forces online, trying to contaminate meaningful political discussions with pro-government memes and commentaries. This has never been covered before in academic publications and will be examined in this chapter.

Methodology

My research analysed Russian meme making from two main angles: practices and motivations of producers (how and why people create political memes), and meanings that these texts convey in the collective digital discourse (what they reveal about the hegemonic political environment and the opposition to it). The main research goal was to understand what roles do Internet memes play in alternative political communication in the Russian-language social networks communication. I was willing to explore whether satirical communication online facilitated alternative political talk, and was instrumental to overcome censorship and serve as coded in-jokes to raise the awareness on political issues. One of the most ambitious aims was to analyse whether memes can connect people and assist further mobilisations around a political cause. However, in the course of my research I realised that shedding light on *resistant* publics alone is limited, as more and more pro-government memes scattered over the Russian-language Internet. Hence, in the course of fieldwork and analysis, I have additionally looked at how supporters of the government employed political memes; what narratives the memes contributed to in the pro-government and resistant communication flows on Russian Twitter.

In order to tackle these questions my research employed mixed methods: content analysis, social network analysis, textual analysis and interviews.

Behind the Scenes

I started my project in 2012 and aimed to explore the role of memes in the digital political resistance in Russia. I was collecting protest memes; I was willing to see the top memes at the peak of political protests in Russia, the 2011–2012. Two main challenges appeared that were highlighted by many Internet researchers (Berg & Lune, 2004; Neuman, 2014): difficulties in searching for imagery, as typing in keywords does not bring you all the images that are related to the subject; and that doing research of the Internet past is a perplexing task as the digital sphere keeps changing every second, and past events and texts get lost in tons of new data. Last but not least, Facebook's privacy policy significantly limited my access to the personal pages and conversations of many protest activists and supporters.

I assessed doing research on Twitter as a feasible approach as it is a public network, and a researcher is not limited by privacy settings. In the absence of advanced automatic tools, I settled to collect data manually and preferably in real time.

I was sitting there calmly (not true), waiting for a new Russian political case study to emerge. I was waiting for a new significant event to happen, so that it could possibly trigger another wave of memes from the politically active Russian users. I could then follow and collect these texts manually and live. In the meantime, I was identifying eminent Russian political activists, journalists, meme sharers and microblogging Twitter stars in order to follow their accounts and stay alert for the next meme-worth case study. While waiting for the new wave of memes to emerge, I detected the popular meme sharers who had been active in the 2011–2012 online protest communication. Then I became able to locate other eminent politicised microbloggers, from pro-government accounts to the liberal media and personal accounts of liberal individuals.

I was much anticipating the Sochi Olympic Games in February 2014 as a controversial event for the Russian public. While the majority of Russians enthusiastically awaited the Games, many liberal journalists were raising concerns on the high level of corruption in spending, and pointed to the potential manipulation of the Olympic rhetoric. They were suggesting that elites could abuse the publicity on the Games to overshadow domestic problems and boost their own popularity. Nonetheless, the end of the Olympics brought a much larger case study than I had expected – the Ukrainian crisis that soon turned into the Crimean crisis and further developed into a large Russian-Western conflict by August 2014. Subsequently, large flows of memes flooded the social networking sites throughout 2014. Luckily, I was prepared to trace them and monitored the popular politicised Twitter accounts that were generating, adjusting and redistributing plenty of memes.

During my participant observation of the political discourse on Russian Twitter throughout 2011–2014, I witnessed the shift from the anti-corruption resistance in 2011–2012 to the combined resistance to the government's corruption *and* its heavy propaganda that marked the public sphere in 2014. Pro-government media became much more persistent in imposing the Kremlin's ideology, and pro-government Twitter users have boosted their activity by sharing more pro-Kremlin texts and posts, memes and links. They were not only endorsing the Russian elites for their domestic and international politics, but were accusing the dissent part of the audience of treachery. The incorporation of these new themes in public discourse has affected the content and style of the oppositional deliberation. Resistant social network users tried to reiterate previous criticism of the corrupt government, but also implement new topics in their discussions. They were pointing not only to the corruption issues, but to media manipulation, boosted discourse on patriotism and stigmatisation of nonconformism. The liberal public also had to resist the allegation of treachery and confront the majority of the Russian population who endorsed Vladimir Putin and his allies.

I have picked the Crimean crisis as my case study as it combined the pro-government efforts in digital indoctrination with the resistant communication by the dissent public. The themes and actors from the alternative political talk of 2011–2012 remained active in 2014, but had to share digital space with the galvanised flows of pro-government propaganda. Furthermore, the Crimean case illuminated new challenges for the style of expression of the resistant public. Pro-government users have actively exploited Internet memes in their politicised communication, thus demonstrating that this vehicle of expression was not confined to the liberal audience and can serve propaganda as much as resistance.

One of the main advantages of my research is that it matched the radical challenges that the Internet communication and political activism faced in Russia in the 2010s. The series of restrictions on the freedom of speech and assembly imposed severe constraints on the deliberation of alternative politics online. Thanks to the recent legislative initiatives, the communication watchdog has received the power to label practically any opposition in Russia as potentially 'extremist' and therefore lawless. My project had aimed to have documented the rise of the protest political communication and mobilisation in the 2011–2012, but eventually recorded its decline to circumscribed deliberation in 2014.

Reflections on Twitter Research

My research primarily sought to explore the *meaning* that meme makers and sharers ascribed to these texts, and the *role* of memes in the political communication online. As these goals were exploratory, my study employed the inductive approach that did not aim to test the existing theory, but generate concepts from the data (Bryman, 2012). Due to the novelty of the studies on Internet memes, I have relied on grounded theory as the most viable method to extract ideas from records and generate conceptual understanding of the ongoing social processes (Neuman, 2014: 177–178). The grounded approach permitted me to be sensitive to my data, engage in constant interaction between practice and theory, understand the phenomenon, create categories from my observations (Neuman, 2014: 177) and harness new concepts out of practice (Lincoln & Guba, 2000; Charmaz, 2014). Comprehension of the context is vital for the grounded method (Neuman, 2014) and essential for addressing my research questions. This study relied on the contextual understanding of the sociopolitical environment of Putin's Russia in the 2010s, which is a very particular setting for media professionals and political activists.

In order to address my research questions, I have utilised both qualitative and quantitative methodology. The qualitative part of this study comprised textual analysis of memes and in-depth interviews with meme sharers. I have chosen qualitative methods for my inquiry in the political expression of Russian social network users as they honoured "an inductive style, a focus on individual meaning, and the importance of rendering the complexity of a situation" (Creswell, 2014: 4). Memes reveal how participants of the digital discourse interpret political reality, and the qualitative approach facilitated accurate comprehension of the subtle nuances of their experiences (Bryman, 2012: 36). Textual analysis of memes and in-depth interviews facilitated the investigation on memes as a social phenomenon and grasped the complexity of human interaction.

I have also exploited quantitative methods of research, such as content and social network analysis, which permitted me to classify the collected data, and substantiate and cross-validate qualitative findings. Content and social network analysis enabled me to categorise the main themes of the Crimean memes and draw a network map of meme sharers on Russian Twitter.

Content analysis refers to the quantitative method of "identifying the information contained within the texts which can be used to identify a reality external to the text" (Alaszewski, 2006: 86). A researcher formalises each category of the text being of interest to her in a set of categories that form a 'coding scheme' (Franzoni, 2004: 4, cited in Alaszewski, 2006: 86). A meme is a multimodal artful text that carries multiple connotations, hence it was challenging to identify memes that evidently addressed the Crimean debate. I acknowledged that they might have done so through ambiguous narratives. I relied on thematic identifiers and validation through contextual knowledge. The primary identifier for the inclusion of a meme in the data was the direct mentioning of "Crimea". Other identifiers were the names of the politicians involved in the crisis (Russian, Ukrainian, European and American officials: Vladimir Putin, Dmitry Medvedev, Viktor Yanukovich, Barack Obama, Angela Merkel and others); the allusion to the "unidentified gunmen" ("volunteers", "self-defence forces", "little green men" or any other euphemism for the pro-Russian troops facilitating the referendum in Crimea) and references to Russian traditional media and journalists who produced many reports on Crimea.

Social network analysis developed in a particular field of academic studies in the 1970s and reflected the growing interest of social sciences scholars in the structure of ties between individuals (Scott, 2013: 1–2). They examined social links through the lens of network and graph theories. With the advent of the Internet, social network analysis emerged and focused on the detection of streams, directions and evolving patterns of communication (Ediger et al., 2010). Social network analysis benefitted this research for two reasons: it permitted to explore the dynamic relationship between like-minded and oppositional users (see how much they retweet and comment on each other's posts), and to inquire whether there were centres and peripheries in their communication networks.

I have imported the names of relevant Twitter accounts in NodeXL, an open-source and free network analysis software and visualisation package for Microsoft Excel. The programme enables the automation of a data flow that harvests network data, processes it through numerous filters and generates network visualisations and reports (Hansen et al., 2009: 1). Having deployed the names of politicised Twitter accounts in the software, I set the data time frame as (UTC) 17/03/2014 00:00 – 21/07/2015 00:00. The time limit was generously set as a year and four months to ensure prolonged and up to date monitoring of the networked relationships between politicised Twitter users.

I have created visualised schemes of networked communication for three groupings: pro-government, anti-government and both groups of users in one display. This attempt pursued the exploratory goal of identifying the structures and intensity of interactions among meme sharers (Hansen et al., 2010: 262); therefore, it did not require supplementary justification of a number of included accounts. In this research, social network analysis served as an additional tool and a trial of applying this method to the study on memes. However, inclusion of a larger sample of accounts and adding more relationship filters would increase the applicability of social network analysis to the research on memes and contribute to future studies on the politicised Russian Twitter.

Utilisation of a mixed method approach helped me to improve the validity and reliability of my research. It enabled me to cross-validate findings from various methods and thus reduced drawbacks of the grounded approach (Matthews & Ross, 2010; Bryman, 2012). For instance, in this research, content analysis exposed the recurring themes (Bryman, 2012), which meme makers were not always able to distinguish in their interviews, and therefore added useful quantitative and qualitative findings on the themes of the Crimean discourse. I sought to utilise explanatory sequential design in my mixed method approach, as defined by Creswell (2015: 6–7): an explanatory sequential design applies quantitative methods prior to qualitative to inform the qualitative phase (see also Matthew & Ross, 2010: 144–145). This approach helped to identify a wide array of themes and narratives in the Crimean Internet memes, and then narrow down the scope of the study to scrutinise a sample of exemplary memes in detail. Besides, the quantitative phase of social network analysis enabled me to detect the major meme sharers with pro- and anti-government views and draw the list of potential interviewees.

The use of Twitter data enabled me to collect hundreds of memes and tweets in the real-time perspective. The texts and profiles of users were publicly accessible. I subsequently benefitted from following the links between different accounts, which enabled me to harvest yet more memes that fitted in the scope of my project. However, the research on Twitter data has a number of limitations that were taken into consideration. A contemporary microblogging network, Twitter operates upon the number of technical algorithms that endorse popular texts and accounts and obscure the marginal ones (Cha et al., 2010; Kwak et al., 2010). This characteristic of Twitter may have challenged the accuracy of locating the networks of sharing and identifying the most popular memes among the resistant Russian publics.

Moreover, the research on Twitter is intrinsically linked to the challenge of "echo chambers". Social media users often follow the accounts of the similar views and interests, thus intentionally and unintentionally forming the opinion and information "bubbles", or "echo chambers" (Gilbert et al., 2009). Twitter's own architecture does not help to overcome this issue, but rather amplifies its problematic influence on the accuracy of data collection. In order to minimise the effects of this hindrance, I conducted the network analysis and held interviews with the prominent meme makers. They allowed me to reflect upon the issues of technology-driven or conscience-driven choices in "liking", "following" and "retweeting". I have spoken to the interviewees about their ideological preferences and favourite accounts, tendency to follow other users due to the ideological similarities, personal sympathies or other reasons. In summary, manual data scrapping on Twitter is a beneficial research approach, yet it is limited in the capacity to provide a balanced picture of the texts and opinions shared; therefore, additional methods such as interviews were added to the study.

In the course of data collection, I have retrieved nearly 2,000 memes (image and texts, and texts) produced within the time frame from February 2014 to April 2015. This interval corresponds with the chronology of the Crimean crisis. The Russian-Ukrainian tension over the belonging of the Ukrainian peninsula started in February 2014 and resulted in the deployment of the pro-Russian forces in Crimea. Then the referendum on Crimean independence (16th of March 2014) led to the declaration of Crimean sovereignty and subsequent swift inclusion of the land into the Russian territory (18th of March 2014). The following polemic in traditional and electronic media proliferated throughout March–April 2014. Post-Crimean debates were still active in a year's time, by May 2015, when the saturation was reached and data collection stopped. The most recent discussions on Crimea and subsequent economic and political confrontation between Russian and the West (from May 2014 to May 2015) contain a broad array of disputes on Russia's international and domestic politics.

Preliminary filtering of my collected data revealed 624 memes that specifically discussed the Crimean annexation and circulated during the peak of the crisis in February–April 2014. These texts formed the core database for the first quantitative stage of the research, content analysis. While it is implausible to attest that the collected memes were representative of all political deliberation on Russian Twitter, they nonetheless exhibited the significant themes, trends and patterns of political communication during the Crimean crisis.

I have focused on the collection and analysis of the memes that comprised an image and a text. It was necessary to specify the type of the researched memes in order to confine the scope of the study and ensure the comparability of texts. The memes that consist of an image with a text employ both visual and textual framing, which makes them more multifaceted and richer than plain visuals or words. Nonetheless, I have also included a small amount of purely textual memes in the sample, when they were expressive enough and added to the main themes of the visual memes with a text.

Exemplary memes from the large content analysis sample of 624 coded texts formed the subsequent sample for **textual analysis**. In order to qualify as "exemplary", a meme had to match one or a few of the following criteria: intelligible references to the recurring rhetoric concepts, common interpretation of these themes, and visual and textual expressiveness (many layers of connotations and popular references). Textual analysis was performed on the sample of 50 texts.

Textual analysis reveals how people make sense of the world. It cannot provide a single truth, as no other methodology can either. However, it can produce a number of informed judgements of the people's sense-making in a particular environment (McKee, 2003), which suits the purpose of this research to examine the contemporary meme making. This method unveils covert connotations, embedded patterns, implied beliefs and possible omissions (Fursich, 2009: 240–241). I followed the principles of textual analysis and analysed memes in relation to the political, social and cultural agenda. In order to do so, I was closely following the political news, blogs and microblogs, and overall media deliberation of the Crimean crisis. It helped me to gain awareness of the political, social and cultural context of the time and place of circulation of memes (McKee, 2003).

The third phase of my research comprised **in-depth interviews** with 15 prominent meme makers. In order to identify suitable interviewees, I had monitored the political debates on Russian Twitter long in advance of the start of data collection and analysis. I was judging the eminence of influential, politically active users by the number of followers, offline reputation (when known), number of retweets by other popular and established accounts, and the number of followers. Then an additional scrutiny of their networks of followers and retweets empowered me to identify other influential political microbloggers. Moreover, private consultations with practising Russian journalists and social media experts enabled me to draw a wider and more comprehensive network of the pro- and anti-government meme sharers.

In-depth interviews were chosen as a reliable tool for the elucidation of personal motivations, experiences and opinions (Bryman, 2012; Creswell, 2015) on meme making and sharing. In-depth interviews permitted encompassing "the *hows* of people's lives (the constructive work involved in producing order in everyday life) as well as the traditional *whats* (the activities of everyday life)" (Denzin & Lincoln, 2003: 62).

Acquiring access to meme sharers and securing their consent to participate in the research was a challenging task. Directly approaching people via Facebook was not effective, as none of the microbloggers responded. However, I applied a 'backyard' research strategy and mobilised my personal networks of journalist contacts in Russia. The 'backyard' method refers to the exploration of the researcher's own organisation or groups of friends (Glesne & Peshkin, 1992). Although I was not interrogating my current colleagues, this term is appropriate to define the method of addressing potential interviewees from the close circle of friends or acquaintances, as it dramatically increases the interviewees' trust and willingness to participate in the research. Moreover, my study advantaged from the 'snowball effect' (Bryman, 2012): a sampling strategy where existing study subjects introduce the researcher to subsequent study subjects among their contacts.

Russian meme makers agreed to talk to me via diverse channels of communication and in different settings, which varied from face-to-face meetings in Moscow and London to email correspondence and WhatsApp chats. Almost half of my interviewees refused face-to-face communication due to privacy concerns. One of them even asked me to make a selfie with a sheet of paper saying "Привет" ("Hi" in Russian) followed by the handwritten name of that person, and send it to him immediately via Twitter chat. Upon me doing so, he loosened and appeared – assured that I was not working for any government watchdog or secret services. I have anonymised the respondents' answers for the sake of their personal safety – in this book, their quotes will appear without their names.

The fact that I was representing a 'Western researcher' could have limited openness and trust of the pro-Kremlin meme sharers. Russian microbloggers with pro-government views frequently express hostility towards Western journalists and academics. I acknowledged this challenge and tried to assure the interviewees in my intentions to analyse their responses with utmost respect and objectivity.

Furthermore, the majority of meme sharers in the sample were male, and I was in a position of a woman asking questions. My identity as a woman interviewing the male interviewees in a rather patriarchal Russian society may have affected their answers – a male researcher could have yielded different responses. Interviewees could be less willing to "explain" things, but probably turn more self-assured and competitive with the male interviewer. In my case, many participants in the sample were eager to demonstrate their knowledge and expertise, and few of them even took a patronising approach.

Subsequently, I took into consideration the importance of treating verbatim accounts of my respondents with high respect to the spoken word. Interviews went through several stages of interpretation and reinterpretation. The initial analysis of the interviews was followed by a second evaluation, when I assessed my transcripts again as tabula rasa and extracted valuable fragments as if no primary analysis had been performed. Then, two variations of analysis were compared and amalgamated. This reflection was necessary to minimise the effect of researcher's bias and stereotypes on interpretation; it enabled me to promote authenticity in the representation of the views of my respondents.

Various findings obtained in three parts of the research were converged in accordance with the "triangulation" effect, which is mobilisation of different methods that secure cross-referencing, objectivity and validity of the project (Gaskell & Bauer, 2000; Matthews & Ross, 2010). This quality measure derives from the triangulation principle in mapping when one determines the distance to the point by references to two other points (Matthews & Ross, 2010: 145). In this book, content and textual analysis relied on the same themes, but illuminated different aspects of the exchange of memes. Content analysis exposed the prevailing topics, while textual analysis explained their contextual connotations and significance for the political discourse. Further juxtaposition with the interview analysis deepened the comprehension of these narratives and revealed the meanings that meme sharers attributed to the memes when producing them. It has also demonstrated how the prominent meme sharers interpreted the memes shared by other people and what roles they ascribed to the circulation of memes in political deliberation.

Ethics. My research concerns the sensitive topic of political resistance in the authoritarian Russian environment; therefore, I had to regard the potential risks for my respondents. The majority of the interviewees in my sample are liberal meme makers who confront the state and may want to conceal their identity. All the participants gave their consent for the quotes to be published and used in academic works in the UK. However, the decision was made to anonymise the microbloggers and experts who gave me interviews – their safety in the unpredictable Russian media climate is the priority. The interviewees will appear under the names Journalist 1, Twitter blogger 1, etc.

All the memes in my data were collected from the publicly available Twitter accounts. Recent scholarship on ethics of Twitter research (Zimmer, 2010; Nissenbaum, 2011; Zimmer, 2015; van Wynsberghe, no date) points to the obligation to elaborate the notion of contextual privacy for the digital era. Twitter is a public space, yet there are still concerns that not all users are aware of the potential utilisation of their virtual self-expression in academic studies (van Wynsberghe, no date). Nevertheless, for the present moment, interactive networks remain an open realm for data scraping. Supporting this, Zimmer (2015) remarks that the US Library of Congress announced in 2010 that it would archive every open tweet appearing on Twitter. Although the decision sparked a debate on the ethics of storing casual individual ephemeral self-expression as the unrestricted records (see Raymond, 2010), it nonetheless additionally validated the status of tweets as public data. For this research, tweets are considered de facto public data on the Internet; their collection and utilisation for research purposes do not require any permission from the users or digital platform owners (van Wynsberghe, no date).

Results of the Meme Analysis: Political Polarisation

Coding of over 600 memes related to the Crimean crisis has enabled the identification of recurring themes. The memes were divided according to the prevailing themes. The most prominent ones were "pro-Russia" (256), "anti-US" (126), "anti-Russia" (121), "anti-Putin" (110) and "pro-Putin" (85).

Content analysis of the main themes has revealed that the majority of memes in the Crimean crisis are focused on Russia and its leader. They either support or criticise the Russian position and activity. They often juxtapose Russia and its president Vladimir Putin to the US and its leader Barack Obama. However, the amount of personalised memes around Putin (pro-Putin – 85, anti-Putin – 110) is much higher than the amount of memes targeted at Obama (just 33). The number of critical memes against Russia almost corresponds with the number of critical memes against Putin (anti-Russia – 121, and anti-Putin – 110), suggesting that **the president often appears as the embodiment of the country and its government**. Moreover, both positive and negative memes about Russia often employ metaphoric concepts, such as references to the allegories of the pan-Slavic family and Russia being a strong wild bear (Figure 5.1).

Pro-Russian memes frequently contain criticism towards the US, and much less often target at other Western countries (anti-US – 126, and anti-EU – 34), suggesting **an interesting rhetorical dichotomy of**

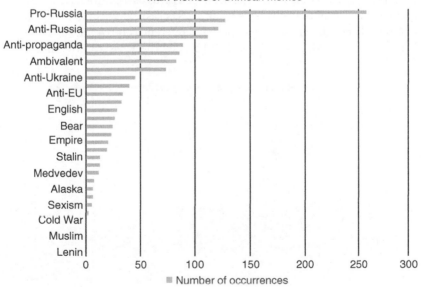

Figure 5.1 Results of the content analysis: Main themes of memes on Crimean crisis in 2014.

'**Russia versus US**'. The overlaps of themes also reveal the combination of narratives in memetic discourses. In the majority of cases (398), memes contained two or three themes (more than half of the sample); this finding corresponds with the high number of memes coded as "ambivalent" (84). The ambiguous character of many memes allowed detecting multiple themes in it, supporting the assumption that memes can be highly equivocal and appeal to various themes simultaneously. Less than one-third (170) of memes in the sample were considered straightforward and focusing to one theme, thus proving that besides being multilayered, memes can also provide a comprehensible direct commentary to the political events. Moreover, the low number of memes with more than four themes (56) further suggested that memes are likely to refer to various themes, but are limited in their rhetorical richness and sophistication.

The most frequent overlaps in the memes' themes exposed how **various polemic narratives were conjoined** in the supportive and critical discourses on Russian action in Crimea. For instance, "Pro-Russia" (256) memes often contained criticism of the US (82 cases), EU (26 cases) and Ukraine (21 cases). Besides, they also relied on the specific endorsement of the personality of Vladimir Putin (50 cases) and promoted the allegory of Russia as a wild mighty bear (17 cases). This amalgamation of themes suggests an intriguing narrative of pro-Russia activists that mostly base their praise for Russia on the opposition to its rivals. They additionally also support their claims by references to the personal strength and wisdom of the leader and links to the folkloric identity of the country (Figure 5.2).

"Anti-Russia" (121) memes also discuss Russian politics through frequent mentions of the country's leader (28 cases). They do not exploit the US, the EU or Ukraine much as positive references (pro-US – 1, and pro-Ukraine – 6 cases), but discuss the abuse by the Russian government in

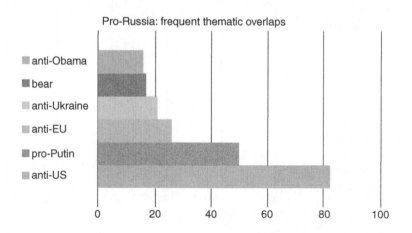

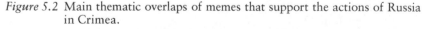

Figure 5.2 Main thematic overlaps of memes that support the actions of Russia in Crimea.

much detail. Two main points of criticism include liberal accusations of corruption and poor management (coded as "resistance" – 13 cases) and manipulative character of state and media propaganda (18 cases). These results may indicate that memetic criticism to Russia often invokes internal problems, while pro-Russian narrative engages external referencing points. Critical meme makers often point to the domestic wrongdoings and link them with the international Russia's activity on Crimea.

Besides, the "anti-Russia" theme often overlapped with "ambivalent" (21 cases). In these cases, a meme was entertaining and commented on Russian action in Crimea, but its ideological stance was unclear. Many memes of that category presented puns and remix of popular culture, resulting in a witticism that could be interpreted either as critical or supportive of Russia. On the one hand, this finding may insinuate that many meme sharers exploited the Crimean case as yet another opportunity to coin jokes. On the other hand, it may mean that political memes are not always explicit in their ideological connotation, and their interpretation may dramatically vary depending on the recipient's views (Figure 5.3).

Memes that personally endorsed Vladimir Putin (85) relied on a similar number of themes as "pro-Russia" memes, but enforced more juxtaposition with the US (26 cases) and Barack Obama (19 cases) in particular. Interestingly, they sometimes employed mentions of the Prime Minister Dmitry Medvedev (7) as a supportive tool. In a relatively significant number of cases (7), pro-Putin memes came from English-speaking users, implying that either Western users adjoined the advocacy for the Russian president, or Russian-speaking netizens deliberately targeted their praise of the leader at the foreign audience. Putin's supporters occasionally appealed to the narratives of empire (3) and patriotism (3), indicating that these rhetorical notions also form a significant part of the pro-Putin memetic discourse.

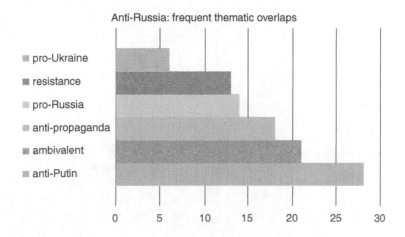

Figure 5.3 Main thematic overlaps of memes that criticise the actions of Russia in Crimea.

Intriguingly, anti-Putin (110) memes also referred to the popular metaphoric concepts, such as Nazism (7) and empire (9), but perhaps with
a different connotation. Besides, anti-Putin memes often contained liberal criticism of corruption and abuse of power (31 cases) and aimed at
deconstructing state propaganda (23 cases). These findings demonstrate
that critical users were more likely to refer to particular cases, words or
events (such as detailed corruption accusations, episodes from television
news, and condemnation of particular activities or speeches) than to
broad juxtaposition of Putin to global political leaders. Furthermore, a
relatively high number of equivocal memes in the anti-Putin selection (13
cases) demonstrate that commentaries on Putin were not always clear in
their ideological connotation, and in many cases the same meme could
be simultaneously interpreted as criticism and commendation of the
Russian president (6 cases). This correlation may indicate that Russian
digital users project and interpret political values on Putin differently,
and interpretations may vary.

Resistance memes (72) were mostly targeted personally at Vladimir
Putin (31). He received nearly twice more critical mentions than the
country's government and its politics in general (13 cases). Resistant
meme sharers frequently pointed to the manipulation of state and media
propaganda (25 cases) and the subsequent brainwashing and deliberation of politics on the Internet (10 cases). Surprisingly, relatively few
memes directly condemned the military activity and called for peace in
Ukraine (3), and only slightly more commented on the notion of "patriotism" (5). These findings illuminate that resistant meme sharers utilised
the Crimean discourse as yet another point of criticism of Vladimir Putin and Russian hegemonic politics; they rarely called for the ceasefire,
but mostly pointed to Putin's involvement in the crisis (Figure 5.4).

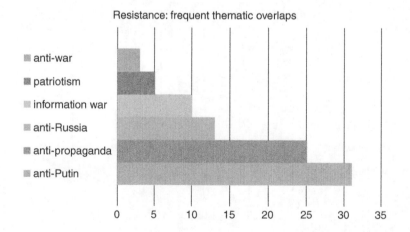

Figure 5.4 Main thematic overlaps of memes that oppose the Russian
       government.

Resistant users exposed the manipulative nature of the patriotic discourse and denunciated it for obscuring the recognition of the existing challenges. For the liberal netizens, "patriotism" means realistic evaluation of the issues and rejection of deceitful rhetoric. The frequent recurrence of the "patriotism" theme in resistant memes highlights the importance of this notion for the Crimean narrative. Over 80% of Russian citizens agree that patriotism should encompass the complete support of the authorities and their initiatives (Ryzhkov, 2015). Criticising patriotism is almost a social taboo in Russia (Ryzhkov, 2015); therefore, liberal publics who object to the propaganda of patriotism embark on a risky endeavour. "Patriotism" and "information war" constitute two of the most debated topics; users from the opposing sides of the political spectrum (pro- and anti-government) utilise memes to share their interpretation of these concepts.

Results of the Meme Analysis: Main Themes and References, from Feel-Good Patriotism to Macho Politics

Based on the classification of main themes and expressive styles of memes, I picked 50 exemplary texts for detailed analysis. The scrutiny of this sample unveils the main angles of political criticism or endorsement in the Crimean discourse on Twitter and identifies the prevailing narratives:

1 **Anti-Propaganda[3] Memes.** Liberal users expose inconsistency of the state rhetoric and media representation of the annexation of Crimea, Ukrainian revolution and Russian resistance; they criticise the manipulation of traditional media and suggest an alternative interpretation of events.

   1.1 Russian Economy
   1.2 Welcome Home

2 **Imperial Ambition.** Pro-Kremlin users reinforce the popular rhetorical concept that Russia has the strength and responsibility to dominate in the region and inaugurate the pan-Slavic 'Russian Empire'; resistant publics utilise memes to comment on the drawbacks of the imperial ambition and the Slavic unity concept.

   2.1 The New USSR project
   2.2 Family Narrative

3 **Russia as a Bear.** A highly popular metaphor depicts Russia as a bear, an unpredictable yet strong and reasonable animal willing to defend its land and offspring. Meme makers apply the allegory of a bear to justify the discourse on Russia's original path in global history and politics and defend its lack of compromise in the international

diplomacy. The subsection *The Olympics and the War* discusses the memes that draw symbolic ties between the Russian feast of sport and the following military campaign in Crimea.

4   **The Rule of Power/Macho Politics.** Pro-government and resistant meme makers deliberate the issues of hard and soft power in domestic and global politics and praise the mounting cult of President Vladimir Putin's personality.

    4.1   Putin as an Action Hero – Militarised Masculinity
    4.2   Putin as the Gang Leader – Criminalised Masculinity
    4.3   Putin as the Embodiment of Russia
    4.4   Sexism

5   **Nazism Allegory.** Pro- and anti-Kremlin netizens apply Nazi labelling to either Putin or his international political opponents, and evoke the stereotypes and scapegoating patterns in rhetoric.
6   **Feel-Good Patriotism.** Pro-government users enhance the state media-promoted style of patriotism that involves uncritical enhancement of the military operation in Ukraine. This sort of social media campaigning utilises methods of advertising and positive branding to make the texts appealing to the networked consumer society.

Anti-Propaganda Memes

Russian traditional and electronic media have produced a colossal amount of coverage on the Crimean crisis. Big professional outlets offered a one-sided interpretation of the events, aggressively endorsed the decisions of the Russian government and dismissed any criticism from its opponents (Kachkaeva, 2015). Social media became the only remaining public site of struggle over meaning and alternative reportage. Yet, even these spaces are not immune to the impact from the state. The Russian government has reportedly hired hundreds of 'Internet trolls' that pollute alternative discussions in the cyberspace with meaningless comments and hate speech (Volchek & Sindelar, 2015). This interruption of the social media discourse has received the name of 'reversed censorship' (Pomerantsev, cited in Bugorkova, 2015), as it does not limit the expression of ideas directly, but makes meaningful discussions hidden and lost in the noise and fights. Despite these and other challenges to the free flow of information and opinion, digital natives used memes to maintain a critical discourse and expose the lies of media propaganda.

Unable to oppose large media corporations with extensive budgets and excellent technical execution of reports, they fight for the truth by dismantling the polished television texts. As the following example (Figure 5.5) shows, opposition users reassemble labels and buzzwords from the official Russian rhetoric and glue them with contrasting images.

Figure 5.5 The meme depicts armed troops as 'tourists'. The tag line says (trans. from Russian): 'Russian tourists are coming to Crimea in large numbers and in orderly manner'.

This juxtaposition of texts highlights the gap between the reality and its mediated version. Russian television was assuring the audience that Crimean people organised the self-defence groups to resist the European and American pressure and preserve independence of the peninsula and keep ties with Russia. These alleged "self-defence troops" appeared in combat uniform and held guns, thus casting doubt on the spontaneous and independent character of this mobilisation. The Russian government denied having sent any professional troops to Crimea and argued that if local people wanted to gather in the name of Russia, it was solely their own will.

On the other hand, Russian media enforced the opinionated coverage of the Ukrainian liberal mobilisation and called it the Western provocation, implying that the US and EU orchestrated the rebellion (Reuters, 2014; Kendall, 2014a; Kachkaeva, 2015). State media referred to the protesters at the main square in Kiev's capital, Maidan Nezalezhnosti, as 'the Maidan fighters'. Journalists labelled them as the recruits of the Western armed forces who receive a solid compensation for spending their time in the protest. Two narratives were developing almost in parallel, prompting the meme makers to comment on the contrast in coverage.

The meme maker experimented with the labels given by the state journalists – he or she swapped around the markers to the images from Kiev and Crimea, respectively. This exhibited the incongruence of the media labelling. 'Maidan fighters' are a group of volunteers who employ random hats as helmets and plates of wood as their armoury, while the 'local Crimean self-defence' is fully equipped in professional military uniform. This popular meme (628 retweets, 128 favourites[4]) unmasks the propagandist tactic of Name-Calling. The dramatic gap between media narratives and reality becomes obvious when the meme maker borrows the components of media discourse and attaches them to the assumed 'real' photographs from the area. Although one cannot check the authenticity of the images, the meme at least questions the validity of assertive labelling in this case.

Furthermore, this meme contains an array of polemic concepts that often function as the rhetorical weapons of contemporary Russian propaganda. There are references to NATO, EU and US as the source of potential threat to Russia (Riabova & Riabov, 2013). These themes borrow from the Cold War rhetoric on Western conspiracy. The Soviet Union ideologists assembled the Cold War propaganda on anti-Americanism and specifically on the conspiracy assumptions that the US was planning to attack the USSR (see Brockriede, 1968). There is another reference in this meme – it points to the terrorism threat. Implicitly, this is also a criticism against the US. Counter-terrorism rhetoric emerged in the American media in the 2000s after the 9/11 attacks in 2001 in New York (Jackson, 2005), and the concept spread out to other Western countries. The meme maker points to the questionable usage of this rhetoric in American politics. The counter-terrorism narrative involves denominating certain individuals, groups, countries or regimes as terrorists or as 'supporting terrorism'; the government can employ this labelling strategy to justify military invasion of other countries and call upon sacrifices inside their own country (Jackson, 2005).

The conjunction of two strands of rhetoric in Russian propaganda yields an interesting result: it accuses Europe of training terrorists. Traditional Western rhetoric links terrorism with the 'clash of civilisations', the dichotomous opposition of progressive Western lifestyle to terrorism groups as the agents of 'barbarism' (Jackson, 2005). Connecting terrorism with Europe indicates a peculiar meeting point of the post-Cold War and counter-terrorism narratives. The US was the primary rival for the USSR, but for the modern Russia it is the collective West that includes the US and Europe. Striving to incite more trepidation in the fellow compatriots (see Kachkaeva, 2015), the Russian propaganda accuses this collective West of conspiracy against humankind: they train terrorists and send them around the globe. The meme maker challenges these claims by showing the shabby-looking Ukrainian protesters. Besides commenting on the exaggeration of Russian propaganda, the meme also touches upon the flexible character of terrorism labelling in the modern-day agenda (see Petersson, 2009; Riabova & Riabov, 2013).

This meme (Figure 5.6) also interrupts the Russian state and media propaganda on the armed resistance in Crimea. It utilises a different principle – it exaggerates the biased rhetoric to the point when it turns into a bad joke. Reflecting on the Russian government's persistent denial of any connection with the gunmen in Crimea, the meme mockingly marks these troops as 'tourists',[5] as if they were voluntary travellers.

One can read this meme differently depending on your political position. The meme sharer is critical of the government and deployed the meme to renounce propaganda. However, the meme is ambiguous. If a person supports Putin and his rule, he or she may perceive this meme as a flattery to the smart propaganda, an appraisal of bold rhetoric that makes Russia influential and blameless at the same time. The hidden meaning of the two-faced rhetoric is that it exercises power: Russian government feels confident enough to lie and laugh in the face of international politicians and call its own troops 'voluntary self-defence'. Calling the armed forces 'tourists' has not transferred much to the traditional media, showing that neither pro- nor anti-government forces found the tag convincing enough. Nonetheless, the term drifted in social networks and even appeared in the job description of an unusual offer that was spotted online. Several recruiting groups used the biggest Russian social network VKontakte (VK) to invite men from 18 to 45 with military experience to go to Crimea as 'Russian tourists' to help decide the fate of the peninsula (Sobytiya, 2015). It remains unclear whether these groups were pranking or actually hiring experienced troops for the Crimean campaign. Nevertheless, the fact that users of social networks appropriated the term means that it has become a euphemism for the pro-Russian troops in the peninsula.

Figure 5.6 The meme juxtaposes two depictions of 'armed forces'. The image on the left says 'Financed by the West, armed by NATO, trained in the terrorist camps of Europe, fighters of Maidan'. The image on the right says 'the spontaneous self-defense of Crimea'.

Memes have a remarkable capacity to absorb cultural codes and references. This meme (Figure 5.7) is multilayered and draws references to many narratives. It suggests how the state media depict the elites and the population of the country: the government works hard to ensure the well-being of the lazy citizens. The Demotivator frame may indicate a witty detail: its black mount reminds us of a TV set, making the meme a symbolic TV screen reproducing the conventional representation of power relations.

However, the image contains another joke and a specific reference inside, like the matryoshka doll. The galley slave on the right has Vladimir Putin's face. Comparing the President with a slave is an old joke, deriving from a 2008 meme. Back then, Putin declared at a press conference in the Kremlin, 'All these eight years I have been working like a galley slave, for all it is worth. I am satisfied with the results of my work' ('Все эти восемь лет я пахал, как раб на галерах, с полной отдачей сил. Я доволен результатами своей работы.') (Putin-itogi, 2012). The quote was misspelled in the media: '(K)ак раб' ('like a slave') became 'как краб' ('like a crab'). Liberal publics coined many jokes about Putin being a hard-working crab (Lurkmore, 2014). This meme functions as a meme in a meme, a sophisticated Russian doll of symbols that links the past with the present. Although the meme does not directly comment on the

Figure 5.7 The meme juxtaposes the depiction of the people and the government on national television. It shows 'people' as a man indulging in vodka and caviar, and 'rulers' as the galley slaves. The tag line says: 'Channel One. The daily news in a nutshell'.

conflict in Crimea, it nonetheless ridicules the notion of 'news' in the environment of 'hybrid warfare' and ubiquitous propaganda. According to the meme, the state media broadcast symbols rather than facts, and affirm the stereotypes that are favourable for the state. The text, therefore, disrupts the convention and probes the availability of unbiased journalism in the Russian media ecology.

Furthermore, many meme makers switch to irrational and artful formats that would expose the bizarreness of the indoctrinated media discourse. In March 2014, the Rossiya-1 channel broadcast a scandalous story. The Kremlin-backed television presenter Dmitry Kiselyov issued an unashamed threat to the US. In his weekly current affairs show, he announced to a massive audience, 'Russia is the only country in the world that is realistically capable of turning the United States into radioactive ash' (Kelly, 2014). The screen behind him showed a graphic mushroom cloud that appears after a nuclear blast. Kiselyov then remarked on the success of the Crimean referendum and affirmed Russian resistance to any outward criticism, which illustrated Kachkaeva's (2015) point that contemporary Russian television does not produce news, but generates an emotion and makes the audience hooked to the overly dramatic storytelling.

A number of liberal users replied to Kiselyov by releasing cascades of witty parodies and imaginative memes in digital networks (Suleimanov, 2014a). Many resistant users seized the opportunity to comment on other themes, such as Putin's international ambition and inability to solve domestic problems. One user tweeted (translated from Russian): 'Russia is the only country in the world capable of turning the United States into radioactive ash, but incapable of building normal roads in the country' (Suleimanov, 2014a: para 9). Other users suggested that Dmitry Kiselyov, who just returned from a family trip to Amsterdam, might consider spending his next holiday in North Korea, as both the US and the EU will probably refuse him entry from now on. In the meantime, pro-government users did not incorporate any other themes, but focused on defending the presenter. They argued that Kiselyov's allegation was not a threat but explanation of what may happen if somebody attacks Russia.

Many meme makers offered doctored versions of the image of Kiselyov swaggering about the radioactive ash. The choice of meme making method illustrates the absurd character of propaganda journalism. By placing Kiselyov in the surreal environment (e.g., when the mental care nurses lead him away (Figure 5.8) or he carries a peacock's tail), the meme makers deem the media agenda as surreal by the way it distorts truth. Absurdity contradicts logic; absurdity is unreasonable, foolish and ridiculous and offers an alternative way to defend a healthy critical mind. As the Theatre of Absurd in the 1950s–1960s broke convention to express a sense of shock at the absence of sensible well-defined systems of values (Esslin, 1965), absurd memes also convey the feeling of disillusionment. Hence, many 'radioactive ash' memes use incomplete communication – no

Figure 5.8 The meme depicts the popular TV host Dmitry Kiselyov being dragged out of his studio by the nurses. The tag line says 'Into radioactive ash'.

clarification accompanies the edited image, and weird laughter becomes the last available resort to protect truth and reason. Following the Theatre of Absurd's principles of applying absurd critically, Kiselyov memes with nurses and peacock's tail disturb the shiny completeness of the conventional television picture, a habitual template of a tidy presenter in a bright-lit studio. By deconstructing the visuals, meme sharers question the transmitted content and the validity of the words and graphs.

Moreover, the reference to a peacock serves as the allegoric commentary on Kiselyov's public demeanour. Comparison to a proud and showy bird inflicts the image of someone who flaunts his or her colours and revels in bragging. The meme casts doubt on the appropriateness of such deportment for the host of a federal news programme; it therefore questions whether Kiselyov's unprofessional and disgraceful claims owe to his personality or the necessity to serve the needs of propaganda. The meme subsequently examines the role of a journalist in the oppressed media environment, when a professional serves as a dependent mediator between the state and the publics. The meme makers point to the irony and idiosyncrasy of such pseudo-journalist employment: Kiselyov pretends to host a personal analytical programme, but lacks autonomy in judgements.

Meme makers can be frank in criticising their own attempts at digital polemic. This meme (Figure 5.9) grasps the essence of hybrid warfare's impact on the social media users and scorns clicktivism. It mocks the enthusiasm and naivety of the 'couch troops', the average citizens who turn to the Internet to express their views and fight the adversaries. Joining the impassioned, frenzied political debates in social networks can be pleasing for one's self-esteem. Getting engaged in these discussions becomes a rewarding and accessible self-identity exercise in contemporary Russia – one can steam off and feel having contributed to the public discussion (Kachkaeva, 2015). This meme also features the postmodern characteristic of self-reference, the custom to represent the world not in the way the author experienced it, but through references to how the author and others had presented the world before (Noth, 2007). The creator of this meme critically remarks on their own practices of digital disputes and on those of their fellow social network users; this is a meme about those who coin memes. The visual language of the meme suggests protective helmets as a metaphor for the prejudices that people carry

Figure 5.9 The meme depicts the people who engage in Internet battles from the comfort of their homes. The coats of arms on the left and right read as 'The couch troops of self-defense. Euro-coach' and 'Couch troops. The slowly reacting forces'. The tag line below reads as 'The fights are continuing'.

with them to their online debates. Many of these prejudices come from the propagandist discourse or the uncritical oppositional discourse. Subsequently, many users join the virtual discussions to promote their own perspective and dismiss any alternative points of view (Kachkaeva, 2015). Two characters in the meme look identical, and only the flags on their heads make a difference. The meme probably suggests that the existence of an open space for a free conversation does not secure a balanced exchange of opinions, and interconnectivity does not shorten the distance between people if they prefer to remain in their own bubbles.

In summary, Anti-Propaganda memes aim at disrupting the hegemonic media discourse and exposing its deceit. They deconstruct elements of state rhetoric and media propaganda and reassemble them to reveal alternative meanings via irony and sarcasm. Moreover, the majority of memes in this category encourage a critical assessment of the 'truth'; despite the exposure to multiple sources of information offline and online, people find it extremely challenging to find truth in the Crimean conflict. Moreover, Anti-Propaganda meme sharers invite us to reflect on the function and morals of journalism in Russia and the journalism code of practice that allows channelling of biased and distorted facts. Resistant users have adopted various defence mechanisms for keeping the sanity of their minds from propagandist journalism: rational, absurd and self-referential humour. Anti-Propaganda memes further explore the merit and consistency of political debates online; they critically point to the incongruity of clicktivism and warn of techno determinism, suggesting that citizens bring their offline prejudices to shared digital spaces. Meme makers subsequently question the possibility of candid representation and interpretation of events during wartimes, either on the television or on the computer screen.

Russian Economy Memes, or When Memes Point to the Structural Issues

Resistant meme makers have implemented other strategies in opposing state propaganda. Anti-Propaganda meme sharers exposed the inconsistencies in media representations of the Crimean crisis. Other users pursued a more ambitious task and discussed how the discourse on the peninsula fits the broader rhetorical narratives that had flourished before the Crimean campaign, but obtained new interpretation during the 2014 events. Two main prevailing propaganda themes arose from the content analysis: assertion of the thriving Russian economy, and the mythological narrative of the Russian empire in the process of regaining its power.

Many memes commented on the financial outcomes of annexing Crimea. In 2014, media and experts were divided on the economic benefit of incorporating the peninsula into the Russian territory. A few of them calculated that the region's development would cost Russia a total of 30 billion dollars up until 2025 (Shokhina, 2014). Other experts claimed that Crimea was primarily a strategic appropriation for Russia: the country secured control over the Black Sea and did not have to pay rent to Ukraine for keeping naval bases there (Shokhina, 2014). Nonetheless, when Crimea was cut off from the Ukrainian infrastructure, Russia had to invest huge sums in building power stations and transport links in a short period. Many financial experts agreed that obtaining Crimea was a strategic and ideological move with severe economic consequences. Despite initial public approval of the peninsula's annexation, by the end of 2014, 60% of Russians sensed that the level of life would decrease in Russia because of the Crimean events (Levada-Centre, as cited in Parfyonova, 2014).

Memes on the Russian economy aim at drawing a link between Russian welfare and politics. The primary meme format of opposition publics here is Demotivator, the suitable expressive vehicle to compare optimistic forecasts and assumptions with reality.

One of the Twitter users accompanied this meme (Figure 5.5) with a tweet 'Vladimir region sent 14 tons of humanitarian aid to Crimea'. The image exploits the iconography of canonical Russian landscapes displayed in museums. The photograph of the rural landscape in the meme reminds us of classic paintings produced hundreds of years ago, thus pointing at the continuously troubled existence of the Russian periphery.

Another version of the meme (Figure 5.10) employs the same image, but with a more satirical tag line: 'In the epicentre of stability'. This meme

Figure 5.10 The meme shows a gloomy landscape and a tag line 'In the epicentre of stability'.

attacks the trademark propaganda concept – the virtue of 'stability'. The Russian authorities have persistently referred to stability as one of the primary achievements and treasures of the country's management: they often warn of the turbulence of an economy and invite the population to worship stability instead of change or improvements (Belkovsky, 2003). The meme agrees that stability does indeed exist in many parts of Russia, but it takes the form of stagnation and scarcity. This observation casts doubt on the overall merit of the politics that presents stability as an accomplishment.

Framing a meme as a painting is uncommon for Western meme makers and seems a local Russian peculiarity. Existing research on memes (Burgess, 2008; Milner, 2013; Shifman, 2013) does not identify remix of a classic painting as a specific meme layout. The rising popularity of the pattern in Russia perhaps owes to the famous Russian idiom 'kartina maslom'. It literally means 'oil painting', but people use it ironically to express one's shock or amusement by what she sees. @ElenaMikhailova included the idiom as one of the tags next to the meme. The other tag is 'Crimea is ours!'

Another popular layout of Russian Economy memes is matching expressive portraits of Russian citizens with motivating slogans or trending catchphrases. They fit into the global rendition of the classic Demotivator meme: the clash of the image and text produce a shocking effect and confront the slogan. Russian Demotivators on socio-economic issues display the average Russians who support the president, and criticise their blind conformism to the corrupt regime. Instead of looking for an improved level of life, citizens applaud ideological gestures with negative economic consequences (over 80% of the population approved of Putin's activity in 2014 (Levada-Centre, 2014, cited in Parfitt, 2014)).

One of the drawbacks of the Russian Economy memes is their limited capacity to share data. The meme format facilitates locating the issue, but restricts argumentation: unlike the exceptional meme with statistics, the rest of the texts mostly call for an emotional reaction rather than rational consideration of facts. Russian Economy memes oppose government propaganda by remixing recognisable symbols of the promulgated discourse ('Crimea is ours') with disturbing visuals. The meme makers subsequently condemn the rhetorical concept of 'stability' and suggest that it deceitfully masks the lack of progress. Surprisingly, this group of memes also draws on the historical perspective and employs the framework of a classic painting to emphasise the continuity of the poor management and sparse living conditions of rural Russia.

Welcome Home Memes

The idea that Crimea is coming home, returning to the place where it belongs, was very popular in public speeches and the mass media in 2014. The main Russian search engine Yandex returns 1 million pages when typing in Russian 'Crimea has returned home'. Major television channels and newspapers used this slogan and narrative in their news reports on Crimea (Khudikova, 2014; Purim, 2014). Vladimir Putin applied this framing in his annual broadcast 2015 New Year address to the nation, asserting, 'Love to the Motherland is one of the most uplifting feelings. It expressed itself fully in the fraternal support to Sevastopol and Crimea, when they decided to return to their home' (RT, 2014b: para 5). This narrative not only legitimises the Russian actions in Crimea, but designates the case to an almost mythological realm. **The Crimean narrative fits the classic fiction narrative of 'Voyage and Return',** one of seven basic plots of human culture (Booker, 2004). The protagonist goes on a mysterious and dangerous journey, overcomes multiple threats and returns with trophies or an invaluable experience. The Biblical Parable of the Prodigal Son and Homer's *Odyssey* are among the examples of this plot in world culture (Figure 5.11).

The liberal public criticised the homecoming rhetoric. They used memes to confront the notion of the 'return' of the peninsula and insisted that Crimean people should think twice about whether to celebrate their new country.

Figure 5.11 The meme shows the map of the Crimean Peninsula. The first part of the tag line on the top says 'The Russians in Crimea were constantly told: 'If you don't like it here, get out!'. The second part of the tag line in the bottom says 'And finally, the Russians said: Fine, convinced, we are going to Russia'.

Ukrainian-speaking users were among the critical voices that commented on the 'homecoming' narrative. One of them, a very popular resistant account @EuromaidanPR,[6] used an edited Soviet poster to make a point (Figure 5.12). While propaganda paints Russia as a happy home for Crimea, the Ukrainian-speaking users here feel like somebody has robbed *their* home. The change of angle from one 'home' to the other invites the audience to reflect on the legitimacy of the homecoming narrative. There is an important motif of invasion in this image. The original poster comes from the 20th-century USSR placard against alcoholism – the original text said 'A drunk father is a tragedy for a family!'. The iconography suggests a conflict; even those not familiar with the provenance of the poster can understand the drive of a mother to protect her homes and family from invaders. Power relations in this narrative imply mercy for the vulnerable individuals, a woman and her children. The meme maker introduced the Russian president's face in the poster, and he personifies the attack on Crimea. The allegory is direct and explicit: the meme maker depicted Russia's activity in Ukraine as Vladimir Putin storming an innocent peaceful home.

Meme makers who attack the homecoming narrative operate on the symbolical level: they carry off to earth the mythological exaggeration of the state discourse and contaminate it with touches of reality. They also offer conflicting mythology to counteract the Prodigal Son-like story of the Russian propaganda. By dissolving the celebrated concept

Figure 5.12 The meme depicts a woman with a child holing a door against the invader who has the face of Vladimir Putin. The tag line is in Ukrainian and it says 'Sir! Go to your own place! This house is not yours!'.

of returning home, they question the applicability and flexibility of the notion of 'home' in three dimensions: Russians, Ukrainians and Crimeans have opposing opinions on what to define as 'home' for the disputed peninsula. Moreover, the Russian-speaking Twitter public inquires whether it is the right time for 'Prodigal Son' to return 'home' as Russia is struggling with domestic issues and may not be the most welcoming homeland for new territories and populations.

Imperial Ambition, or How the Centuries-Old Narrative Achieved New Dimension Online

The term 'Imperial ambition' defines a country's desire to create an empire and project power over neighbouring states (see Chomsky & Barsamian, 2010; Galeotti & Bowen, 2014). The Imperial Russia idea implies that the country has the obligation to reinstate its long-standing glory and global significance. The state, therefore, demands sacrifices from its citizens in the areas of comfort, safety and financial stability for the benefit of the awaited political magnificence. The authorities invite the population to evaluate their living conditions not by the global standard, but by the unique local paradigm, thus making the government practically unaccountable (Dubin, 2014). In Crimean memes, the rhetoric of **Imperial Ambition appears in two main instances: as the enhancement of the Soviet myth, and as a softer narrative of the alleged familial ties** between Russia, Ukraine and the Crimean population in particular.

The New USSR Project

The following meme (Figure 5.13) illustrates how digital publics respond to the imperial narrative. The meme proposes to return Russia to its Soviet borders. The tweet says, "Russia is not getting angry. Russia is concentrating. It is time to get things together!"

The map of the Soviet Union carries a Soviet slogan borrowing from the first verse of a 1923 popular song 'Aviators' March'. It used to be the official hymn of the Soviet Air Forces, and is well known to the population. This meme indicates that the myth of the Soviet prosperity is becoming increasingly popular in the 2010s. Levada-Centre (2014) reports that 40% of Russians assess the economic and political system of the USSR as 'almost perfect'. Sociologist Lev Gudkov (2014) believes that people's longing for the USSR owes to the gaps in collective memory. Russian citizens have forgotten the real-life conditions and remember mostly positive key points such as a free healthcare system, housing and public utilities available in the Soviet Union. The ruling elites endorse the romantic vision of the Soviet past: television frequently broadcasts movies of those times that promote an idealised portrayal of the society. Between the end of the 1990s and the beginning of the 2000s, there was a

Figure 5.13 The meme shows the map of extended territory of Russia with the tag line 'We were born to make the fairy tale come true!'.

short wave of media reports, investigations and public discussions on the de-sentimentalisation of the Soviet era. It has not affected public opinion in the long-term perspective and on a deeper level. Prokhorova (2015) believes that the de-idealisation required more repetition, introduction to the school curriculum and establishment as the state's official standpoint.

The population's tendency to sentimentalise the Soviet past may also signify an unexpressed criticism of the current government which is unable to provide the same availability and quality of public services. The majority of pro-Soviet publics reside in small towns and villages (Gudkov, 2014) and often depend on the infrastructure remaining from the USSR. Old Soviet factories and enterprises may be the only job providers for the whole town. The population from peripheral areas, Gudkov (2014) notes, are frightened that they would not be able to survive in the market economy and dream of a strong socialist state; they are willing to pass responsibility for their well-being to the authorities and hence idolise the Soviet system of distribution of goods.

The meme (Figure 5.14) contains a curious reference to the realm of a myth – the verse mentions the 'fairy-tale' that should be made true. The meme maker is self-contradictory as he or she classifies the Soviet dream as an unattainable myth yet still demands the revival of the USSR. The

Figure 5.14 The meme shows a drawing of Vladimir Putin looking in the mirror to find Joseph Stalin in the reflection.

map creates an intriguing symbol here: it serves as the verifiable evidence that Moscow's dominance over such a colossal land was once a historical fact. If the USSR happened before, the meme maker implies, it can happen again. The presence of a map turns the idea real and presents the possibility as the completed act.

The majority of memes represent the USSR in memes through symbols, as either a map or a flag. For instance, a Ukrainian opposition user @Dbnmjr published a meme containing a Russian flag that conceals the flag of the Soviet Union underneath. This framing may attract manifold interpretations. Many Russians yearn for the USSR's reunion, while the citizens of the ex-Soviet countries detest the 'back to the USSR' rhetoric. Notably, memes promoting the New USSR idea rarely specify which ex-Soviet states should be absorbed. Clarity on the geopolitical victims of reunion may repulse users from those countries and invoke their opposition to the memes praising the New USSR.

Reinforcement of the Soviet myth may play against the current government. Several memes (see, for instance, Figure 5.14) on imperial ambition encompassed the figure of Joseph Stalin, a very controversial figure in Russian history. In 2013, almost 50% of respondents positively evaluated the role of Stalin in the country's history (Levada-Centre, 2013). The Soviet dictator also led the rating of the most distinguished persons of all times, beating the likes of Lenin, Marx, Peter the Great, Pushkin, Putin and Great Patriotic War commanders (Levada-Centre, 2013). Only 25% of Russian people treat Stalin negatively, with disgust or fear.

Sociologists admit that the attitude towards the Soviet leader is gradually becoming positive over the years (Ria, 2013). The meme (Figure 5.14) creates a fertile soil for debate. It does not explicitly reveal the author's attitude towards either Putin or Stalin. We observe a confident and demanding Joseph Stalin confronting an awkwardly looking Vladimir Putin from the mirror. The meme consists of a cartoon; there is no text to shed the light on the author's intentions. What makes it a meme is this ambiguity of interpretation – one has to take into account the knowledge of context and their personal political preferences to decode the meaning. The account that circulated this meme defines itself as Ukrainian, hence the meme is most likely to vilify Putin and the Kremlin.

Although the meme slates Putin as the successor to the notorious dictator, it can also serve as the endorsement of this controversial 'inheritance'. Those in favour of Stalin may admiringly notice that Putin adopted many traits of Stalin's political strategy: from rigid vertical hierarchy of governance to the cult of personality. Those condemning Stalin as the oppressor would find it alarming to see him equated to Putin. The third interpretation would be to see Stalin as a much more powerful historical figure, an aspiring role model for the current Russian president. The fourth interpretation is that Putin is obsessed with Stalin and fantasises of following in his footsteps so passionately that he starts envisioning Stalin in the mirror.

The juxtaposition with Stalin sheds light on the potential trajectory of Putin's public representation. Travin (2015) claimed that Vladimir Putin had to decide on a rebranding strategy for his public persona after he turned 60 in 2012. The Russian leader faced a challenging choice on whether to stick to the 'Macho' image, or invest in either 'The Wise Elder' or 'The Saviour of the Motherland' identity. According to Travin (2015), Putin chose the last title and utilised the Crimean crisis as an opportunity to earn it.

Alaska Memes. Memes that discuss the possibility of returning Alaska to Russia form a special strand. It can be attached to many other narratives (for instance, Macho Politics), but is mostly related to the Russian imperial ambitions. The Kremlin justified the annexation of Crimea as the 'correction of a historical mistake'. Bloggers suggested applying the same pattern to Alaska, the American state that used to belong to the Russian territory (Tetrault-Farber, 2014). Tsar Alexander II sold this land to the US for $7.2 million in 1867. It is unclear whether politicians or pro-Kremlin journalists started the Alaska memes, yet the narrative has been present in political speeches, media publications and social networks (Tetrault-Farber, 2014). Putin acknowledged the Alaska narrative, but did not elaborate on it in his public appearances. However, a woman asked the President about the possibility of annexing Alaska during his traditional broadcast open line with the nation in 2014. Putin joyfully remarked 'Faina Ivanovna, my dear, why do you need Alaska?' (Ria, 2014), thus closing the topic with everyone laughing.

A common trait of Alaska memes is that users realise the mock character of the claims to 'bring Alaska back'. Jubilant and lighthearted memes help the users to overcome fear regarding sanctions and global tension that followed the Crimean annexation. Netizens turn the appropriation of Crimea into a mythological act, a folkloric joke; they scorn the real consequences of the event and exaggerate the phantasmagorical dimension. They brag about snatching Alaska, Kiev, the Moon and other lands with the same facility. Alaska memes interpret global politics as a reality game or a show, where Putin always wins. This framing invites the Russian public to celebrate being on the winning side.

Family Narrative

Meme makers widely exploited the themes of brotherly unity and pan-Slavic camaraderie both in pro-government and critical texts. The ambition to dominate the global political arena drives the Russian authorities to propagate the concept of Russian patriarchy over other countries. To do so, it draws parallels with traditional family ties. Hegemonic Russia often identifies itself as the 'older sister' or 'older brother' to demarcate the country's hierarchical status in relation to neighbouring countries and diplomatic partners. A high-ranked Kremlin-related diplomat Andrey Kortunov elucidated the subtle gender connotations of these family-related metaphors:

> Who are we now for the Chinese? Perhaps, older brother no longer... They have a notion of "older sister". Older brother is the one you necessarily have to obey, while older sister is the one you respect and whose advice you follow, but must not conform to. I think now we are "older sister" for China.
>
> (Kobzev, 2015)

The evolution of the 'older brother' in the 'older sister' rhetoric symbolises Russia's attempts at projecting soft power instead of hard power over influential counterparts.

The Russian public rhetoric has also progressed from patriarchal to neo-patriarchal in recent years (see Snyder, 2003, as cited in Stein, 2005). In opposition to the dominant, conservative, highly hierarchical state with rigid traditional gender roles and an unyielding family order, the neo-patriarchal state tolerates more flexibility. Neo-patriarchal narratives exhibit a smoother, gentler version of traditional masculinity: media portray men as caring fathers and husbands, compassionate protectors and sympathetic caretakers (Snyder, 2003, as cited in Stein, 2005: 604). An overly dominant conservative male conveys aggression, while a neo-patriarchal man consents to a compromise. When transferred to politics, these notions correlate with hard power and soft power (or at least a softer version of hard power, for authoritarian regimes). Memes that appeal to fraternal bonds communicate soft power. Instead of issuing a direct order to obey, the Russian state validates its involvement in the conflicts of other countries through sympathy, concern and a familial responsibility.

This meme (Figure 5.15) presents Russia as a caring and commanding Mother. Big and strong, dominating other actors in the image even in size, she authoritatively calls home not only Crimea, but also Alaska.

Despite the efforts of the Family narrative apologists, resistant meme makers denigrate the caring nature of the neo-patriarchal Russia. They used the same style – the circle-shaped simple drawings – but painted Russia as the demagogue and assailant; they cast doubt on the idea of a family reunion and called the Crimean operation an act of robbery instead. This meme (Figure 5.16) points to this forced relationship.

Figure 5.15 The meme depicts a scene between little balls that represent Russia, Ukraine, Crimea and Anarchy (red and black). Russia calls for Crimea as for a child and urges it to come home immediately. Then Russia starts calling for Alaska.

Figure 5.16 The meme depicts Russia and Ukraine as little balls. Russia calls to Ukraine by saying 'Ukraine, wait! Aren't we brothers?'. In the next scene, it forces Ukraine back with a gun and reinstates 'Brothers, I said!'.

This meme remarks that Russia's influence over Ukraine is dramatically limited. The meme implies that Russia can keep the 'little brother' attached only by means of violence and threats, 'hard power' instead of 'soft' persuasion. Russia has a prolonged tradition of perceiving Ukraine as part of its own territory and political influence over the neighbour has been 'an existential imperative' for Moscow for centuries (Bogomolov & Lytvynenko, 2012). According to the Chatham House's analysis (Bogomolov & Lytvynenko, 2012), Russia of the 2010s possesses limited socio-economic resources for projecting authority over Ukraine. The lack of pertinent instruments of control prompts the exploitation of national myths around the 'common future' of the ex-Soviet states. Such ideological apparatuses as the Russian Orthodox Church, the media and non-governmental organisations have access to the Ukrainian public due to the common language and historical influence: the majority of Ukrainians speak Russian fluently and many churches belong to the Moscow Patriarchate. These institutions are capable of deploying narratives on the might of pan-Slavic unity to the Ukrainian people, acting as the enforcers of 'soft power'.

Nonetheless, the Kremlin of the 2010s cannot afford a soft power rhetoric. A country has to retain a significant political and economic authority to appear invincible and influential to the foreign states (Nye, 2004, as cited in Bogomolov & Lytvynenko, 2012: 2). The power struggles in Ukraine over 2013–2014 have divulged the growing ineptness of Russia to oppose the soft power of the EU and US; the failure of Moscow's diplomatic schemes resulted in the success of the Maidan protests in Kiev and a complete change of rulers in Ukraine. The loss of influence exhorted Moscow to the open execution of 'hard power' and the physical capture of Crimea. Russia's endeavours to resuscitate the narratives of familial bonding and a common past are now stumbling upon a watershed, the Crimean case. The meme emphasises the gap between two dimensions of power that Russia projected over Ukraine and an inability to switch between them without damage.

Ukrainian users resisted the Family narrative by suggesting the concept of a Broken Family. One of the most popular memes started as an offline poster. Someone hung the image of two hands, the damaged Ukrainian and the augmented Russian, and asked in Ukrainian 'Brothers?'. This contestation of the popular myths shows how people use memes to discuss politics on a metaphorical level. Unlike Welcome Home meme, the case of Family memes demonstrates that people can intervene in the archetypal concept and challenge them. They don't need to ground them in facts and examples from real life, but question the validity of the outdated 'fairy tale'.

The study of the Imperial Ambitions narrative manifests a fascinating amalgamation of the Orthodox Church's doctrine of the Imperial Russia, the myth of the Soviet prosperity, the demand for neo-patriarchal state hegemony and Moscow's failing attempts at projecting soft power in global diplomacy. References to religion are relatively rare, but the pro-Soviet sentiments of the idealised life under the Communist authoritarian rule are ubiquitous. Pro-Kremlin meme makers express their longing for the stable, prosperous superstate. However, this public demand may in fact conceal the unacknowledged request for better management of the country. Memes reflect the recurring message of the state rhetoric that ideological dominance is more important than the material needs of the population. The Russian government has a remarkably high approval rating, which confirms the triumph of the patriotic rhetoric within the country. Pro-government social network users express their approval of conservative gender roles, vertical social hierarchy, rigid discipline and traditional family. Intriguingly, pro-government memes frequently link the two components: a stable superstate and patriarchal society. This finding is particularly interesting, as the Soviet Union required women to be equal counterparts to men in labour and social duties. Nevertheless, this trend towards equality does not appear in the memes, which mostly celebrate the mythological, idealistic comprehension of the traditionalist social order.

Many memes discuss the inconsistency of Russian imperial claims and familial narratives on Ukraine. They also point to the gap between the domestic worship of the Soviet myth and international denunciation of hard power and patriarchal ideologies. Twitter users remain divided in their evaluation of the current Russia's level of affluence on the global arena. Liberal meme sharers also expose the lack of clearly identified alternatives to the remnants of Soviet ideological and social system: contemporary Russia struggles to design an original identity on the global arena and still refers to the glory of the USSR and ambitions of the Cold War era.

Russia as a Bear

The Olympic Games in Sochi in February 2014 seemed to have called a temporary 'ceasefire' in the exchange of political memes. Although the liberal public kept criticising the government for corruption and minor issues, they paid much respect to the Olympics and did not ridicule the organisers or sports federations – patriotism won over protest (Walker, 2014b). Eighty-one percent of respondents felt more proud of their country thanks to the Games in Sochi (Levada-Centre, 2014, as cited in Poroshina, 2014). Even the leaders of political resistance praised the professional organisation, the beauty of the opening ceremony and the achievements of the winning Russian athletes.

One of the well-known memes on Sochi and Crimea (Figure 5.17) looks like the work of an English-speaking user and seems more appealing to the Western rather than Russian publics. The meme uses advertising techniques and advances an ironic rebranding of the Games. It involves three official mascots of the Sochi Olympics: polar bear, hare and leopard (Olympic.org, no date). The meme implies that the Kremlin may have used the Olympics to turn the public attention away from the Russian military campaign in Ukraine. Mascots here may represent the unidentified gunmen in Crimea. It can also mean the failure of the Games as the festival of good spirit and sport. In this case, the meme may imply that people would remember the Sochi mascots as the symbols of war, not peace. The supporting tweet points at the Russian reputation abroad and says, 'Bear, Bunny, and Leopard are taking a field trip! #Crimea #Крым #война #war'. Russia has made such a big and costly effort to modernise its economy and reputation by means of holding the Games (Fedyashin, 2014), yet the following Crimean crisis may have destroyed all this good work.

Pro-Russia accounts also included the Olympic mascots in their memes, but utilised them to conjoin the narratives on the Olympics and Crimea. They hailed the military success together with the achievements in sports. Sport and war share a similar semiotic system, and the elites have articulated and mobilised the tropes related to sports in many

Figure 5.17 The meme mixes the official mascots of the 2014 Sochi Olympic
          Games with the drawing of a tank. It replaces the logo of the Games
          with the words 'Krim.ru' ('Krim' is the Russian way to say 'Crimea').

armed conflicts (Jansen & Sabo, 1994). Power holders have frequently
deployed sports/war rhetoric for nation building. In the Crimean case,
two narratives mingled into one to bypass the social divisions and political discrepancies of various groups in society and buttress loyalty to the
ruling elites (see Jansen & Sabo, 1994).

Many Olympic memes present Russia in the form of a bear. The
year 2014 marked a conscious revival of that centuries-long emblem of
Russia, and memes help to shed light on the reasons why.

The portrayal of Russia as a land of bears first appeared in the writings
of 16th-century Western explorers. They reported that these wild animals
had been wandering freely in the streets of Russian settlements. Although
Russian fairy tales and folklore frequently feature a bear, the stereotype
of depicting Russia as a bear in politics came from abroad. Western political cartoonists of the 18th century first rendered Russian emperors as
bears (RT, 2010). Since then, both international and local cartoonists,
writers, journalists, philosophers and politicians persistently articulated
the metaphor to lay emphasis on Russia's nonconformity, unpredictability and confrontational demeanour (De Lazari, 2012; Riabova, 2012).
De Lazari (2012) draws a socio-historical explanation for the domestic

regard of the allegory. He blames the Soviet social oppression for inflicting hatred towards discipline and order on the Russian mentality. The trauma of collectivism, negligence of personal freedom and economic independence made people perceive the state and the law as an enemy. Russian philosophers and writers insisted on the importance of the Internal Law (moral values, religion) for Russians over the External Law (social contract, judicial system and welfare state) (De Lazari, 2012: 276). A bear is an allegory of a wild spirit, a creature strong enough to resist pressure and retort violently to any attack and threat to its land or breed. The connotations of power and safety make the bear metaphor alluring for Russian collective identity. However, Riabova (2012) notes that the West mobilises a bear as a symbol of Russia more than Russia does for itself, and often in a negative sense.

The USSR government employed the bear in an attempt to rebrand the country in global discourse. They made an amicable bear 'Misha' a mascot of the 1980 Summer Olympics in Moscow: this bear was not the wildlife barbarian, but resembled a benign teddy bear. Organisers of the 1980 Games closing ceremony ended the show with a meaningful detail – they let the giant inflatable bear fly away in the Moscow skies. For many people this was a symbolic farewell to the hostile tension of the Cold War: Russia let go of being tumultuous and feral; the bear metaphor is outdated and deserves to rest in peace (Platoff, 2012).

The revival of the bear metaphor for the Olympic Games in Sochi, where a bear reappeared as a mascot, creates a surprising continuity between the 1980s and 2010s. The post-Cold War environment of the last century was marked with the desire to cease the hostility and establish a global balance, while the rise of 2012 marked a new round of tension between Russia and the West. The 1980 Olympic bear promoted peace and the 2014 Olympic bear has high chances to be associated with war (Koshkin, 2014). The perpetuation of the bear trope in the war/sports narrative indicates that the bear still functions as the allusion to Russia's hard power and reminds us of the Cold War-like antagonism between Russia and the rest of the world.

This very popular image (Figure 5.18) appears in many memes related to the Crimean crisis. In most cases, the photo alone makes a statement, in other versions users add a commentary. The meme of a nonchalant bear surrounded by the symbols of Russian national glory (from the traditional music instrument balalaika to a tank) articulates the narratives of the Russian special path of development and unconventional standpoint in global politics.

The exchange of sanctions between Russia and the West resulted in a partial economic isolation for Russia. Nevertheless, the cultural isolation has become even stronger. In December 2014, Vladimir Putin deemed the economic turbulence in Russia as 'the price to pay for our natural desire to self-preserve as a nation, as a civilisation, as a state' (Kremlin,

Figure 5.18 The meme depicts a bear surrounded with stereotypical symbols of Russia, a tank, a bottle of vodka, a Kalashnikov gun, a balalaika and the ushanka hat. The tag line says 'Waiting for the sanctions'.

2014a, para 3). Putin notably and proudly included a bear metaphor in his speech. He gave a highly allegorical address to the crowd of 1,200 Russian journalists gathered in Moscow's World Trade Centre. The annual meeting with the press coincidentally followed the collapse of the rouble a few days before. Putin reassured his guests that the economy would rebound and compared Russia to a bear protecting his taiga.

> (S)ometimes I think that maybe it would be best if our bear just sat still. Maybe he should stop chasing pigs and boars around the taiga but start picking berries and eating honey. Maybe then, he will be left alone. But no, he will not be! Because someone will always try to chain him up. As soon as he is chained, they will tear out his teeth and claws. In this analogy, I am referring to the power of nuclear deterrence. As soon as – God forbid – it happens and they no longer need the bear, the taiga will be taken over. <…> And then, when all the teeth and claws are torn out, the bear will be of no use at all. Perhaps they will stuff it and that is all. So, it is not about Crimea but about us protecting our independence, our sovereignty and our right to exist. That is what we should all realise.
>
> (Kremlin, 2014a: para 4)

Putin's speech both explains and mystifies the analogy with the bear. He portrays him as a reasonable creature protecting his land; his hostility is the direct result of the pressure from the outside. At the same time, Putin draws a parallel with nuclear deterrence, looping in the Cold War narrative of nuclear threat (see also Sen, 2014). Reference to the bear's control over nuclear weapons suggests that his enemies should refrain from pressure. This speech points to the bear's unpredictability and relates to the classic centuries-old allegory of a bear for Russia. The 2014 Putin address squandered all the rhetoric efforts of the 1980s bear rebranding.

Bold framing of the bear memes (expressive photo or laconic cartoon with minimum text) implies that many Twitter users endorse and approve Putin's vision. The bear serves as a positive self-representation of Russian self-defence – celebrated inside the country and feared from the outside. It signifies an important shift towards the rule of power as opposed to the rule of law, liberalisation and compromise.

The bear rhetoric has another particularly significant function; it fosters the atmosphere of threat and danger surrounding Russia from the outside, but describes the decision makers as the indomitable guardians of their people. The new wave of approval of the bear metaphor indicates the population's content with the government's course to hard power and harsh actions. Russia appears in memes as a bear either waiting for an attack or succeeding over weaker adversaries. Bear memes also fit into the Russian Imperialism discourse – they present the animal as a solitary custodian of the forest, a fierce fighter for his land and offspring. The controversial nature of the bear symbolism – sturdy and fair, yet unpredictable and savage – stimulates the domestic endorsement of Russia as a special character in global politics. By promoting the narrative on Russia as a bear, the authorities reserve the right to implement unreasonable and erratic measures inside the country and disobey international diplomatic principles. They may call for sacrifices for the preservation of the 'sieged land'; the bear protects his environment by all means, not only those approved by civilisation. This rhetoric assigns the blame for internal issues to external enemies and presents the elites as mighty guardians of their people.

The Rule of Power/Macho Politics

Content analysis of the Crimean collection has revealed a strong pattern – plenty of memes depict the Russian leader and his allies as members of a gang or a group of lads. Machismo discourse is closely linked to the authoritarian politics when power and domination prevail over rules and negotiation. Many pro-government users make Vladimir Putin personify Russia; these two have become interchangeable actors in recent political memes. The missing distinction between the leader and the state owes to two peculiarities of the Russian politics: centralisation of power and the tradition of the leader's cult of personality. By 2015, Vladimir Putin had evolved as a leader who is 'revered, even feared, to the point where no one will contradict him; aloof, isolated, a digital hermit who is never out of touch; broadly supported, but very narrowly advised by an ever-tighter group of confidantes' (Walker, 2014a: para 2). The president has sweeping control over the parliament dominated by the highly loyal Edinaya Rossiya party; Moscow appoints local governors and faces little opposition at the regional level.

Soon after Putin's election as the president in 2000, his portraits appeared on the shelves in many bookstores. Vladimir Putin was the first Russian leader to restore the features of the cult of personality that Joseph Stalin had previously established (Cassiday & Johnson, 2010).

Max Weber outlined three types of leadership: traditional, rational-legal and charismatic (Rees, 2004). Charismatic leadership entails integration of the social and political institutions around the alluring figure of a leader; either mass adoration or fear secures the collective veneration of the leader's personality and subservience to his power (Rees, 2004). Joseph Stalin was a prominent example of a charismatic leader who centralised power, secured a rigid vertical hierarchy and built his prestige on the myth of his extraordinary personal talents and skills. The late Soviet leader Nikita Khrushchev coined the term 'cult of personality' ('kult lichnosti') in 1956 at the 20th Congress of the Soviet Communist Party; he started the notable course to the deformation of the cult of personality and condemned the despotic regime of Stalin as the abuse of power.

The Russian audience of the 2010s has witnessed many popular attempts either to restore Stalin's popularity or dismiss him as a violent tyrant responsible for taking hundreds of thousands of lives (see Rees, 2004; Cassiday & Johnson, 2010). Putin's cult borrows few traits of Stalin's worship yet lacks the sacramentalisation (Rees, 2004) that it had during the Soviet times. Ideological state apparatuses such as the media and cultural institutions refrain from portraying Putin as a godly man; instead, they present him as the man with excellent talents and skills yet obeying to God and church. The communist regime appropriated many concepts and principles from the Orthodox Church, forging the cult of the head of the Communist Party as the living god. Similar to Stalin, Putin promotes his own personal cult to unite the society around it and offer 'psychological and emotional reassurance, a focus of stability and unity, in a world of uncertainties' (Rees, 2004: 13). The Russian president's public persona has many facets that can please various strata of the population: they span from the military action hero to the assertive gang leader.

Putin as an Action Hero – Militarised Masculinity

The post-Soviet reality comprises the strong influence of global technological advancement, the Western consumer culture and local restoration of the leader's cult of personality. Cassiday and Johnson (2010: 686) suggest that two pervasive cultural practices shape Putin's cult: nostalgia and consumption. The ongoing myth of Soviet grandeur stimulates positive public regard towards the charismatic leader. Putin has also established an effervescent public image of an action hero, a physically strong and energetic male whose representation borrows many details from consumer and pop culture (Travin, 2015). The media largely featured the Russian president's machismo escapades, from hunting to diving to the seabed to discover there the antic amphorae. These public appearances contained many traits of popular stereotypes and visual icons from the film industry, linking the public persona of Putin to the characters of action movies. Besides, Putin's exaggerated and demonstrated physical health responds to the nostalgic longing for the strong and dominative rule of the Soviet leaders (Goscilo, 2012). After the unreliable and physically unstable Boris Yeltsin in the 1990s, many Russian citizens expressed their desire to have an authoritative figure in top administration (Bjelica, 2014) and return to the vertical hierarchy in the government and society (Belkovsky, 2003).

Russian audience mainly endorses Putin's mediated machismo, while the Western public express mixed attitudes, from mockery to adoration (see Williams, 2013; Weil, 2014). The enthusiasm over sexualised public appearances of Putin has reached even Western social media users – they, not Russians, mostly produced memes celebrating the physical abilities of the Russian leader. Many Western memes depicted Vladimir Putin as a boxer in a ring with Barack Obama (Figure 5.19).

Figure 5.19 The meme portrays Vladimir Putin and Barack Obama as the protagonists of Rocky IV movie, where the Soviet boxer Ivan Drago faced the American boxer Rocky on the ring.

They reimagined Rocky Balboa's fictional fight with Ivan Drago in Rocky IV (1985), where Sylvester Stallone and Dolph Lundgren played the main characters.

In many memes in the collected data, Putin appears physically stronger and even much taller than the American president does. American writer Josh Weil (2014) speculates that the Russian president enchants the Western audience with his ruthless energetic activity and ability to 'do things'. Putin's actions may not be democratic, yet they show a decisive active man in power. The use of the frame from the box office hit about Rocky acts as a popular reference.

In the formulaic film that celebrated the American dream (Arnold, 2013) the hard-working Balboa overcame many obstacles and defeated the fearsome Soviet boxer Drago. However, if the audience is not familiar with the plot, the overwhelming physical presence of Drago-Putin in the meme suggests his victory. Another peculiar finding about Rocky's meme is the return of the Cold War symbolism. Hollywood movie culture offered reassuring narratives to the American population; producers utilised Rocky's opposition with Drago as the allegorical explanation of the nerve-racking conflict between two superpowers (Arnold, 2013). Memes involving references to Rocky Balboa amplify the gender politics of crude brutal masculinity. At the same time, one can read the metaphor of boxing as a compromise between soft and hard power, a meeting point between war and sport. Those who fight in a boxing ring confront each other with passion and often brutality, but retain respect to the opponent. Overall, the memes on Rocky Balboa indicate that the audience perceives the new wave of confrontation between the US and Russia in two instances: as a familiar encounter (reference to the past) and a spectacular duel (reference to the personification of global politics).

The fictionalisation of Vladimir Putin's charisma mobilises parallels with other movie characters, and one of the most frequent appearances is James Bond. The memes operate on the visual iconography of the British secret service agent and refer to Putin's past as the officer of the Soviet secret service KGB. This reference exemplifies another ambivalent trait in Putin's forceful masculinity – besides acting simultaneously as a father and a lover, he also tethers two types of war roles: as an open warrior and a secret agent.

War discourse as the display of muscle and influence has been especially efficient in Putin's public identity. His antiterrorism military campaigns in Chechnya increased his popularity in the 2000s. The two last times Putin's rating was remarkably high (80%), were in 2000 and with the wars in Chechnya and Georgia, respectively (Levada-Centre, 2014, cited in Parfitt, 2014). Parfitt (2014) accordingly observes that Putin's popularity jumps up when he performs strong-minded energetic actions.

Putin as the Gang Leader – Criminalised Masculinity

The political memes of the 2010s not only amplify the traits of Putin's cult, but also enrich them with a new component, the 'criminalised' variation of the masculine identity. Mafia discourse has a mixed perception in Russia. Many people negatively associate it with the dangers of the wild 1990s and at the same time positively link with insuperable power and an attractive dominant masculinity. The rise of mafia culture in the 1990s–2000s reflected fundamental changes in the country. The decomposition of the USSR in the 1990s led to the emergence of 'violent entrepreneurship' (Volkov, 2002): lawless individuals proliferated in the ruins of the Soviet economy. The market sank into deep depression, and nearly 40% of Russians were living in poverty by 1993 (World Bank, cited in Milanovic, 1998).

Private business had to develop under pressure from criminal gangs. They consisted of ex-sportsmen and the enforcers who offered protection from competing mobs and corrupt police (Koltsova, 2006). Nearly every business in the country had to pay an interest rate to a chosen ring. The boundary between state and non-state agents of violence was blurred. Only later on, by the end of the 1990s did Russian mafia godfathers adapt to the market economy and converted to executives and politicians (Koltsova, 2006).

Many ex-gangsters invested in media outlets and upheld the glamorised media representation of organised crime. Besides, Volkov (2002) noticed a general trend among Russian journalists towards romanticising criminals – media professionals would rather call them 'mafia' than 'organised crime'. The choice of term is important. The members of the audience who were not familiar with the ugliness of the organised crime envisaged mafia in the terms of movie images. Mafia discourse has been notably infiltrating Russian television and films since the early 2000s. Many popular TV series and films (see, for instance, Brother (1997), Brother 2 (2000), Banditskiy Peterburg (2000), Brigada (2002) and Bummer (2003)) tell the stories of the talented likeable youngsters who frequently disobeyed the law and succeeded in criminal business. Although a few critics have accused these dramas of aestheticising mafia culture and violence, the movie industry awarded them prestigious prizes.

The popularity of mafia culture affected the norms of public behaviour, fashion and slang. Many Russian politicians and celebrities, including Vladimir Putin, have been notoriously exploiting prison and mafia slang since the late 1990s (Yaroshevsky, no date). For instance, in 1999 Prime Minister Putin made a famous comment about air strikes on terrorists in Chechnya, promising to hunt them everywhere: 'Even if we find them in the toilet. We will rub them out in the outhouse' (Brown, 2012). Putin mobilised a harsh slang expression 'mochit v sortire' ('rub them out in the outhouse'), which is not used in literary Russian (Yaroshevsky, no date). An established philologist Chudinov (2001: 34) suggests that the deterioration of the linguistic norm expresses the public accord that one has to be a criminal to survive in modern Russia. Conversely, Krongauz (2014) points out that Putin normally speaks in literary Russian, but uses occasional slang to provoke the audience and draw their attention to specific statements. In propaganda studies, this practice is classified as the Plain Folks rhetoric technique when the leader deliberately turns to colloquial vocabulary to shorten the distance and establish bonds with the public.

The utilisation of colloquial slang and mafia jargon may serve as the linguistic ornament for Putin's machismo. Slang normally buttresses the conservative gender rhetoric and tends to denote women in sexist derogatory terms (Grossman & Tucker, 1997). A political and environment activist Evgeniya Chirikova (2015) accordingly notes that the proliferation of prison and criminal slang promotes the corresponding lawless norms of public behaviour and reflects the collective trauma of the USSR's detention system. Eighteen million Soviet people passed through the gruesome experience of the forced labour camps of the Soviet era, known as Gulag (Gulag History, no date), many of them guilty of no crime. Between 1928 and 1953, Joseph Stalin sent to the camps his political enemies, rich peasants with all their families, eminent military officers and doctors, priests and dissident intellectuals, and many other innocent people, forcing them to starve, die of harsh climate conditions and illnesses and exhausting manual labour (Gulag, 2015).

This long-term exposure to the fear of arrest and prison experience has gravely affected the Russian population: many people have prison survivors in their families or know somebody who does. The prison's 'kingpin' is the centre of absolute power for other convicts, he communicates supremacy and violence, and there can be no debate or compromise. Chirikova (2015) suggests that the Russian nation lives in the 'forced labour camp mentality', which explains the neurotic conformism to the state and relentless circulation of criminal slang. 'It became clear why there is so much thieves' talk in a fairly stable and prosperous society. It varies from the songs and words that parents neglectfully use when talking to their children, to the prison norms of behaviour, which imply that to "scam" or cheat on somebody is an indication of smartness and audacity, but not the asocial behaviour' (Chirikova, 2015: para 9).

Memes often present Putin and his allies as a gang. Figure 5.20 depicts Russian Prime Minister Dmitry Medvedev, Ukraine's ex-president Viktor Yanukovich and the Russian president Vladimir Putin as a group of friends. The textual component has references to mafia symbolism as much as the visual elements – masculine postures and dark coats resembling mafia's trademark dark leather jackets. The user added a third

Figure 5.20 The meme depicts Vladimir Putin, Dmitry Medvedev and ex-president of Ukraine Viktor Yanukovich walking in the park. The tag line says 'No worries, Vityok, we will figure it out!'.

component – a tweet – adding to the mafia connotation of a meme. The tweet said (translation from Russian) 'We figured it out. Now, Vityok, you ought to pay us interest rate for the job. Give us Crimea'. By 'figuring it out' the meme sharer probably means the anti-government protests in Kiev and the EU's pressure – they disturbed Yanukovich's rule and made him flee Ukraine. Russian leaders welcomed Yanukovich in Russia and offered him protection in the Russian territory.

In the context of the enduring popularity of mafia culture, Putin's criminalised masculinity becomes one of the facets of his public persona. The meme above expresses strength and authority. The audience may enjoy perceiving three leaders as a united gang living by their own principles. On the other hand, the meme can act as a criticism to Putin and his allies who allegedly apply criminal methods to global politics. There can be a third interpretation – the group may look comical to the audience due to the inequality in heights and the difference in facial expressions.

Putin as the Embodiment of Russia

Putin's macho discourse has obtained not only new connotations, but also new platforms of circulation in the 2010s. The president's communication team has successfully expanded the media strategy to incorporate the online realm (Goscilo, 2012). One of the most active pro-government accounts @Pravdiva_pravda publishes memes almost every day. Many of them reaffirm Putin's rhetorical identity of an authoritative confident leader who represents the interests of all nations (Goscilo, 2012).

The tendency towards close identification of Putin with Russia becomes especially vivid in memes with juxtaposition. The following meme (Figure 5.21) audaciously compares Putin to…Israel.

There are three particularly interesting features in this meme. First, it juxtaposes a state and a human being, instead of comparing two countries or two leaders. This is just more evidence of how inseparable Putin and Russia are becoming in the public consciousness. Second, the meme uses slang that helps to recognise mafia culture. 'Nicking' Crimea is not the same as negotiating for it. The word 'отжать' ('nick') belongs to the lad and mafia slang and appeared in many discussions on Crimea in traditional media and social networks. Russian/Soviet dissent poet Lev Rubinstein commented on the linguistic connotation of the expression: 'They nicked Crimea in a blokey way, as they know it. But I saw it as a typical robbery during a fire' (Volodarskiy, 2014). When studied together, these two peculiar traits of a meme (identification of Putin with Russia and the linguistic reference to mafia politics) evoke a third feature. The meme maker identifies Russia with a 'bloke' who prefers the rule of power to the rule of diplomacy.

Figure 5.21 The meme juxtaposes the efforts of Israel that has been 'fighting with the Arabs for 60 years over a piece of land' with the success of Vladimir Putin who 'nicked Crimea in one month'.

Figure 5.22 is a rare example of a meme that touches on Putin's private life. It employs an uncommon format of a mobile phone screen. Imagining for a moment how Putin's smartphone would look like creates an interesting effect. The image is almost interactive – it makes you want to unlock the screen to see what else Putin's phone is hiding. Yet for now, the only texts visible are those related to the Crimean crisis. The locked screen's one-sided communication from Barack Obama is a metaphor of the international power relations around Crimea, it reaffirms that the Russian president is in control and the American leader is frustrated. Putin's self-composure represents his uncompromising stance in negotiations. Fifty missed calls from Obama signify the latter's trepidation and further endorse Putin's hard power and Macho Politics. According to the meme maker, this poise is a winning one as it makes your enemies afraid.

The meme further elaborates on the macho depiction of Putin. Reading between the lines (behind the lock screen, in this case) is a more intriguing task than making sense of displayed messages. One may wonder why Putin has his own portrait on the lock screen: is he an egomaniac or the meme maker could not think of any personal picture he or she would

Figure 5.22 The meme imagines the screen of Vladimir Putin's phone. It features the portrait of the Russian president and panicky messages and missed calls from the ex-leader of the US.

dare to present as Putin's wallpaper? Would it be his unknown partner or grown-up daughters who never appeared in public? The straightforward character of the image actually poses more questions than it hides. To a certain extent, it unveils the constructed character of Putin's public profile – almost everyone is able to reproduce stories of Putin's macho acts, yet his private life is a blank page where many truths are concealed. This lack of personal information complements the representation of the Russian president as the lone hero, an irreplaceable and passionate patron of his people.

Sexism

The visual and linguistic depiction of forceful (often militarised) masculinity coexisted in many memes with the sexualised representation of women. Meme makers often objectified women and emphasised that men should be in charge of conducting politics, while women can serve as either a trophy or a decorative background to their battles.

@vezhlivo's meme (Figure 5.23) places an attractive female figure in front of the heavy state-of-the-art vehicle to pursue two goals: praise the macho splendour of military men and validate the deployment of forces to Crimea. A woman supposedly welcomes the arrival of the heroes; she is not involved in the operation, but poses passively next to the tank. The accompanying tweet 'Beauty will save Crimea' is hypocritical and further diminishes the woman's role – the image explains that her beauty does not affect the future of the peninsula as much as weaponry and gunmen do. Men in power justify their actions by the needs to protect the weak, women and children.

The approach of portraying women in the media as objects has been criticised by feminist media scholars (Mulvey, 2009; Byerly & Ross, 2008; Gill, 2007; Carter, 2014). The media frequently depict women as the objects of sexual desire (Carter, 2014; Ross, 2014). Another belittling pattern of representation is placing a woman in the position of a victim, which has been prominent in the news discourse in both Western and non-Western societies (Byerly & Ross, 2008: 40–43; Gill, 2007: 121–124). Byerly and Ross (2008: 42) refer to this phenomenon as 'the media's fascination with the fragile female form and her vulnerability to violation'.

However, when the political regime demands the propagation of patriarchal values, such as, for instance, the case of the unification of Germany in 1990, the media emphasise the societal role of women as mothers and wives (European Commission, 1999). Similarly, the US authorities promoted a comparable celebration of protectorate masculinity and caring femininity after the attacks at the World Trade Center on 9/11 in 2001 (Godfrey & Hamad, 2014). The media claimed that the state was responsible for the protection of its citizens and amalgamated

Красота сласёт Крым

Figure 5.23 The meme depicts a young woman next to the tank; the tag line says 'Beauty will save the world'.

this narrative with the reinforcement of patriarchal gender framing. '(T) he role of the masculine protector puts those protected, paradigmatically women and children, in a subordinate position of dependence and obedience' (Young, 2007: 116, as cited in Godfrey & Hamad, 2014: 170).

Authoritarian regimes persistently amalgamate discourses on sex and power (Sperling, 2014). Sexualisation has two instances: 'the extraordinary proliferation of discourses about sex and sexuality across all media forms, as well as [...] the increasingly frequent erotic presentation of girls', women's and (to a lesser extent) men's bodies in public spaces' (Gill, 2007: 256). Wouters (2010) adds that public discussions on sex and the right of an individual to take control of their sexual choices benefit the emancipation of women. Yet, Gill (2007) and Krijnen and Van Bauwel (2015) argue that the media tend to endorse traditional masculinity in the discourse on sex: they 'contribute to a context in which individuals' choices are structured towards a sexual agency while letting them think they are all individuals' (Krijnen & Van Bauwel, 2015: 164). It is specifically evident in the authoritarian male-dominated media ecology where the media impose predetermined sexualised roles on men and women (Sperling, 2014). Russia's case proves that women's activities and responsibilities in this perspective lie within the domestic realm, while men's agency and domination expand to the extra-domestic level.

The memetic representation of the only notable female Crimean politician adds more understanding to the sexist phenomenon of the Crimean discourse. Digital citizens exploited the manga visual language to create memes of the Crimean Prosecutor General Natalya Poklonskaya (see Figure 5.24). This young woman has become popular in the Russian cyberspace for her wide round eyes and baby face that conflicted with her solemn statements. The fame expanded to the global level, and even Japanese users created numerous fan clubs of Poklonskaya on the Web (Fredericks, 2014).

Memes with Poklonskaya rarely discuss her professional skills and background, but superficially lay emphasis on her uniform and title to emphasise her sexual appeal. Natalya Poklonskaya did not approve of the fandom and notably reacted with embarrassment, reminding her admirers that she is a high-level attorney with serious duties and responsibilities, 'not a Pokemon or something' (Broderick, 2014). The refusal to be 'something' expresses her rejection of objectification. Despite this

Figure 5.24 The meme juxtaposes the Crimean Prosecutor General Natalia Poklonskaya with the similar-looking manga character.

statement, Poklonskaya nonetheless conforms to certain aspects of conservative gender roles. For instance, she confessed that she deliberately exploited gender stereotypes to secure a job with the Crimean newly appointed pro-Russian Prime Minister. She deliberately came to his office on the 8th of March, which is a state holiday – International Women's Day in Russia. 'I came to see Sergey Valeryevich (Aksyonov) specifically on the 8th of March to ensure that he accepts me. A real man cannot reject a woman on the 8th of March; and he let me in', Poklonskaya confessed (KrymInform, 2015: para 2).

The sexist memes portray Poklonskaya as the object whose future depends on the decisions of male actors. Vladimir Putin has acquired the peninsula with the attractive trophy on it, the charming Prosecutor General. The rising number of memes link filthy Putin with the wide-eyed Poklonskaya and serve as yet another example of the promotion of 'action-oriented machismo'. Sexist narratives that proliferate in contemporary culture and media often rely on the simplified scenarios of gender relations that are omnipresent in folklore and classic fairy tales (Fraser & Nicholson, 1994; Byerly & Ross, 2008). Russian memes on Poklonskaya uphold this point by framing the Crimean annexation as the plot of the hero defeating his enemies and seizing the princess as a prize.

The sexism of Crimean memes strengthens the leaning towards the Rule of Power in Russian politics. Pro-government users approve of the leader's macho bravado and subsequently authorise conservative gender relations. Memes exhibit how the public rhetoric on 'traditional values', family and patriarchal social order shields the discourses on criminalised authoritarian politics and objectification of women. Any transferral from 'tradition' immediately receives the label of deviation. According to the Kremlin, the worst nightmares of the Russian society, such as revolution or homosexuality, come from disobedience to the norms and customs. Putin's anti-gay law during the Olympic Games, for instance, banned 'propaganda of non-traditional sexual relations' (CBS, 2014), laying a strong emphasis on the virtue of tradition. Sexist memes expose the prevailing societal stereotypes as much as they comment on political power struggles; the two are intrinsically united and praise the neo-patriarchal political order and conservative gender hierarchy.

Nazism Allegory

Various actors have employed Nazism rhetoric in the discussions on Crimea: from politicians and experts to the state and opposition media. They all exploit Nazi labelling as a classic rhetorical tool, a one-fits-all insult that is not limited to wars or particular countries. Nonetheless, Nyhan (2006) noted that opponents are more likely to compare each other to Nazis on disputes of foreign policy rather than on other political subjects. Proving this, British Prime Minister David Cameron recently compared Russia to Nazi Germany because of its actions in the Ukraine, marking the annexation as an example of 'a larger state bullying a smaller state' (Swinford, 2014). The American former secretary of state Hillary Clinton was more specific in her condemnation: she compared the Russian offer of issuing passports to ethnic Russians outside the country to Hitler's claim to protect ethnic Germans from oppression in other states (Rucker, 2014).

Nazi labelling has an inflammatory power in any dispute (Godwin, 1990), and the digital realm is no exception. The Internet users exhaust Nazism rhetoric in the most casual conversations. Mike Godwin (1990: para 3) coined the Rule of Nazi Analogies and suggested that the more heated the discussion becomes, the more likely someone would throw in the Nazi label as an obscenity: 'As an online discussion grows longer, the probability of a comparison involving Nazis or Hitler approaches one'. The flexible character of this label leaves room for manipulation and constant renegotiation – one can define what constitutes 'Nazism' according to their political preferences.

Vladimir Putin ignored his Western colleagues' remarks and issued his own Nazi-label for the Ukrainian authorities. The shelling of Eastern Ukrainian cities by Ukrainian troops reminded him of Nazi Germany's shelling of Soviet cities, including Leningrad (RT, 2014a). In fact, the Russian government employed Nazi rhetoric before, and flexibly adjusted it to fit into various agendas. After the 9/11 terrorist attack at the World Trade Centre in New York, Russia issued a statement calling terrorism 'a Nazism of the 21st century' (Simons, 2006: 8). In the mid-2000s, Putin often alluded to the horrid outcomes of the Nazi regime to emphasise the unity of suffering among Russian and European countries. In 2005, the year of the 60th anniversary of the Great Victory, he spoke publicly about the necessity to reconcile, to overcome mistrust and establish cooperation between nations to fight Nazism, racism and xenophobia (Simons, 2006).

In 2013–2014, Putin's government exploited the Nazism threat in mass propaganda to invoke hatred towards the anti-government protests in Ukraine. By the time of the Crimean annexation the Russian television had educated the audience on the figure of Stepan Bandera. The Ukrainian political leader of the nationalist movement, he declared the independence of Ukraine in 1941. According to Russian media, Bandera has a questionable reputation for allegedly collaborating with the Nazis. Powell (2014) suggests that Bandera sought Hitler's help in gaining independence for Ukraine in 1941, but ended up being arrested by the Nazis.

The Kremlin used Bandera as a nickname for the neo-Nazi – 'banderovets' was the newly adopted term. When anti-government protests in Kiev succeeded and Ukraine obtained a new government in 2014, the

Russian media began associating the new administration with Bandera followers (Syomin, 2014). Vladimir Putin included many references to the neo-Nazi and Bandera in his address to the nation after the referendum in Crimea. He emphasised that 'nationalists, neo-Nazi, Russophobes and anti-Semites' (Putin, 2014: para 4) executed coup d'état in Kiev and now rule in the country. Putin mentioned that the new government of Ukraine was plotting legal action against the Russian minority and added 'We can all clearly see the intentions of these ideological heirs of Bandera, Hitler's accomplice during World War II' (Putin, 2014: para 5). The Kremlin thus offered its services to defeat the assumed new wave of Nazism and presented itself as the saviour of the Russian minority in Ukraine.

Russian sociolinguist Maksim Krongauz (2014) points out that the rhetoric of hatred replaced reasonable argumentation in the Crimean crisis. By introducing ritual, emotionally charged appellations for enemies, such as 'banderovets' and 'neo-Nazi', the state formed a new ideology which is strongly in demand in the absence of other established state doctrines. Linguistic clichés offer shortcut solutions and opinions that can arise in doubtful situations (Krongauz, 2014). The newly invented 'public threat' of the Bandera neo-Nazis, on the one hand, fits in the old collective fear of fascism, but on the other, supplies new enemy figures for the confused public.

One of the sophisticated memes attacking the Russian Nazi-related propaganda came from @Dbnmjr. Supposedly a Ukrainian user, he has published plenty of popular anti-Russia and anti-Putin memes throughout and after the Crimean crisis. This one is a text without images; it is called 'An average day of a banderovets'.

> Yesterday morning I woke up in my extremist bed, brushed my fascist teeth, had a cup of Lvov coffee made of crushed St George ribbons; went to work at Bandera gestapo; got bored at lunchtime and brutally beat up a defenceless "berkut" who was picking field flowers by the road; on my way home drew a swastika on all of the neighbourhood's synagogues; treaded the sprouts of Slavic unity down with a bloody boot; had a dinner, shouting "Beat the Moskal!"; watched a gay parade in Berlin on TV; kissed Shukhevich's portrait on the cheek and went to sleep. This was my day.

The author created an Orwellian exaggerated image of a neo-Nazi, an absurd conjunction of media buzzwords and symbols assorted in an amusing manner. The decoding of the text requires knowledge of both the Russian and the Ukrainian context. 'St George ribbons', for instance, refer to the symbolic ribbon that used to be part of military decoration in the USSR. Since the 60th anniversary of the Russian Victory Day (May 9, 2005), the state launched a campaign to encourage civilians to wear the ribbon as an act of commemoration and remembrance. During the 2014 tension with Ukraine, the St. George ribbon also became known as the symbol of pro-Russian separatism (Biggs, 2014).

'Defenceless "berkut"' refers to the Ukrainian government's special police forces, Berkut – the name has become synonymous with police brutality in Kiev protests (BBC, 2014c). The phrase 'treaded the sprouts of Slavic unity down with a bloody boot' links this meme with the narrative of the Russian Imperial Ambition and mockingly denounces Russia's aspiration to install command over other Slavic countries.

'Beat the Moskal!' means 'Beat the Russian!' as 'moskal' is a Ukrainian nickname for Russians. Roman Shukhevich was the military ally to Bandera. Altogether, this mock diary presents a utopian perfect Enemy as depicted by Russian propaganda. The meme, therefore, reveals the absurdity and the exaggerated, hysterical character of the emotionally charged labels coming from the television screen.

Another wave of resistance against Nazi-related Russian propaganda appealed to humour and reason. Many users claimed that the Kiev protesters of 2013 were not even familiar with the figure of Stepan Bandera and his nationalist ideology. It was largely due to the Russian media that Russian and Ukrainian citizens learned about the neo-Nazi threat and became afraid of pro-Bandera activists (Alifanov, 2014). This meme (Figure 5.25) exposes the constructed character of the Bandera rhetoric and the imposed fear. A popular anti-Russian meme maker @Dbnmjr posted the meme and then got retweeted by @gruppa_voina, an account held by Pussy Riot members.

The meme is not explicit. It invites the audience to laugh at the similarly sounding surnames of such a variegated group of popular characters. Yet, putting these faces and names together may suggest that Stepan Bandera was not a household name at least for Russians until 2013; people frequently misspelled his surname and misidentified him in social network debates.

Moreover, there are three fictional characters and only one real person in the group of people with Bandera-sounding names. This may imply that propaganda reimagined Bandera, and his mediated persona belongs to the realm of fiction and popular culture. The meme may also tease the clumsy choice of a propaganda object – Bandera's name is easily confused with other, more popular characters. Moreover, looping in the popular fictional con artist Ostap Bender adds another connotation to this narrative. The most loved charlatan in the Russian literature and film first appeared in the book *The Twelve Chairs* written by Soviet writers Ilya Ilf and Yevgeniy Petrov in 1928. The inclusion of Bender in a meme points to the deceit of popular propaganda and calls for a critical reading of its symbols.

The resistant publics also used the Nazi rhetoric, but against Putin. They associated Russian president Putin with Hitler. This Demotivator

КОРОТКАЯ КЛАССИФИКАЦИЯ ДЛЯ «ЧАЙНИКОВ»

БАНДЕРОВЦЫ

БОНДЕРОВЦЫ

БЕНДЕРОВЦЫ

БИНДЕРОВЦЫ

PORNOLITICA

Figure 5.25 The meme provides the classification of the similar-sounding nick-
names. The text says 'Short classification for the dummies: The
Banderovets, the Bonderovets, the Benderovets, the Binderovets'. It
distinguishes the followers of the popular actor Antonio Banderas
from the followers of the controversial Ukrainian wartime politician Stepan Bandera, and from the fans of the fictional characters
Ostap Bender and Mr Bin.

(Figure 5.26) employs a photo of the gate of the Auschwitz concentration
camp and draws a parallel between Hitler's occupation of Europe and
Putin's annexation of Crimea. The meme maker deconstructs the narrative of 'Putin's tourists' in Crimea and develops it into a Nazi discourse.
He or she argues that soldiers came not to bring peace, but to turn the
peninsula into a war zone or concentration camp.

Generally, Nazi memes do not require much knowledge in order to
be decoded, yet several anti-Putin memes included supplementary information for reflection, such as the concept of the Russian World in this
meme. This idea stems from Vladimir Putin's public rhetoric and implies
the Russian cultural and moral superiority over other nations. Putin announced his vision of the 'Russian world' by the end of the television
marathon with the nation in 2014 (Kremlin, 2014a). He introduced the
term 'a person of the Russian World' defining this abstract individual as
a broad thinker and apologist of high moral principles, who is concerned

Figure 5.26 The meme uses the photograph of the German concentration camp
and the photo of a modern soldier. The text says, 'Dear travelers!
Welcome to the resorts of Crimea', and the text in the bottom says
'Travel agency "Russian world"'.

about the world beyond his private space. The president counterbalanced
Western values of personal gain and individual success to the Russian
values of patriotism and sacrificing oneself for one's friends, nation
and Motherland (Kremlin, 2014a: para 5). The concept of the 'Russian
world' infers that a Russian has the moral responsibility to care for the
well-being of other nations; the ambiguous targeting of this responsibility seems to worry the meme maker. The author of this Demotivator
compares 'Russian World' to the Nazi project of global dominance and
imposing one's rules and beliefs over others. Nazism labelling often co-
incides with the narrative of imperial ambition, raising intriguing questions on the borderline between the nebulous humanistic responsibility
to help thy neighbour and intruding on one's privacy or sovereignty.

Meme makers further elaborate on the fear of nationalism and imbal-
ance of power. They draw historical comparisons and make a link between Hitler, Putin and the leader of ex-Yugoslavia Slobodan Milosevic
(Figure 5.27). 'Ruthless manipulator of Serbian nationalism' (Traynor,

Figure 5.27 The meme compares Adolf Hitler, Slobodan Milosevic and Vladimir Putin. Hitler says 'Let's protect the Germans!', Milosevic says 'Let's protect the Serbs!', and Putin says 'Let's protect the Russians!'. The pictures in the bottom show the aftermath of Hitler's and Milosevic's actions – genocide graves and a trial in Hague. The meme poses the question in the right hand side in the bottom, 'Will Russia follow the path of the Greater German Reich and "Great Serbia"?'

2006), the ex-president of Yugoslavia founded his media-enabled propaganda on the dehumanisation of other ethnicities living along the Serbs: he called the Croats fascists, the Albanians rapists and terrorists, and the Muslims of Bosnia Islamic fundamentalists. Milosevic became the first European head of state to be prosecuted for genocide and war crimes; he notoriously used nationalist propaganda to justify cruel ethnic cleansing (Traynor, 2006). The meme that unites Hitler, Milosevic and Putin functions as a highly condensed political activism: it matches documentary photos with expressive images of the dictators and their claims.

The iconography of the meme is powerful – it captures all the leaders in a moment of inspired rage and charismatic performance. The meme

invites people to reflect on the lessons of history, on the direct link between pompous rhetoric and ugly motives; it places Russia in the context
of two other failed 'empires', and hence warns of the misleading propaganda of imperial ambitions.

In conclusion, the comparison to Nazi Germany and Adolf Hitler can
be attention-grabbing and powerful. On the one hand, it refers to a hor-
rendous time in human history and triggers an emotional response from
the audience. On the other hand, drawing a comparison to Hitler and
labelling one as a Nazi has become common place in political rhetoric.
The majority of Nazi memes lack depth and justification of claims. Only
the memes that criticise the Nazi discourse on propaganda offer additional grounds for reflection – they invite the audience to critically assess
information that they receive from the leaders and the state-controlled
media. The Nazi analogy needs supportive arguments to create a complex message. 'A usual day of a "banderovets"' meme is a remarkable example of how one text can absorb many layers of narrative and symbols,
and expose their inconsistencies.

Feel-Good Patriotism

Pro-Russia Twitter accounts habitually borrow plot lines and slogans
from traditional media propaganda. The majority of them reproduce
narratives from television, yell patriotic slogans and fight violently with
virtual enemies, while the minority provide a more unconventional and
sophisticated stance. Twitter user @vezhlivo (which in Russian means
'polite') is exceptionally skilful at branding and serves as an example of digital propaganda that picks ideas from the state rhetoric and
elaborates on them in a creative manner. The buzzword 'polite people'
appeared roughly at the same time as the idea to call military men in
Crimea 'tourists' (see p. 26 for more). The media discourse on the armed
men who facilitated the Crimean referendum engaged the term 'polite
people' to emphasise the delicate and considerate manners of the troops
in question (Shevchenko, 2014).

Opinions are still divided whether this catchy term came from. Apparently, it was the source in the Crimean police who claimed that
unidentified gunmen had occupied the local airport and 'politely'
asked the police to leave the building (Politnavigator, 2014). A local
Ukrainian media outlet quoted this. Then, Crimean blogger and journalist Boris Rozhin reposted the news item in his blog and titled it
as 'Polite people have seized two airports in Crimea' (Meduza, 2015);
the meme was born, and soon many iterations of it went viral in the
blogosphere. According to an alternative view, spin doctors came to
Crimea from Moscow and suggested the buzzword (see Shevchenko,
2014). As the popular Russian blogger Ilya Varlamov speculated, 'they
are creating an image of a Russian liberator-soldier wearing a nice new

uniform and armed with beautiful weapons, who has come to defend peaceful towns and villages' (Shevchenko, 2014). Traditional media swiftly appropriated the term from cyberspace. Several media rushed to identify the 'polite people' as Russian troops although the Kremlin denied sending any force to Crimea (Ria, 2015). Vladimir Putin confirmed the deployment of a Russian professional army in Crimea only in April 2014 (Meduza, 2015).

Twitter account @vezhlivo has been posting photos of military men in Crimea since March 2014, supplementing them with sentimental uplifting captions. The author of this book was able to identify the authors of the @vezhlivo account as a collective of three authors, with at least one of them coming from a high-level company providing public relations to big clients. The @vezhlivo co-author claimed that this work was not commissioned by anyone, and came as a voluntary patriotic initiative of the collective, in their spare time.

@vezhlivo has been promulgating the new image of the Russian troops as polite, well intending, brave people coming to protect the weak (Ria, 2015) through the memes published on their Twitter page. This book already used @vezhlivo's meme in the section about sexism – with the young woman posing against a tank. Other examples further glorify the idea that military men do not bring danger, but safety to the society. For instance, @vezhlivo portrays a soldier with a cat (Figure 5.28), thus mobilising this well-regarded Web darling – the cat – to point to the humanity of the Russian troops. The cat here functions as the metaphor for all the weaker creatures in need for protection. The visual contraposition of the relaxed furry animal with the heavy deadly armour boosts the impression of safety: the soldier is on guard and the citizens can enjoy peace.

The meme with a cat was appropriated and deployed in a completely different discourse. Another pro-Kremlin account @anti_maydan appropriated the meme created by @vezhlivo to criticise the Western media for their coverage of the Crimean crisis (Figure 5.29). This is a particularly interesting example of a meme mutation.

What started as a sentimental postcard praising military glory turned into a harsh condemnation of media fabrication. @anti_maydan creates another level of meaning: he presents the soldier with a cat as if seen through the eyes of Western journalists. He imagines how they may pervert the image and suggests that global media would blame the warrior for torturing the poor feline in front of the astonished locals.

Two versions of the meme belong to different genres. @vezhlivo is 'selling the product' and applies advertising techniques to promote the mellow, peaceful vibe around the Russian army. @anti_maydan acts as a tabloid and reproduces the scandalous, obnoxious expressive style of the sensationalist media. Besides, one can interpret @anti_maydan's meme from two angles: it may condemn either Western propaganda or

Вежливые люди
@vezhlivo

Вежливое фото дня

↩ Reply   ⇄ Retweet   ★ Favorited   ••• More

Figure 5.28 The meme depicts a soldier caressing a cat that sits on the top of his gun. The tag line says, 'Polite photo of the day'.

local liberal users who largely use Demotivators and subvert media texts through memes.

Overall, @vezhlivo is in a league of its own among other patriotic accounts. It preserves a recognisable romantic style, uses memes to construct a positive identity for the pro-Russian self-defence troops in Crimea (and later – for the Russian army in general). The account depicts military presence in the peninsula in the visual language of advertising and branding, selects expressive photos, often applies soft, pastel filters and matches images with airy slogans. These catchphrases generate a favourable emotional response as they appeal to the notions of safety, peace, protection and fairness (Zaidi, no date). **Polite People memes are a peculiar example of 'soft' propaganda.** They supplement the

Figure 5.29 The meme depicts a soldier caressing a cat that sits on the top of his gun. The tag line says, 'Foreign media are in shock. The camera spotted a polite person who is pulling the poor cat over his gun'.

hegemonic media by offering a non-direct endorsement of the Russian government's activity in the Ukraine. They generate a special flow in the meme exchange on the Crimean subject – non-argumentative, but assertive and sentimental. Congenial design, discreet ideological underlining and branding of this media campaign made the 'Polite People' a household name in Russia, prompting the mass production of Polite souvenirs, which included thousands of T-shirts, mugs and glasses adorned with the words 'polite people'.

What Meme Makers Say – Motivations, Risks and Perks of Meme Making

1   Genesis of political memes in the Russian protest
2   Circulation and role of memes in the Crimean crisis

3   Personal motivation for meme making and sharing
4   The potential of Twitter for alternative political activism in Russia
5   Memes that help to let off steam and receive comfort (slow-burn resistance).

I held interviews with the most popular politically active meme makers and sharers of the Russian segment of Twitter. The analysis of their responses allowed the identification of a number of recurring themes as well as discrepancies, which demonstrate that meme exchange is a contemporary, evolving digital practice that requires further research.

Among 15 speakers interviewed, two express pro-government sentiments, and the rest either openly confront the government in their daily expression on Twitter or criticise it occasionally, when triggered by any specific events.

The pro-government meme sharers will appear as Pro-Government Meme Maker 1 and Pro-Government Meme Maker 2. They have tens of thousands of followers on social networks and either praise the military glory of Russia and the Crimean campaign, or harshly criticise the critics of the Kremlin.

There are 13 anti-government meme sharers. Their popularity varies from over a million to tens of thousands of followers on Twitter. I will refer to them as Resistant Meme Maker 1, 2, etc. There are also several high-profile liberal journalists in the sample. They have been vocal about criticism to the Crimean campaign. They are active on Twitter; they are experts in the field of social media and especially how the media extend their presence to the networked platforms; and they have contributed exclusive insights to this book. I will refer to them as Digital Journalist 1, 2, 3 and 4.

I have been lucky to conduct an interview with a popular critical political cartoonist – I will refer to him as Cartoonist.

Without compromising the privacy and safety of the meme makers in Russia, I can disclose that majority of them belong to creative professions – they work or have experience in the media, public relations. Several meme makers come from the field of business or higher education.

Genesis of Political Memes in the Russian Protest

The majority of interviewees agreed that memes became visible and influential in Russian politics in 2011–2012, when the first large anti-government protests took place. They attribute the attractiveness of this new media format both to the peculiarities of shape and content. The playful form of a meme organically derived from the entertaining, casual expression of the social media banter.

During the protests, social network users filled popular general meme templates (such as Demotivator, Image Macro and others) with criticism of the government. **Memes were a familiar and casual language for the**

digital natives, who carried this habitual format of online expression down to the streets and transformed it into posters.

> Memes evidently gained political weight in the 2011–12 protests. It is explainable. The accumulated people's fury at injustice emanated in the form of angry jokes. Citizens actively shared them to express their point of view again and again.
>
> (Digital Journalist 1, personal communication, 1 May 2015)

Anyone was able to go online, generate or borrow a joke and then fuel the digital discussion with it within minutes. Many interviewees highlighted the imperative power of memes in channelling emotion. Bold, rude and stinging texts transmitted the vehemence of people's annoyance. Internet memes on Twitter often served as the digital 'passwords' or markers that vaguely distinguished the audience of traditional media from the audience of social networks.

> They [Navalny,[7] @KermlinRussia and other prominent liberal bloggers - AD] sent the message to the audience that appreciated memes, "Guys, I am the same like you, we are on the same page". This worked especially well because it demarcated the digital audience of memes from those people who perceive not only memes, but the whole Internet as a hostile environment.
>
> (Digital Journalist 1, personal communication, 1 May 2015)

Curiously, even pro-government meme sharers concede that memes formed a refreshing emblem, or a branding element, of the 2011–2012 resistance. They, nonetheless, accuse the resistant users of manufacturing memes on purpose, not spontaneously. They see memes as the deliberate weapons of an organised campaign.

> If one assesses [the 2011–12 memes] by the principles of media technologies, he or she would admit that they were manufactured with competence. Alexey Navalny, who promoted and animated many of those memes, is primarily a public relations specialist. He is by no means a politician, but a public relations and new media expert. He knew how to pull all of this off. However, the memes have soon turned against their creators. <…> People understood the quality of the 2011–12 protests and the motives of the organisers. All these memes, as saggy balloons, went from our life to the scientific papers, Wikipedia and history.
>
> (Pro-Government Meme Maker 1, personal communication, 5 June 2014)

Liberal journalists and bloggers also render homage to the leading liberal politician Alexey Navalny for his exemplary employment of memes in raising the political awareness of citizens. A blogger-turned-politician, Navalny has been utilising memes as the Internet jargon that helps to draw attention to his large investigations into state corruption. Moreover, Navalny has notably exploited memes to establish contact with the digitally savvy crowds.

> An image always works better than a text. Navalny has become popular thanks to the blogosphere, people began paying attention to his account and support him with "likes". This environment was very attractive due to the use of humour.
>
> (Resistant Meme Maker 2, personal communication, 10 July 2014)

'*People share memes to pass the idea without using their own words*' (Digital Journalist 2, personal communication, 10 May 2014). Memes allowed resistant users to find like-minded people on the digital realm. At the same time, they enabled them to protect their privacy. Users were able to draw a distance between their identities and the messages they passed; a meme sharer could always say that he or she only redistributed a meme, but did not originate it. This practice became an often-necessary precaution in the highly censored environment of Russia of the 2010s.

Since the early 2010s, Twitter and memes have celebrated informal communication among liberal publics. Interviewees bring to the attention the example of the most popular informal Twitter account of a news media in Russia in the early 2010s – Lenta.ru's famous @lentaruofficial. The Twitter channel of the leading news website, it was active in sharing oppositional news and perspectives during 2010–2012. The media was shut and the editor-in-chief was ousted, when the website became too critical of the Kremlin. The whole editorial team left the outlet in protest, and in support of the editor-in-chief. Russian audience longed for a human touch and sincerity in journalism. The Twitter account of Lenta.ru celebrated informality and authenticity, and Internet memes became one of the means of expression for the resistant crowds. It contributed bold sarcasm, politically incorrect jokes and Internet memes to raise the awareness of the audience on political issues. It also included news from the opposition activists and thus maintained the flow of alternative information and communication that largely fuelled the 2011–2012 protests.

> We shared our endless conversations and laughs in the office with the audience, made it our brand. This helped us to turn from the potbellied people with cabbage in their beards, as they may have imagined us, into likeable dudes just like themselves; the dudes who also sneer and laugh at the news.
>
> (Digital Journalist 3, personal communication, 26 June 2014)

What Twitter-savvy journalists were, in fact, doing was providing an immediate analysis of the news. In order to make an informed joke on Twitter, a journalist has to understand the topic first. The genre of the independent analysis has almost vanished in the restricted Russian media environment, hence ironical Twitter insights of the likes of @lenta-ruofficial occupied this niche.

The editorial team widely employed memes as the bridge between the website's experts and mixed audience of social networks. The staff of Lenta.ru followed the standards of professional objective journalism on their main website, but allowed subjectivity and interpretation on Twitter, aiming to encourage critical thinking in the audience.

Besides, journalists point to Twitter's capacity of channelling sentiments; the microblogging platform became an important tool for the collective experiencing of joy and grief. The informal opinionated Twitter feed made the journalists seem trustworthy in the eyes of the liberal users: 'People want live communication, not a robotic sharing of the web link. Editorial staff appeared on Twitter as a human being, a likeable lad, a "warm", not a cold media' (Digital Journalist 2, personal communication, 10 May 2014).

Many meme makers agree that protest communication in social networks facilitated the shaping of the civil society. Thanks to the digital mobilisation and the following Bolotnaya square protest in 2011, both the liberal public and the government realised that the active citizens who demanded a change in politics existed and were relatively large in number.

> The Internet has played a crucial part in it [establishment of the civil society - AD]. An excellent proof to this is the recent Kremlin's crusade on the Internet and the freedom of speech. Before this crusade, they killed TV Rain,[8] suggesting that independent television had also played a significant role in the Bolotnaya protest. Yet the Internet was way more influential.
>
> (Resistant Meme Maker 1, personal communication, 26 August 2014)

For the 2011–2012 protesters, memes acted as the beacons that denoted one's belonging to the stratum of digital citizens and avid users of social networks. High digital literacy and habit to utilise the Internet as the source of alternative information and opinion were important characteristics of the 'angry townspeople', the driving force of the 2011–2012 demonstrations (Kiriya, 2012). Moreover, there are indications that the Bolotnaya square manifestation was to a large extent the march of successful city dwellers; many belonged to the middle and upper middle classes.

First protest at the Bolotnaya square gathered many businessmen, with the monthly salary of $10,000.

(Resistant Meme Maker 2, personal
communication, 10 July 2014)

The government reacted furiously to both the online and offline activity of the Russian protesters. Interviewees believe that the Kremlin has declared war on protest mobilisations and treated opposition as a state traitor:

We were told that the Presidential Administration was shocked by this rally, it was as extraordinary for them as if a domestic cat started talking. They thought "We gave it food, cleaned its litter box, and it suddenly raised the voice at us! Look at it, the cat is complaining that the system is unfair and needs corrections!" We are in touch with Kovalchuk's[9] circle, these people dub the protesters "the Bolotnaya trash".

(Resistant Meme Maker 2, personal
communication, 10 July 2014)

The Russian political system is a closed one and rejects any external influence. Only those political elites inside it are capable of having an impact on it. In order to understand the nature of this vacuum, one has to analyse the Russian mentality. We are a highly hierarchical nation. The Russian character perceives authority on the metaphysical level, not by chance, the tsar was distinguished as the top power, obeying only to God. This tendency has not eroded but bolstered over time.

(Resistant Meme Maker 3, personal
communication, 15 September 2014)

During the 2011–2012 protests, the government started persecuting not only liberal media, but also individual users with popular Twitter accounts for their political activity. This increase in state pressure has further demonstrated the significance of individual political communication in social networks. The meme makers are sarcastic:

There are no risks in leading a protest account except for the hazard of being fired or beaten in the porch of your own house. They almost fired me from the university in 2012, but with the help of TV Rain, we defended justice.

(Resistant Meme Maker 1, personal
communication, 26 August 2014)

The popularity of their accounts would never protect Twitter users from the attacks of the government: as the account holders reveal, the elites are not afraid of public opinion and could suppress any alternative media or individual account at any time. For these reasons, most meme makers remain anonymous and hide under pseudonyms for many years.

> We are not fooling ourselves that nothing could ever happen to us. I do not know whether they consciously keep us free or are just busy to take any action against us. We are indeed the biggest satirical account on Russian Twitter, but any person can write a post that would be better than ours and receives more "likes" and shares. We are not a newspaper, not a media. Eliminating us does not eliminate the problem. It is not the communication that is the issue, but the reality. There will remain a large number of people who reside online, monitor the reality and write about it.
>
> (Resistant Meme Maker 2, personal
> communication, 10 July 2014)

Other meme makers reveal similar reasons for staying in the shadow. They are unsure what to expect from the state that puts pressure on its enemies, and the criteria of becoming one are extremely vague. One of them admits to going online in Russia only in public places so that the government's watchdog cannot locate his mobile phone. Others, on the opposite, use various IP addresses and never log in from the publics spaces.

> People are in fear. After Bolotnaya square, everyone became very frightened. The authorities probably would not kill you (who cares about you!), but they can accuse you of something and send you to prison. You would spend there a couple of years, maybe two or more, depending on your luck. You could attempt to appeal to the Human Rights Council or whoever else, to no avail. Others would be boiling over Twitter and call for different actions, but with no result. …I would not personally want to go to prison, but I have already spent some time in detention, so I know what it is. I know that I would survive there. The only thing that worries me is that I have a family and in the worst case scenario I would send them away for protection.
>
> (Resistant Meme Maker 4, personal
> communication, 1 September 2014)

Circulation and Role of Memes in the Crimean Crisis

The escalation of the Crimean crisis has widely affected the distribution of sarcastic commentary and memes in social networks. In addition to restricting freedom of speech and assembly, Russian authorities tried to curb the memetic communication on the Internet. **Meme making and sharing have become an increasingly menacing public activity.**

Satirical communication and parody created more inconvenience to the state during the Olympic Games in Sochi. As the fascinating insight by the Internet expert (Digital Journalist 4, personal communication, 26 June 2014) reveals, the ruling elites despise the Web's vernacular of the liberal users. They are not sure how to contain the digital satire that includes memes. For them, satirical jokes on Twitter are an obstacle that the propaganda machine cannot constrain. The state had declared war on the derisive digital communication by the start of the Sochi Olympics in early 2014:

> There was a ground-breaking meeting with top media managers in the Kremlin right before the Olympic Games in Sochi. They were strictly instructed on the topics and tone of media coverage. They were allowed to speculate on the stolen money or bad preparation, but by no means could the media use irony and sarcasm in discussing the authorities. The current government does not allow any mockery. I cannot answer why. "Why" and "Why the fuck" are two main questions striking in my head every day when I read Russian news.
>
> (Digital Journalist 4, personal communication, 26 June 2014)

Mockery has become forbidden, as the shallowest and lighthearted memes are now on the government's radar. As one of the interviewees revealed,

> Even in the USSR you were able to ridicule the authorities, but not in the current regime. During the Sochi Olympics we [journalists working at Lenta.ru - AD] received a call from the very top: they demanded the deletion of a meme from our Twitter. It was called "Mishka-Razorvishka and Zayka-Narezayka [Bear-Ripper and Hare-Cutter – AD]."[10] There is no analytical or logical way to explain this madness. They are just messed up dudes with a total absence of humour.

Digital experts explain the crusade on memes and satire by the spontaneous and liberating nature of this style of communication; the government goes amiss in the attempts to comprehend the inner logics and spirit.

> The government is not as much afraid of memes as offended by them. The authorities find it insulting that somewhere there are people who make good jokes and mock the state. The elites fail to confront these people in their environment. It is impossible to "produce a meme" that would silence the opposition therefore they put pressure from above.
>
> (Digital Journalist 1, personal communication, 1 May 2015)

Besides, the Crimean campaign not only triggered new disputes between pro-Kremlin and anti-Kremlin publics, it became an apple of discord inside the opposition crowds. Meme makers believe that the government deliberately challenged the liberal unity by appealing to patriotic feelings of the resistant circles.

> The government constantly poses questions to the nation by its actions. For example, the annexation of Crimea was one of these questions. Imagine that before Crimea there was an X number of protest public in Russia. What Putin, or the authorities did, they posed this question. Do you approve of the annexation of Crimea or not? Many of Putin's opponents among my friends and good mates contemplated: "Putin is not that bad, apparently". Therefore, they forced the opposition public with different political preferences and leaders, supporting Navalny or whoever else, to respond to this question, either approve or denounce. <...> Currently Putin enjoys colossal support among Russians as he successfully exploited the imperial ambitions, insisted that everyone hates us and created the enemy image. The society will eventually wake up, but it is hard to predict when.
>
> (Resistant Meme Maker 4, personal communication, 1 September 2014)

Personal Motivation for Meme Making and Sharing

The acknowledgement of the plausible jeopardy in leading a protest account affects the users' self-identification. The majority of interviewed meme makers persistently reject any ties to traditional organised politics. **They declare independence from any instituted ideology and prefer to frame their own political views in civil terms.** This rejection of political activism is emblematic and signifies self-censorship and fear of prosecution.

> I do not consider my account political, it is actively civil. When you call a thief a thief, it is not politics.
>
> (Resistant Meme Maker 1, personal communication, 26 August 2014)

> I have a wide scope of political interests and take interest in both Russian and European politics. I tend to cling to the right-wing liberal doctrine, but in general, it would be best to describe my ideological position as the priority of personal rights and freedoms of the citizens, limited government's involvement in economy and denunciation of the Byzantine and Oriental practices of nepotism and idolisation of the authority. I am a supporter of the regular change

of the government; without power shift the authorities turn corrupt and become a problem.

> (Resistant Meme Maker 5, personal
> communication, 9 September 2014)

> I would assess my political stance as libertarian, and I have felt this way since the age of 15. Before having moved to Moscow, I had resided in a city where people had two favourite pastimes: complaining about life and recalling how wonderful it was under communism. Nonetheless, very few were trying to generate an actual change, and those 3–4 individuals I knew finally moved to Moscow and succeeded there. This is why I get furious when I think of the Russian laziness, passion for freebies and irresponsibility. Each person is the host of their fate and this is my life credo.
>
> (Resistant Meme Maker 6, personal
> communication, 10 September 2014)

This observation sheds light on the importance of the Soviet myth for the conservative public. People find comfort in *'recalling how wonderful it was under communism'* and respond well to the efforts of contemporary Russian propaganda in reviving the myth of the idyllic life in the USSR. However, none of the liberal meme sharers interviewed expressed any positive sentiment towards the Soviet times.

A legendary liberal Cartoonist (personal communication, 13 August 2014) also prefers to define himself as ideologically neutral, despite harsh criticism of Putin in his works: *'I feel like a sniper on the vigil: whoever raises his head, gets the shot'*. He created a variety of highly recognisable and sharp cartoons denouncing Putin's actions in Crimea and his post-Crimean rhetoric.

Resistant meme makers refuse to declare loyalty to any party or mobilisation. They do not see themselves as political activists, but rather impartial journalists.

> We will always remain in opposition no matter what, this is how our minds operate. If tomorrow Navalny or whoever else is elected as a president, we will keep whacking so that people keep "pulling their hands off the kettle". This is the function of journalism. Your body does not report every minute that your right hand feels truly marvellous, but it sends you a signal when you burn your left hand. In this moment you do not care about the right hand, but of the other one that is in pain! We will keep writing critically on anyone in power.
>
> (Resistant Meme Maker 2, personal
> communication, 10 July 2014)

Even those few who try to convert their online popularity into civil campaigning achieve minor results. With bitterness, meme makers point to the lack of constructive support and coordination among politically active popular Twitter users. They argue that liberal publics engage in clicktivism and fail to mobilise resources for offline activism.

> People are not afraid to join our mobilisation online, but it takes us nowhere. Writing posts is one thing, most of us do it well and even without grammar mistakes, but it is a dead-end road.
> (Resistant Meme Maker 4, personal communication, 1 September 2014)

Contrary to this singular ambition to unite and mobilise resistant crowds, many other meme makers gave up on the idea of gathering protest public for offline mobilisation. They blame lack of trust in the established politicians of the Russian opposition and therefore absence of appealing leaders for the liberal public. Politically active microbloggers also share their disappointment with the results of the 2011–2012 political activity – the government did not respond to the criticism in a constructive manner.

> The euphoria of 2011–12 halted when people learned that there were no easy ways, and it was not enough to go out in the square with a poster. The falsified Presidential election brought Putin to reign again (actually, even if they were fair, there was no alternative to him). Protests continued with no clear goal or perspective and soon diminished. People lost the motivation to go, got tired, angry and confused.
> (Resistant Meme Maker 2, personal communication, 10 July 2014)

The insights of meme sharers illustrate that the liberal public in Russia experience difficulties in the pursuit of political goals. In the absence of opportunities and trustworthy organisations, social network users dwell in the realm of individual accountability and self-assigned obligation. With no aim to mobilise anyone, they nonetheless seek to spread an alternative message and raise the political awareness of other users.

> This project [the critical Twitter account - AD] was created by three people who follow the political news in Russia and abroad. Several years ago, we started noticing the growing Kafkian character of the news from Russia. <...> As all three participants of the project are devoted to the liberal values, the country's throwback to the close-minded conservatism after 2011 brought disappointment. We decided to respond to it with the special satirical Twitter account where we could show our criticism through satire and humour.
> (Resistant Meme Maker 5, personal communication, 9 September 2014)

Meme makers agree that the yearning for the fair deliberation of politics coalesced with the need for individual self-expression. Their contribution to the liberal resistance borders on creative, even artistic self-actualisation.

> I am enchanted by the possibility to condense a smart/deep/witty idea in 140 symbols. This challenge gives me shudders, jokes apart. I am not willing to expand to larger formats, as there are already established masters who I would not dare to compete with. Navalny's posts are almost pieces of art, not to mention Bykov's[11] opuses that are 100% art. I am trying to shoot a joke as if it was my last one, so that there was nothing to add or cut. When I succeed I receive an array of subsequent jokes from the followers, and many of them make me envious.
>
> (Resistant Meme Maker 1, personal communication, 26 August 2014)

> My expressive style is callous, occasionally angry, but unchangeably doomed, dystopian, touching a sore spot, which is quintessential for a Russian citizen. One need not forget that we are a tough Northern nation accustomed to living in unforgiving climate; we prefer bitter laugh to joyful tears.
>
> (Resistant Meme Maker 3, personal communication, 15 September 2014)

Meme sharers divide on whether to define memes either as creative artworks or as mundane Internet vernacular. Some of them insist that production and distribution of memes are not a privilege of the creative professionals or intellectual elites. Social network users of all backgrounds and skills can discuss any possible subject by the means of memes. Pro-Government Meme Maker 1 (personal communication, 5 June 2014) supports the point and adds that people in all epochs enjoyed '*simplification, labelling and brevity*'.

There is yet another motivation that turns Twitter users into satirists and meme makers. The professional activity of some of them involved close collaboration with high-ranking Russian officials. They were providing business and media marketing services for them and could see the corrupt Russian political system from within. Besides the urge for self-expression and voicing political criticism, they wanted to ridicule their clients and break the cycle of cynical hypocrisy in the business of political media relations.

> I was working in a PR agency and realised that four out of five of my clients were state officials. These people have a very specific approach and a completely different system of values. They are not interested in real communication, but only desire to flash before Putin,

get their foot at the door of the offices of higher bureaucrats. You cannot rely on logic when you negotiate with these people, and this is very exhausting.

For example, a person owns a badly functioning television operator company; it consists of two broken networks and employs one and a half persons. However, these people would spend enormous money on buying a ticket to the event with Putin; through their connections, they would receive the state investment money and spend them to their own liking. People of this breed throw events and promise to the others that higher officials would attend; thus, they sell the ticket to other bureaucrats for incredible prices. They aim at selling a Potyomkin Village[12] to the state; this is how this business operates. I am more than aware of the rules of this game and utterly detest them. [Our account] was born as a "fuck" to all these people.

(Resistant Meme Maker 2, personal
communication, 10 July 2014)

Intriguingly, pro-government users share similar motivation for leading their Twitter accounts as anti-Kremlin users. They also feel responsible for the fate of the country, for supporting the good forces and fighting the disruptors. They disclose that they wanted to promote the preferred ideology and communicate with the like-minded public.

I consider Twitter a formidable political weapon for the overthrow of power and mobilisation. <...> My aim on Twitter is, on the one hand, to unite patriots, and on the other hand, attract the support of like-minded people for my activity, even in the shape of retweets. <...> It would allow me to create a bank of followers and then push forward my ideas, demand something and open a non-governmental organisation. <...> During the Second World War, there was the Foundation of the Russian, or USSR, Defence. I, as a patriot, want to open the equivalent foundation, but devoted to the Red Army in its current state.

(Pro-Government Meme Maker 2, personal
communication, 10 September 2014)

We have been working in media and public relations for a long time, but have not planned any organised campaigns around the Crimean situation. At the same time we, as the people competent in the subject (the Internet, blogs and social networks), saw that there was a clash of two and more propaganda machines. I personally craved to do something less classical in the sense of contemporary political propaganda in the Internet.

(Pro-Government Meme Maker 1, personal
communication, 5 June 2014)

Pro-government's meme makers' interpretation of 'patriotism' means loyalty to the government and pursuit of the national foes. Similar to resistant meme makers, the loyal ones equally acknowledge the need to express their passion about their native country. One of them does it through propagating hatred towards the enemies of the state. Often, they are the liberal targets suggested by the state propaganda.

> Patriotism includes everything that concerns the support of your country, your Motherland, and you can do it by all possible means, be it war, friendship, clans or sections. I am fully championing Putin's and the Kremlin's politics, I have bought all T-shirts with the depiction of Vladimir Vladimirovich.
>
> (Pro-Government Meme Maker 2, personal communication, 10 September 2014)

> We are citizens of our country and wanted to help Russia not for the sake of counter-propaganda, but to present the situation as we saw it. We aspired to depict the Crimean event as we comprehended it: as the peninsula's return home, to Russia. <...> In brief, it is a positive representation based on the pride for Russian people, the Russian army and sincere feelings of the Crimean citizens who have returned home.
>
> (Pro-Government Meme Maker 1, personal communication, 5 June 2014)

Pro-Kremlin meme sharers identify with state propaganda in their vision and goals, yet differ from it by offering more personal motivations. The cases of pro-government social network users exemplify how individual users interpret and amplify the indoctrination that comes from the media. One of them propagates combative patriotism, while the other appeals to soft unobtrusive persuasion. Remarkably, pro-government users concur with the opposition public in exhibiting a high level of concern over the country's future and perceived personal responsibility over it.

The Potential of Twitter for Alternative Political Activism in Russia

The majority of meme makers are cautious in their judgements of Twitter's potential in addressing the society at large, and this corresponds with the statistical data on the network's popularity. Only 3% of all Russian Internet users engage with Twitter day (Russian Search Marketing, 2017). From the positive perspective, **the majority of meme makers hail Twitter for its capacity to inform and raise awareness.** Russian Twitter has a younger audience than other social media and communication is informal thanks to the similar age and interests that members share (Digital Journalist 2, personal communication, 10 May 2014). Others see it as a premium platform for at least two reasons: (1) *'almost all the journalists use Twitter, spending there much time and discussing the social and political situation'*, and (2) *'opinion leaders also reside on Twitter, and they pass the information further down'* (Pro-Government Meme Maker 1, personal communication, 5 June 2014).

Twitter can become instrumental in reaching opinion leaders who would disseminate the message in their circles and then popularise it among the larger masses. Many interviewees lauded Twitter for its networking power. Unlike other popular social networks based on the principle of holding a certain relationship with other individuals (a friend, a colleague, a family member, etc.), Twitter encourages you to follow accounts out of interest for their content. Many meme sharers seek to locate the like-minded Twitter users and establish reliable communities that can further their political engagement:

> I am inclined to assess social networks as the instrument which can be used as the uniting tool for people in search for a change. They are not only useful for coordination during mass events; a person may go to social networks and see that he is not alone and there are thousands of people with the same ideas and aspirations. It would encourage him to be braver, act bolder and, in summary, all these activities can generate political changes.
>
> (Digital Journalist 1, personal communication, 1 May 2015)

> This environment [interactive media] has become very attractive due to the use of humour. The people who inhabit it do not seek violence or coup d'état, they are not criminals, but seemingly affluent citizens. Viral pictures, gags and memes are full of irony, and irony indicates reasonable judgement and comprehension of the situation. This is an intellectual sphere. A marginal alcoholic will hit you with a bottle, while educated people would rather make jokes in strained circumstances.
>
> (Resistant Meme Maker 2, personal communication, 10 July 2014)

The pressure from the government, however, has constant influence on both the shape and the utilisation of social networks for political debates.

> Previously all Russian political discourse was based on LiveJournal, which has recently experienced a dramatic loss in popularity. The fall of politicised LiveJournal came as the direct result of the Russian state's pressure. The authorities have been deliberately and persistently destroying this platform by all means, from frightening

the bloggers and filing lawsuits for particular blog posts to polluting the discussion with verbal rubbish. A cohort of specially trained people close to the Federal Agency for Youth Affairs was releasing massive floods of nonsense in the blogosphere.

Currently, the most intellectual political debates happen on Facebook; VKontakte has a more lumpen and young audience that mostly enjoys the so-called "shitstorms", and Twitter functions as the quick dissemination tool for on-the-spot information. However, you can also utilise Twitter to tilt with a federal politician or editor-in-chief of a big pro-Kremlin media (many of them are quite active specifically on Twitter).

(Digital Journalist 5, personal
communication, 15 June 2014)

In addition to the state monitoring, the other challenge emerges for Twitter community building. The fragmentation of publics: Russian networks tend to divide into niche streams of communication, making liberal discourse more dispersed.

Very soon there may only remain niche platforms. I predict that Russian cyberspace will fleetly mimic the Chinese one: Chinese bloggers can also discuss something and then get a prison sentence. People get detached easily. Remember how soon the audience neglected the anti-terrorist operation in Dagestan[13]: first, the media reported on it every day, people were eagerly reading the news and then it became part of the routine. When they detain terrorists on a daily basis, the narrative gets boring. The same happens with the news of the Russian nightmarish existence – the audience gets used to it and consents. In Russia a state official receives promotion for his project to block Twitter, while in any reasonable country he would be fired.

(Digital Journalist 3, personal
communication, 26 June 2014)

The majority of social network users in Russia, including older citizens and dwellers of smaller Russian cities and towns, visit top social network Odnoklassniki (translates as 'Schoolmates' from Russian), while Facebook, Twitter and Instagram are mostly successful in big cities (for instance, twice more people on average use them in Moscow than in the rest of Russia). Resistant meme makers call Facebook and Twitter primary platforms for the aggregation of opposition crowds, but always complain about the limited popularity of these boards among a larger audience. Liberal activists either need to access larger crowds on their mainstream platforms, such as Odnoklassniki, or remain locked in the more loyal, but limited circles of Twitter and Facebook spaces.

The gap between the digital opposition public and the rest of the audience is a tremendous problem. We discussed this issue with Navalny and he insisted on going offline and printing traditional newspapers for the non-digital public. I argued that those people whom he wants to access are already online, but reside not where we do, but on the neighbouring sites such as Odnoklassniki and Vkontakte. These citizens are very close, but we do not know how to reach them.

(Resistant Meme Maker 2, personal communication, 10 July 2014)

I think there is a noticeable close-knit community of opposition users on Twitter. If you look at the number of Navalny's followers, you can estimate the size of this clique as hundreds of thousands. However, even half a million are a drop in the ocean, less than one percent of the country's population.

(Resistant Meme Maker 5, personal communication, 9 September 2014)

Twitter has partially replaced independent media in Russia. It has become an open battlefield of viewpoints that supplanted traditional journalism. The latter had proven unable to perform this function. According to Soldatov and Borogan (2015), the erosion of journalism had a direct impact on the migration of analytical discussions to Russian social networks. Ousted from established media platforms, journalists relocated their writing to blogging and microblogging spaces: 'A phenomenon was born: highly opinionated, sometimes brilliantly written journalism that was highly critical of the Kremlin, spurring the government to find new methods to drown them out' (Soldatov & Borogan, 2015: para 7–8). Many of the Twitter satirists found themselves regular producing journalism content – supplying their followers with news, opinion and analysis on a daily basis.

Unfortunately those Russian media that used to be liberal have experienced a massive degradation in the recent years. <...> Many interesting and burning news arrive in the daily newsfeeds, but barely receive any deeper analysis or commentary in the media. This is why Twitter has turned into a highly important tool of raising awareness.

This transformation of the media sphere has affected our account's format. Initially we tried to be funny and not post too often, but in the last year, our account has grown into a steady bulletin of the most significant, from our point of view, news of the day. We comment on many of them in a jokey form, but also present some as they are without adding any humour at all.

(Resistant Meme Maker 5, personal communication, 9 September 2014)

Not by chance, the juxtaposition format is one of the most popular ones when meme makers criticise media propaganda. This approach allows presenting facts in a different light and exposing the distortion of truth.

> We had a number of operational formats that always worked. For instance, the Bolotnaya square protester is sentenced to 6 years of colony for the overthrown toilet cabin and the police officer guilty of rape is just suspended for 2 years; we push these two stories towards each other, and this is it. We used Pussy Riot's sentence in our memes multiple times. People who were sentenced to 10 years for stealing borscht were juxtaposed with the state officials who stole 300 billion on construction and received promotion in the following years. We were contrasting the absurd that surrounds us in the news.
> (Digital Journalist 3, personal communication, 26 June 2014)

The majority of meme makers strongly believe that the Russian media have fallen victim to state pressure and self-censorship and no longer serve as reliable sources of information. The government keeps expanding its censoring efforts to cover not only professional, but interactive media and networks. The state encourages anxiety and paranoia by implementing ambiguous laws, for instance, the one on extremism prevention in the digital space. The nebulous definition of 'extremist' reporting makes this legislation prone to abuse by any executive: *'All these laws are not written to have an actual impact on things, but to provide tools to prosecute a politically undesirable blogger'* (Resistant Meme Maker 7, personal communication, 11 December 2014).

> The state nonetheless is not capable to keep up with technological progress, <...>. Schizophrenia is spread through our society; the lack of universal laws and rules makes everyone nervous.
> (Resistant Meme Maker 2, personal communication, 10 July 2014)

These findings illuminate the importance of Twitter as an information hub merged with a discussion platform for Russian liberal users. In the absence of truthful sources of news, social network users adhere to their social networks' flows of data, hand-picking reliable accounts and creating what Negroponte (1995) and Sunstein (2001) called the 'daily me', the information package where a person chooses and mixes components according to personal preferences. In the Russian media environment, the necessity to create such a package comes from not only individual interests, but also restrictions on free circulation of information.

Besides dissemination of information and commentary, there is a third highly precious component that makes Twitter so appealing to politicised publics – interactivity, the ability to relate to others, tweet or retweet, link and comment. Meme makers praise Twitter for the opportunity to 'get involved' in the events: *'Many prominent opposition leaders have narrowed their communication down to writing solely on Twitter. It gives a fascinating effect of involvement in the events and allows the immediate spread of information'* (Resistant Meme Maker 6, personal communication, 10 September 2014).

Yet, the interactivity is overshadowed by the polarisation of users. They mostly stick to their echo chambers and – even when tempted through memes – would hardly get curious of the opinions that are not similar to theirs: *'The black-and-white thinking reigns in the Internet; separate segments live in isolation from each other, cherish their own ideas and consider the opponents wrong'* (Pro-Government Meme Maker 1, personal communication, 5 June 2014).

Moreover, the state media have excelled at indoctrination, and even digitally savvy users familiar with Twitter and alternative discourse are predisposed to preserving the pro-government point of view. This begs the question whether people come to the Internet with the predetermined ideas – instead of harvesting news and opinion from there. This may be particularly the case in Russia, where the national media are controlled by the government. Sociologists (Volkov & Goncharov, 2014: 14) confirm that a sheer 5% of the population retain news only from the Internet and do not watch television, while others employ the digital space as the supplement to the daily portion of traditional media. Furthermore, Volkov and Goncharov (2014: 14) came to a surprising observation that even those citizens who absorb information from at least four different sources (including electronic ones) do not turn any more critical in their judgment than an 'average' television-addicted Russian. These findings contradict the previous assumption of the liberal press (see, for instance, Gazeta, 2010) that people were likely to develop a critical political stance by garnering news from the Internet.

Resistant Meme Maker 2 (personal communication, 10 July 2014) confirms from an own experience that availability of digital resources does not mean that one would use them to harvest alternative opinions. He or she would more likely settle on soothing ideas or feelings:

> There is a lovely story of our friend Maya Usova whose mother complained that television and newspapers were all saying the same thing and she was confused whom to believe. Maya suggested that she picked her news from the Internet. In a few days her mother calls and says "Now I get it all!" and enthusiastically blethers about reptiloids, underground bunkers[14] etc. When a person jumps from one extreme to the other, exaggerations occur. When a person holds a rigid system of values, he or she is more resistant to manipulation; the inner filter sifts the incoming facts and opinions. Reconfiguration of one's values is a long and complex process.

Furthermore, the Internet realm offers not only open and uninhibited deliberation of politics, but holds plenty of manipulative and distorted discussions. Fake news, fabricated video and audios, trolls and fake accounts complicate the pursuit of a meaningful information on social media.

> Social media are the ultimate space where you can discuss politics and learn news first. You receive news on Twitter faster than from any news agency. However, when a video, say, from Ukraine appears, one should not trust it and boil over. Fabricated news come from both sides, and you need to get confirmation of authenticity first, and only then disseminate the video, and reproduce the buzz around it. I am very suspicious these days.
>
> (Resistant Meme Maker 4, personal communication, 1 September 2014)

In the 2010s, the Russian government has utilised advanced tactics in the distortion of opposition discourse in social networks. Many users have noticed the emergence of multiple pro-government accounts that were flooding the discussions with either hate speech or thousands of similar comments. These bundles of text interrupted valuable threads and conversations. This practice, known as the pro-government 'trolling', is a newly acquired state strategy of controlling digital deliberation. Internet trolls are users on the payroll who load electronic media and social networks with praise of the Russian authority; they negatively label Putin's enemies (see also Fanaylova, 2014). Pomerantsev (cited in Bugorkova, 2015) defines trolling and fabricated discourse as 'reverse censorship': instead of curbing communication, the government overloads it with hate speech and gossip that obscure authentic arguments. Digital Journalist 4 observes that Russian authorities have never allocated as much funding to the Internet manipulation as in the 2010s. They try to censor social network communication from the inside by commissioning paid users and attempting to mimic the style of the uninhibited Internet debates.

> The state does not know how to manage Twitter. They have the experience of imposing control over traditional media, but not the digital sphere. They tried to promote pressure groups and influential bloggers, but these efforts failed. Then they filled the cyberspace with Internet bots paid 80 roubles[15] each. Now they are considering shutting down the global Internet in Russia and creating a local version called Cheburashka.
>
> (Resistant Meme Maker 2, personal communication, 10 July 2014)

Nonetheless, many interviewees disagree with attributing much significance to this practice. They claim that the experienced social network users would immediately notice the artifice of paid trolling.

> If the government-funded Internet troll centres exist, their work seems a shallow waste of the state money. What goals do they pursue? Publishing blog posts? Polluting opposition hashtags with rubbish? All this activity is a meaningless hustle that does not influence anything and cannot change anybody's opinion or position. These trolls only supply extra work for the moderators of the Internet forums who are obliged to sweep this rubbish out.
>
> I am noticing the planting of pro-government memes out of the corner of my eye and do not remember if any of their memes turned successful.
>
> (Digital Journalist 1, personal
> communication, 1 May 2015)

From a more sceptical perspective, not all users are capable of distinguishing toxic accounts from authentic ones. Besides, people tend to follow popular accounts favoured by other people and join busy threads of comments. They are not aware that the number of followers may be fabricated. The Pro Government Maker 2 (personal communication, 10 September 2014) confesses:

> I can obtain one million followers in a day; I have a service that automatically generates retweets. I can fabricate 500–600 new followers today. They are bots. If you see a person with 200,000 followers, there is a possibility they are not real people. Half of my followers are real, the rest are bots. I made them before the account became "the comrade Stalin". I am against this, but I also have a personal account as a blogger and participated in a contest that required me to fabricate a large amount of followers.

Several meme makers share a positive view on the future of civil protest online. They want to believe that, while recent Russian laws restrict offline mobilisations, online mobilisations can still occur. The meme makers often note that liberal resistance needs more offline triggers that would mobilise resistant publics: the actions of the government that may incite fury or disappointment and motivate people to join online deliberation. If more offline triggers arise, a virtual dissent can find the way into the streets.

> There is much fear in Russia nowadays, but this fear is not eternal. Social networks can mobilise people online and offline. I am sure

that we will see many protests and manifestations resulting from the communication on social networks.

(Resistant Meme Maker 5, personal
communication, 9 September 2014)

Memes Help to Let Off Steam and Receive Comfort (Slow Burn Resistance)

The role of political memes in the Russian virtual resistance has changed dramatically over just a few years. Having emerged as the expressive language of the digital protesters in the 2010s, memes travelled to the offline posters during the Bolotnaya square and Sakharova square manifestations, turning from casual jokes into condensed and humorous political claims. Later on, memes have evolved into a tool of continuous political communication in digital networks – a vehicle for the quick transmission of a concept or idea, used by different sides of the political spectrum.

Meme makers agree that the format of a meme is easy to consume and therefore has more chances to reach people than, for example, lengthy blogposts or opinion columns. Social network users are too busy:

> The simpler the idea and the brighter form it takes, the quicker it affects your mind. It is the main principle of neuro-linguistic programming. People who invented Twitter were fully aware that 140 symbols are quite enough to form a specific mind-set. <...> I doubt that more than 1% of people read serious political or economic analysis, the human race is much simpler.
>
> (@Resistant Meme Maker 6, personal
> communication, 10 September 2014)

> Memes exist for the same purpose as anecdotes. Political satire is, on the one hand, a pleasant and unhindered way to let off steam, express one's indignation or wrath, but on the other hand, a specific lens that can often convey the essence of a political event much sharper than ten highly intellectual newspaper columns.
>
> (Digital Journalist 5, personal
> communication, 15 June 2014)

In the current sociopolitical environment, liberal users of social networks praise memes as one of the few remaining mouthpieces of political communication. Under increased surveillance over the digital sphere, **opposition publics use memes as the vehicles to express grievances and to let off steam**. Unable to permeate the public space dominated by the hegemonic media, SNS users share memes to maintain an alternative flow of ideas and opinions.

Satire and humour permit keeping a sane mind when reading Russian news bulletins. If you stay serious perceiving all that stuff, there are not many options left for you, either a suicide or a mental institution.

(@Resistant Meme Maker 5, personal
communication, 9 September 2014)

Tweets will not solve problems. Yet if sharp humour helps someone to see differently from how the television instructs, it would be a significant achievement.

(Resistant Meme Maker 4, personal
communication, 1 September 2014)

The production and spread of memes often function as the coping strategy for liberal users who struggle to reconcile with the disturbing political reality. The degree of comforting stands in direct proportion with the degree of deceit in traditional media. The intensification of emotional pressure from media propaganda propels users to coin more absurd memes and thus release their rage and despondency.

Many people think that laughing at Hitler is wrong and makes us forget how gruesome and serious the story of Nazi Germany was. I disagree. When you turn the likes of Dmitry Kiselyov into a joke, you find a coping mechanism. It is easier for me to perceive all this absurd in the form of a joke, turn the absurd into a bigger absurd and somehow reconcile with it.

(Digital Journalist 2, personal
communication, 10 May 2014)

The habit of liberal users to instantly react to any government initiative with a satirical commentary and memes can sometimes turn against them. Curiously, in 2014–2015 Russian authorities had proposed a high number of the odd laws that immediately gained attention from social network users. The absurdity of the initiatives stimulated citizens to respond with memes and compete for the creation of the best joke. Frenzied debates on the bizarre government actions clouded other important legislative measures. **The innovation of the Russian elites lies in distracting social network users in the age of memes;** digital inhabitants take the challenge to express themselves on the entertaining topic in the public eye and often miss important news behind the weird ones.

State Duma's trashy laws play the role of distraction and hide from people that Rotenberg has obtained yet another company[16]. An amendment here, an amendment there – little laws steal your money and freedom. Everyone is discussing the penis on a 100-rouble banknote,[17] meanwhile State Duma is deciding how to withdraw the accumulative part of pension in 2015. <...> Blogosphere takes this bait. This is how human's psychology works: put your hand on a hot kettle and you will immediately react and pull it back.

(Resistant Meme Maker 2, personal
communication, 10 July 2014)

Simultaneously, memes are not limited to silly humour or absurdity, they are open to different sorts of humour including more complex and demanding wit. Meme makers recall the examples of their friends with postgraduate degrees and high-level jobs that are able to coin the silliest memes and deploy them to the Internet, to much success. In other cases, the meme makers can create more sophisticated jokes that require a deeper knowledge of a specific context, but even in this case, the meme finds its audience.

The spontaneous nature and essential anonymity of memes proliferate the equality of social network users: anyone could design a successful meme and witness its rise to fame. Memes arise spontaneously, but meaningfully, as they probably hit the right spot in the public perception of a particular person or situation. Memes are blueprints of trending themes.

Although some creative individuals may be more successful in creating amusing texts and attracting large numbers of followers, they cease owning memes as soon as they travel beyond the borders of the initial account. *'No one holds a patent on a good joke. All are equal, you cannot trace the author. Three thousand monkeys can type Hamlet'* (Digital Journalist 2, personal communication, 10 May 2014). Anonymity of memes is also a strong asset when it comes to censorship – by spreading memes with no authorship details, dissent users protect their identities and evade any scrutiny by the vigilant state.

The majority of meme makers doubt that memes can trigger and maintain a steady political discussion. Only very few smart and timely memes can draw attention to certain topics and encourage a debate. Cartoonist (personal communication, 13 August 2014) declares that only in a rare number of cases his works elicited a meaningful argument that even affixed users with the opposing political views:

> A cartoon can arouse a hundred comments and go viral. I have witnessed my cartoons encourage a good debate five or six times. These were about the public opinion and the statistics that 90% of the nation approve of Putin. Social network crowds are mixed, so participants from both parts of the spectrum took part in the heated debate.

Other meme makers also recall a few examples of when memes encouraged a substantial discussion – in the most meaningful cases, social network users even exchanged links to additional analytical pieces to provide their opponents with new food for thought. Nevertheless, meme sharers perceive these instances as the exclusions from the rule.

Besides, memes are limited in their potential to trigger a meaningful discussion as various users read memes differently. Understanding of a meme depends on one's intellectual level, education, digital literacy and comprehension of the context. Moreover, in the most peculiar cases, users even notice how their personal perception of the same meme can change over time.

> Sometimes memes are so terribly unfunny that it makes you laugh, and then you find them horrible again, and then you laugh about it, finding amusement not in the joke itself, but in the context of your perception dynamics.
>
> (Digital Journalist 2, personal communication, 10 May 2014)

The short expiry date of a meme and its direct dependence on digital 'fashion' present a constraint for the meme's bonding capacity. Meme makers point to the volatility of memes' 'reputation': an incompetent misappropriation can repulse the digitally savvy public and ruin the worth of a meme as the 'inside joke'. Contrary to this, the conservation of a meme inside a close discourse diminishes its chances to evolve and appeal to the more general public. This dichotomous nature of memes' dependence on digital vogue and context makes them unstable communication equilibriums:

> By the time you coin a political slogan that exploits a fresh meme the audience might already be tired and sick of it (or will get tired in a few weeks). An expired meme <... > makes users wince. In a half a years' time, no one would be able to remember why the meme seemed so amusing. The other issue is that memes are not always clear to the audience. When you pick an extremely fashionable meme and attempt to use it for your purposes, you may need to spend quite a lot of time explaining its meaning. Explaining the jokes is always a deadly idea.
>
> (Digital Journalist 1, personal communication, 1 May 2015)

Conclusion

Meme makers have become the new journalists, civil activists and political protesters at the same time. The vague structure of the Russian political system and lack of established social institutions and platforms of negotiation with the state make the Internet the only vibrant site of the public discussion. Highly censored traditional media produce multiple propaganda flows, and liberal citizens resist via social networks. They employ the ambiguous digital folklore, the Internet memes, to share their grievances and disrupt propaganda's deceit. By exploiting these interactive, adjustable communication vehicles, social network users articulate their alternative view at the reality and invite other users to reflect, juxtapose and accept different truths.

The format of a meme has evolved to become instrumental in these circumstances. The quick medium that offers a half-baked joke and a layout to fill, a meme facilitates one's self-expression and disclosure of criticisms to the state. The most important functions of memes in the contemporary Russian media environment are raising the awareness of digital publics, directing their attention to the burning political topics and providing mental self-defence against the aggressive indoctrination of the state. Additionally, as the majority of meme makers agree, political memes allow to let off steam, locate the like-minded individuals and restore confidence in one's principles and aspirations.

Contrary to this, memes have proven feeble in triggering or maintaining a substantial discussion. Their short-lived nature and reliance on agenda make them a wobbly building brick of the virtual deliberation. Memes can facilitate political discussions in the established bonded communities, but appear inefficient in linking individuals or groups. Russian Twitter demonstrates low capacity in uniting protest public in sound communities. Digital dissidents indicate a high level of self-censorship and caution – they persistently reject any engagement with political activism and refer to their accounts as civil mouthpieces. This tendency towards detachment from organised politics exposes a lack of trust in established political structures, freedom of speech and disappointment with the existing systemic opposition. Politically active social network users emphasise the prevalence of personal responsibility over any group affiliation; they reside in the individual realms of independent Twitter accounts.

The practice of meme making and sharing stands on the edge of artistic self-expression and articulation of active citizenship, the necessity to voice one's opinion and confront injustice. This peculiar equilibrium explains why memes attract very diverse crowds of people – they are not limited to either art or politics, entertainment or activism, but amalgamate various discourses. The accessibility of memes to citizens of different social backgrounds links them to the carnivalesque resistance. Anonymous, entertaining and easily consumable, most memes travel in between various communities. Meme making is not restricted to creative elites, as anyone can craft a successful joke and encourage artistic contributions from other users. This means that memes provide the ever-flexible possibilities for the change of power relations, they are not fixed or limited to elites or intellectuals.

The Russian government attributes much influence to memes, as the recent legislative measures and pursuit of meme makers illustrate. Memes remarkably irritate the state that struggles to handle spontaneous mockery and counterbalance it with fabricated texts. The authorities have deployed massive forces online, trying to contaminate meaningful politicised discussions with pro-government memes and commentaries. Yet, digitally savvy users report that artifice is notoriously visible in the realm of memetic exchange.

From the alternative perspective, memes are not as much the language but the blueprint of the collective digital identity, a Polaroid of the Twitter sphere in any given moment of time. Memes sensitively ingest the existing moods and trends in society and politics; they vigorously echo the main points of the offline agenda in the virtual space. Memes cannot survive without public demand; they represent public request and interest in certain types of information or debate in the present moment. Memes facilitate the communication of complex political issues to larger publics. This practice fits into the changing pattern of media consumption – people prefer laconic concentrated texts to long explanations, and memes have the capacity to pass the message in a condensed and entertaining frame.

Overall, the analysis of the memes, meme mutation and interviews with prominent Russian meme makers and sharers illustrate that the role of memes as discursive weapons is constantly evolving. The challenges of the restricted media environment that puts increasing pressure both on traditional and new media, on the one hand, curb the outreach of liberal microblogging, but on the other hand, encourage the liberal accounts to sustain alternative discourse by all available means. Social network spaces are becoming the ultimate sources of uninhibited data and commentary. Although many liberal users perceive memes as pleasurable additions to the meaningful textual discourse, they nonetheless affirm their potential in addressing apolitical crowds, infiltrating casual conversations and providing symbolic manifestation to the burning resistant debates.

Meme Metamorphosis. How Memes Mutate and 'Change Sides' While They Travel

Memes are not living creatures. They have no agency. It is the people who use them according to their goals and likings. One of the ambitious tasks every meme researcher is facing is tracing the evolution of a meme – how it changes from one shape to the other, while preserving recognisable features of the 'original'. This task has proven challenging – primarily, because it is hard to trace an image that keeps changing. Image search does not have the capacity to return the results with the chain reactions of meme transformations. Determined nonetheless, I opted for the manual tracking of several popular memes of the Crimean crisis.

I have found the mutated versions, the people who spread them, and analysed how the memes literally changed sides and fell to the opposite sides of the political spectrum, when adjusted.

This was an experimental non-representative and non-replicable approach, which nonetheless highlighted a number of trends in Russian politicised meme sharing. These tentative findings suggest areas of future research on the Internet memes and provide evident examples of chains of memetic transformations that illustrate the adaptive nature of memes and ways people alter their meaning in different contexts.

This test study has revealed that, at least in Russia, **instead of contributing their alterations to the same thread, individuals tend to publish the adjusted memes to other networks,** personal and group accounts; uploading to meme aggregators and humorous websites. This research includes two case studies on the highly popular Crimean memes that enjoyed rampant circulation on the Web, hence their trajectories were more visible than those of their less prolific counterparts.

The 'February-March' meme (see Figure 5.30) emerged in social networks in early March 2014, soon after the end of the Sochi Olympic Games and along with the start of the Crimean campaign.

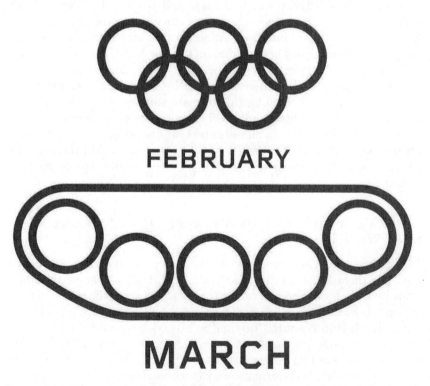

Figure 5.30 The meme juxtaposes the symbol of Olympic Games, the five Olympic rings, with the schematic drawing of a tank's caterpillar track.

The very process of following the trajectory of this meme turned into an industrious investigation. The meme was first located on the personal Facebook web page of a public figure, television celebrity Rovshan Askerov. He had obtained the text from the entertaining Facebook portal and Web magazine Theories of the Deep Understanding of Things. This website has a large community of followers (over 130,000), and a few of them shared their doctored versions of the meme and additional memes, fitting in the narrative linking the Olympic Games and subsequent war. Other sharers included Facebook communities of art posters and gags (Alt, Ctrl, Del, 275,940 followers, and That's Messed Up, 13,233 followers – see Appendix for more detail). Uneven popularity levels of the sharers did not indicate any recurring patterns of dissemination: prominent and minor accounts, personal and group pages both distributed the meme. Still, the larger distributors attracted a larger audience and higher number of comments; many individual users added their own modifications of the meme to the discussion.

In several cases, clicking on the image provided the original source of publication. By expanding the investigation to other group pages on Facebook, I was able to identify the entertaining community That's Messed Up (over 13,000 followers and 160,000 mentions). The distribution of the February-March meme on this page attracted more memes on the subject of war and the Olympics. Although **users did not adjust the February-March meme, they nonetheless contributed other related texts**. At this point, tracking of the February-March meme revealed no other significant alterations and came to a dead end. The other memes with different images and stories brought new angles to the discussion – they were popular and cohabited the social networks, next to the February-March meme. This raises the question whether we need to look at memes as a chain of mutation or see them in the midst of their meme threads. Social media platforms do not preserve inclusivity for a single meme and its mutations, they rather offer a marketplace of visual images (Figure 5.31).

The analysis of the meme travel proved that memes pass through communities and individual pages and are not limited to either interpersonal or intergroup communication. Netizens can also enrich the discourse by adding other related memes to the conversation, and hence broaden the scope of ideas and invite reflections from others. The dispersion and aggregation of memes in social networks can facilitate the accumulation of ideas in a shared virtual space, but **memes do not seem to stimulate the community formation**. The correlation of various memes in one thread creates an interesting mixture of ideas, but there is no evidence that people take these viral texts as a starting point to form bonds with each other or discuss politics any deeper.

My second case study of meme travel analysis also placed Russia-related memes in a global context, but incorporated more Russian users. The second case, Doors meme (see Figure 5.32), contains a little text and is comprehensible without a dictionary. However, it exhibits a slightly

Figure 5.31 The screenshot from Facebook's community That's Messed Up, users add new memes in the comment thread started by the February-
March meme (Figure 5.30).

different role of a meme – users employed the meme as the discursive
weapon, dramatically remixing it to change the ideological content, and
use in political activism.

The original Doors cartoon is the allegory of the US invasion of other
countries. It portrays the male figure of a figurative Uncle Sam, symbol of
the US, who walks from door to door that are labelled as 'Iraq', 'Syria',
'Libya' and others; flames and blood are coming from these rooms. The
protagonist is shocked to meet the Bear, the metaphoric representation of
Russia, greeting him from the Ukrainian door. There are two main versions of the Doors meme that first circulated in Russian social networks;
one belongs to the unknown, perhaps Western cartoonist, and the other
is the work of the Russian cartoonist Vitaly Podvitski (Figure 5.33).

Figure 5.32 The 'Doors' cartoon by Vitali Podvitski depicts a bear that greets a person dressed in the US flag-like coloured suit. The bear represents Russia that stepped in to protect Ukraine from the US influence.

Figure 5.33 The new version of the 'Doors' cartoon that became a meme. This time, US is depicted as the death that knocks on the doors with the names Iraq, Libya, Ukraine.

Both versions of the meme travelled through Russian and English-speaking accounts on Twitter, receiving multiple alterations. Some users have turned it into a comic, while others have completely overthrown the ideological argument, revolving the satire against Russia (Figure 5.34).

The circulation of the Doors meme encouraged an array of opinions on the Crimean crisis and the roles of Russia and the US in it. Users utilised memes to point at the previous debates on the abuse of power by the US and eventually linked it with the current dispute on the abuse of power by Russia. Versatile mutations of the meme exposed the ambivalence of this rhetoric tool. They proved that ideological content is not static in it, but can transform through a quick remix. The bare replacement of

Figure 5.34 Yet another version of the 'Doors' carton, where the invader is portrayed in the colours of the Russian flag. Previously opened doors with the blood stains on them read as Caucasus, Chechnya, Dagestan, Abkhaziya, North Osetiya. The only closed door is Ukraine.

labels on the doors and painting various flags on Death's contours alternated the whole content and twisted the targets of criticism. Besides, this meme's flexibility to adjustment exposed the conversational power of the cartoon format – users adapted this professionally executed coded text and applied it as a rhetoric weapon.

Tracing down the provenance of the Doors meme brings us to the earlier crisis, the Israeli-Palestinian conflict. Apparently, the meme was not created by the Russian cartoonist, but originated in the Middle East. According to the Israeli blogger David Guy, the Doors meme derives from the anti-Israel Internet campaign of 2013 (see Figure 5.35; Guy, 2013; Rothrock, 2014). There was also another version of the cartoon that blamed the aggression at the Wahhabi movement, the ultraconservative version of the Islam that dominates Saudi Arabia, and had no mention of Israel and the US (Guy, 2013).

The roadmap of the Doors meme journey includes individual Twitter accounts, the Twitter feeds of established media sources, independent electronic media, local Russian social network VKontakte's page and the Israeli blog for advocates. The broad scope of platforms demonstrates the meme's potency in surmounting the limits of individual and public spaces.

Figure 5.35 Another version of the 'Doors' meme depicts the invader as death with the US flag and Israel's emblem on the clothing. The previously opened doors bear such names as Iraq, Libya, Sirya, Tunisia. The closed door is Egypt.

The limitation of this fluidity is the constant change of audience: digital crowds were unlikely to trace the metamorphosis of a meme and witness the transfiguration of discourse, given the diversity of the meme's voyage. In conclusion, the analysis of the Doors meme travel validated the high capacity of memes for trans-platform circulation and rhetorical metamorphosis. There are no proofs that memes conjoin digital users in a debate. Nevertheless, the study on the Doors example suggested that memes could be encouraging for individual creativity and expression of political position through memes. This insight informs that **memes are more likely to link ideas and narratives than individuals**: they bypass the margins of the established groups and virtual communities and flourish among larger digital crowds.

Notes

1 The currency exchange rate was calculated from the average 2012 figures.
2 The full text of the Law on Extremism (officially known as Article 282 of the Criminal Code) can be found at www.russian-criminal-code.com/PartII/SectionX/Chapter29.html.
3 The naming of this category may not be perfect. Any persuasion based on the labelling of people and events, omission of facts and selective presentation of truth technically is classified as propaganda. However, this notion fits into the scope of the book as it terms the efforts of Twitter users to disrupt the narrative of the mainstream, state-affiliated media and their distortion of information in Russia.
4 From here onwards, the amount of retweets and favourites refers to the numbers obtained in February 2015, when the analysis of data took place.
5 The search on the provenance of the term has proven to be difficult. The quest for the 'Russian military tourists' and other variations of the idiom (in Russian) in the main Russian search engine Yandex did not harvest any substantial results. Those publications that labelled pro-Russian forces in Crimea as 'tourists' appeared only in minor media, mostly local publications and Internet outlets with a relatively small audience.
6 @EuromaidanPR is a popular pro-Ukrainian anti-Russian Twitter account with over 40,000 followers. It defines itself as '#1 independent citizen media about #Ukraine' and tweets many times a day, providing news and images on the Russian-Ukrainian war conflict.
7 Alexey Navalny is the leader of the Russian political opposition. Before founding his own party, he used to work for other liberal parties, combining this with the career of a lawyer. Navalny gained recognition in the 2010s with his highly popular sarcastic blog and acclaimed crowd-sourced campaign against corruption. The politician extensively exploited the Internet's interactivity, inviting legal expertise and financial input from his followers to pursue the bribe takers in the government.
8 TV Rain is a large independent television channel that broadcasts online and via cable networks. In 2014, it fell under the state pressure for their reports on corrupt officials, and major cable operators withdrew the channel from their packages, hindering the channel's income and future.
9 Yury Kovalchuk is the Russian billionaire who allegedly belongs to Putin's close circle of friends.
10 The meme ridicules the official mascots of the Sochi Olympics, the Bear and the Hare, and includes reference to the corruption of the Russian Olympic

committee and, perhaps, aggressive methods of the Russian government in reaching their goals. 'Ripper' and 'cutter' insinuate the methods of stealing from the Olympic budget and the ways the Kremlin deals with rivals.

11 Dmitry Bykov is one of the eminent liberal journalists and a writer. He contributes to the most prolific media and acts as one of the leaders of the opposition.

12 'Potyomkin village' is an idiom referring to the fabrication of results to present to the higher authority. The expression derives from the name of Katherine the Great's duke who installed fake happy villages on the way of her carriage so that she would perceive Russia as a joyful and prosperous country.

13 The interviewee probably refers to the eight-month counter-terrorist operation in the Russian republic of Dagestan in 2014. However, he may also mean either of any other counter-terrorist operations conducted by Russian Special Forces in Dagestan in 1999, 2005 and 2008–2009.

14 The interviewee refers to the sensationalist journalism and user-generated websites that focus on conspiracy theories and pseudo-scientific investigations and reports. Reptiloids are reptile-looking aliens, and underground bunkers are probably related to the fear of nuclear threat and secret shelters.

15 The equivalent of one-pound sterling, or less than two dollars.

16 Arkady and Boris Rotenberg are Russian billionaires who allegedly belong to Putin's inner circle and used to be his sparring partners in martial arts. They are known to seize the most prestigious state contracts (including a 7-billion-dollar worth construction deal for the Sochi Olympic Games) and own dozens of companies, including the offshore ones.

17 In 2014, one of the Russian parliamentarians proposed to withdraw the image of male genitals from the 100-ruble note. The object of the outrage shows the façade of the Bolshoi Theatre, adorned with a world-famous sculpture of a chariot driven by the Greek god Apollo. Apollo's intimate parts caused Russian MPs moral panic. Liberal journalists called this move a ridiculous manipulation of the popular discourse on 'traditional values' (Lipman, 2014).

Bibliography

Alaszewski, A. (2006). *Using Diaries for Social Research*. London: Sage.

Alifanov, V. (2014). Likbez* from the Russian journalist: How media "created" the banderovets**. *StopFake.org*, 29 April 2014. Available at: www.stopfake.org/en/likbez-from-the-russian-journalist-how-media-created-bandervicev/ (last accessed March 2015).

Arnold, G. B. (2013). *Projecting the End of the American Dream: Hollywood's Visions of US Decline*. Santa Barbara: ABC-CLIO.

Aron, L. (2012) *Russia's Protesters: The People, Ideals, and Prospects*. American Enterprise Institute for Public Policy Research. Report, 9 August 2012. Available at: www.aei.org/publication/russias-protesters-the-people-ideals-and-prospects/ (accessed April 2016).

Asmolov, A. (2012) Vlast' Dolzhna Ponyat, Chto My Zhivyom v Drugoi Realnosti [Authorities have to understand that we live in another reality]. *Moskovskiye Novosti*, Interview, 28 March 2012. Available at: www.mn.ru/politics/20120328/314447137.html (accessed July 2014).

Baker, P. and Glasser, S. (2007) *Kremlin Rising: Vladimir Putin's Russia and the End of Revolution*. Washington, DC: Potomac Books.

Banditskiy Peterburg: Advokat (2000). [TV miniseries] Directed by Vladimir Bortko. Russia: 2-B-2.

Bateson, I. (2014). Russia's Ukrainian minority under pressure, Al Jazeera, 25 April 2014. Available at: www.aljazeera.com/indepth/features/2014/04/russia-ukraine-crisis-minority-under-pressure-20144231041321 54242.html (last accessed March 2015).

BBC (2012). *Russia Internet Blacklist Law Takes Effect*, 1 November 2012. Available at: www.bbc.co.uk/news/technology-20096274 (last accessed August 2016).

BBC (2013). *Ukraine Suspends Preparations for EU Trade Agreement*, 21 November 2013. Available at: www.bbc.co.uk/news/world-europe-25032275 (last accessed February 2015).

BBC (2014a) *Russia Lenta.ru editor Timchenko fired in Ukraine row*, 12 March 2014. Available at: www.bbc.co.uk/news/world-europe-26543464 (last accessed April 2016).

BBC (2014b). *Ukraine Crisis: Timeline*, 13 November 2014. Available at: www.bbc.co.uk/news/world-middle-east-26248275 (last accessed February 2015).

BBC (2014c). *Ukraine's Berkut Police: What Makes Them Special?* 26 February 2014. Available at: www.bbc.co.uk/news/world-europe-25895716 (last accessed March 2015).

Belkovsky, S. (2003). Mif o stabilnosti i natsionalnyi proekt, *Pravda.ru*, 26 September 2003. Available at: www.pravda.ru/politics/authority/kremlin/26-09-2003/38648-belkovski-0/ (last accessed August 2015).

Bell, D. (1976). *The Coming of Post-Industrial Society: A Venture in Social Forecasting*. New York: Basic Books.

Berg, B., & Lune, H. (2004). *Qualitative Research Methods for the Social Sciences*. Boston: Pearson.

Biggs, C. (2014). Kyiv Ditches Separatist-Linked Ribbon As WWII Symbol. *Radio Free Europe/Radio Liberty*, 17 March 2015. Available at: www.rferl.org/content/russia-ukraine-st-george-ribbon-wwii-commemoration/25375013.html (last accessed March 2015).

Bjelica, S. (2014). *Discourse Analysis of the Masculine Representation of Vladimir Putin*. Master's Thesis, Freie Universität Berlin. Available at: www.academia.edu/11590578/Discourse_Analysis_of_the_Masculine_Representation_of_Vladimir_Putin (last accessed April, 2015).

Bogomolov, A. & Lytvynenko, O. (2012). *A Ghost in the Mirror: Russian Soft Power in Ukraine*. Briefing Paper. Chatham House. 1 January 2012. Available at: www.chathamhouse.org/publications/papers/view/181667#sthash.KJQILPMF.dpuf (last accessed August 2016).

Booker, C. (2004). *The Seven Basic Plots: Why We Tell Stories*. London: Continuum.

Borenstein, E. (2004). Survival of the catchiest: Memes and postmodern Russia. *The Slavic and East European Journal*, 48(3), 462–483.

Brigada, (2002). [TV mini-series]. Directed by Aleksei Sidorov. Russia: Avatar Film.

Brockriede, W. (1968). Dimensions of the concept of rhetoric. *Quarterly Journal of Speech*, 54, 1–12.

Broderick, R. (2014). The Internet can't stop making gross fan art of Crimea's "cute" new attorney general. *BuzzFeed*, 24 March 2014. Available at: www.

buzzfeed.com/ryanhatesthis/the-internet-is-making-gross-fan-art-of-russias-cute?utm_term=.ery0WeedM#.twz6l33dG (last accessed August 2016).

Brother (Brat), (1997). [Film]. Directed by Aleksei Balabanov. Russia: CTB Film Company, Gorky Film Studios, Roskomkino.

Brother 2 (Brat 2), (2000). [Film]. Directed by Aleksei Balabanov. Russia: CTB Film Company.

Brown, A. (2015). Internet memes mocking Vladimir Putin are now ILLEGAL in Russia. *Express*, 14 April 2015. Available at: www.express.co.uk/life-style/science-technology/570122/Russia-Vladimir-Putin-Memes-Banned-Ban-Remove-Sadimir (last accessed July 2015).

Brown, M. (2012). Vladimir Putin: 'the godfather of a mafia clan'. *The Telegraph*, 25 February 2012. Available at: www.telegraph.co.uk/news/worldnews/vladimir-putin/9100388/Vladimir-Putin-the-godfather-of-a-mafia-clan.html (last accessed February 2015).

Bryman, A. (2012). *Social Research Methods*. Oxford: Oxford University Press.

Bugorkova, O. (2015). Ukraine conflict: Inside Russia's 'Kremlin troll army'. *BBC Monitoring*, 19 March 2015. Available at: www.bbc.co.uk/news/world-europe-31962644 (last accessed October 2015).

Bummer (Bumer), (2003). [Film]. Directed by Pyotr Buslov. Russia: CTB Film Company, Pygmalion Production.

Burgess, J. (2008). All your chocolate rain are belong to us. Viral video, YouTube and the dynamics of participatory culture. In Lovink, G. & Niederer, S. (eds.) *Video Vortex Reader: Responses to YouTube*, 101–109.

Byerly, C. M. & Ross, K. (2008). *Women and Media: A Critical Introduction*. Hoboken: John Wiley & Sons.

Carter, C. (2014). Sex/gender and the media. From sex roles to social construction and beyond. In Ross, K. (ed.) *The Handbook of Gender, Sex and Media*. Oxford: John Wiley & Sons, 365–382.

Cassiday, J. A., & Johnson, E. D. (2010). Putin, Putiniana, and the question of a post-Soviet cult of personality. *Slavonic and East European Review*, 88(4), 681–707.

CBS (2014). *Putin: Russia Must "cleanse" Itself of Homosexuality*, 19 January 2014. Available at: www.cbsnews.com/news/putin-russia-must-cleanse-itself-of-homosexuality/ (last accessed August 2016).

Cha, M., Haddadi, H., Benevenuto, F. & Gummadi, P. K. (2010). Measuring user influence in Twitter: The million follower fallacy. *ICWSM*, 10(10–17), 30.

Charmaz, K. (2014). *Constructing Grounded Theory*. London: Sage.

Chernikova, N. (2014). Aifon v karmane vatnika. *The Village*, 23 April 2014. Available at: www.the-village.ru/village/business/story/157495-iphone-v-karmane-vatnika (accessed April 2016).

Chirikova, E. (2015). Lagernyi mentalitet. *Activatica.org*, blog entry, 24 August 2015. Available at: http://activatica.org/blogs/view/id/1114/title/lagernyy-mentalitet (last accessed August 2015).

Chomsky, N. & Barsamian, D. (2010). *Imperial Ambitions: Conversations on the Post-9/11 World*. New York: Macmillan.

Chudinov, A. (2001). Rossiya v metaforicheskom zerkale. *Russkaya rech* (1), 34–42.

Clement, C. (ed.) (2012). *Gorodskie dvizheniya Rossii v 2009–2012 godah: na puti k politicheskomu*. Moscow: Novoe Literaturnoe Obozrenie.

Confino, M. (2013). *Russia Before The 'Radiant Future': Essays in Modern History, Culture, and Society.* New York and Oxford: Berghahn Books.

Creswell, J. W. (2014). *Research Design: Qualitative, Quantitative, and Mixed Methods Approaches.* Thousand Oaks: Sage publications.

Creswell, J. W. (2015). *A Concise Introduction to Mixed Methods Research.* Washington: SAGE.

Dahlgren, P. (2006). Doing citizenship: The cultural origins of civic agency in the public sphere. *European Journal of Cultural Studies, 9*(3), 267–286.

De Lazari, A. (2012). Pochemu Evropa boitsya russkogo medvedya. In Ryabov, E. & De Lazari, A. (eds.) *Russkiy Medved: Istoriya, Semiotika, Politika.* Moscow: Novoe Literaturnoe Obozrenie, 274–282.

Denzin, N. K. & Lincoln, Y. S. (2003). *Collecting and Interpreting Qualitative Materials.* 2nd Ed. London: Sage.

Dmitriev, M. (2012). Political values in 'Putin's Russia': A Q&A with Mikhail Dmitriev, Interview with Lev Aron. *American Enterprise Institute*, 12 May 2012. Available at: www.aei.org/publication/political-values-in-putins-russia-a-qa-with-mikhail-dmitriev/ (accessed April 2016).

Dobrokhotov, R. (2012). Chto Zapreschayet Novyi Zakon o Mitingakh? *Slon.ru*, 6 June 2012. Available at: http://slon.ru/russia/chto_zapreshchaet_novyy_zakon_o_mitingakh-796475.xhtml (accessed July 2014).

Dubin, B. (2014). Nam nesti vsyu tyazhest rasplaty, Interview by Maria Shubina. *Colta.ru*, 21 August 2014. Available at: www.colta.ru/articles/society/4319?fb_action_ids=10152682093622094&fb_action_types=og.recommends (last accessed April 2015).

Eckel, M. (2007). Russian extremism law casts wide net. *The Washington Post*, 3 September 2007. Available at: www.washingtonpost.com/wp-dyn/content/article/2007/09/03/AR2007090300470.html (last accessed August 2016).

Ediger, D., Jiang, K., Riedy, J., Bader, D. A., & Corley, C. (2010). Massive social network analysis: Mining twitter for social good. In *2010 39th International Conference on Parallel Processing*, 583–593.

Edwards, J. (2008). Defining the enemy for the post-Cold War world: Bill Clinton's foreign policy discourse in Somalia and Haiti. *International Journal of Communication, 2*, 830–847.

Eggert, K. (2015). Kommentariy: Likhyie 90-ye skoro mogut stat slavnymi. *dw.com*, 26 September 2015. Available at: www.dw.com/ru/%D0%BA%D0%BE%D0%BC%D0%BC%D0%B5%D0%BD%D1%82%D0%B0%D1%80%D0%B8%D0%B9-%D0%BB%D0%B8%D1%85%D0%B8%D0%B5-90-%D0%B5-%D1%81%D0%BA%D0%BE%D1%80%D0%BE-%D0%BC%D0%BE%D0%B3%D1%83%D1%82-%D1%81%D1%82%D0%B0%D1%82%D1%8C-%D1%81%D0%BB%D0%B0%D0%B2%D0%BD%D1%8B%D0%BC%D0%B8/a-18742021 (last accessed August 2016).

Esslin, M. (1965). Introduction. In *Penguin Plays-Absurd Drama*. Available at: www.samuel-beckett.net/AbsurdEsslin.html (last accessed April 2015).

Etling, B., Alexanyan, K., Kelly, J., Faris, R., Palfrey, J. & Gasser, U. (2010). *Public Discourse in the Russian Blogosphere: Mapping RuNet Politics and Mobilization.* Cambridge: Berkman Center for Internet and Society, Harvard University. Available at: http://cyber.law.harvard.edu/sites/cyber.law.harvard.edu/files/Public_Discourse_in_the_Russian_Blogosphere_2010.pdf (last accessed April 2016).

European Commission (1999). *Images of Women in the Media*. Brussels: Commission of the European Communities.

Fanaylova, E. (2014). Trolling, Instrument Voyny, Svoboda v Klubakh Podcast. *Radio Svoboda*, 13 July 2014. Available at: www.svoboda.org/content/transcript/25452526.html (last accessed September 2015).

Fedyashin, A. (2014). The real political takeaway from the Olympics: The West needs to get over the cold war. *The Guardian*, 24 February 2014. Available at: www.theguardian.com/commentisfree/2014/feb/24/sochi-olympics-west-not-over-cold-war (last accessed March 2015).

Fraser, N. & Nicholson, L. (1994). Social criticism without philosophy: An encounter between feminism and postmodernism. In Nicholson, L. (ed.) *Feminism/Postmodernism*. New York: Routledge, 19–38.

Fredericks, B. (2014). Crimean AG becomes anime sensation. *New York Post*, 24 March 2014. Available at: http://nypost.com/2014/03/24/crimean-attorney-general-becomes-japanese-anime-sensation (last accessed August 2016).

Fukuyama, F. (2006). Identity, immigration, and liberal democracy. *Journal of Democracy*, 17(2), 5–20.

Fürsich, E. (2009). In defense of textual analysis: Restoring a challenged method for journalism and media studies. *Journalism Studies*, 10(2), 238–252.

Galeotti, M. & Bowen, A. (2014). Putin's empire of the mind. *Foreign Policy*, 21 April 2014. Available at: http://foreignpolicy.com/2014/04/21/putins-empire-of-the-mind/ (last accessed March 2015).

Gambarato, R. & Medvedev, S. (2015). Grassroots political campaign in Russia: Alexey Navalny and transmedia strategies for democratic development. In *Promoting Social Change and Democracy through Information Technology*. Hershey: IGI Global, 165–192.

Gaskell, G. & Bauer, M. (2000). Towards public accountability: Beyond sampling, reliability and validity. In Bauer, M. & Gaskell, G. (eds.) *Qualitative Researching with Text, Image and Sound: A Practical Handbook for Social Research*. London: Sage, 336–351.

Gazeta (2010). *Internet Protiv Zomboyaschika*. 21 December 2010. Available at: www.gazeta.ru/comments/2010/12/21_e_3473009.shtml (last accessed September 2015).

Gilbert, E., Bergstrom, T. & Karahalios, K. (2009). Blogs are echo chambers: Blogs are echo chambers. In *System Sciences, August 2009*, 1–10.

Gill, R. (2007). *Gender and the Media*. Malden: Polity.

Gladarev, B. (2012). "Eto nash gorod!": analiz peterburgskogo dvizheniya za sokhraneniye sotsialnogo naslediya. In Clement, C. (ed.) *Gorodskie Dvizheniya Rossii v 2009–2012 Godah: Na Puti k Politicheskomu*. Moscow: Novoe Literaturnoe Obozrenie, 23–145.

Glesne, C. & Peshkin, A. (1992). *Becoming Qualitative Researchers: An Introduction*. White Plains: Longman.

Godfrey, S. & Hamad, H. (2014). Save the cheerleader, save the males: Resurgent protective paternalism in popular film and television after 9/11. In Ross, K. (ed.) *The Handbook of Gender, Sex and Media*. Oxford: John Wiley & Sons, 157–173.

Godwin, M. (1990). Meme, Counter-meme. *The Wired*. Available at: http://archive.wired.com/wired/archive/2.10/godwin.if_pr.html (last accessed March 2015).

Gorham, M. (2012). Putin's language. In Goscilo, H. (ed.) *Putin as Celebrity and Cultural Icon* (Vol. 80). London: Routledge, 82–104.

Goscilo, H. (ed.). (2012). *Putin as Celebrity and Cultural Icon* (Vol. 80). London: Routledge.

Grossman, A. L. & Tucker, J. S. (1997). Gender differences and sexism in the knowledge and use of slang. *Sex Roles, 37*(1–2), 101–110.

Gudkov, L. (2014). Commentary. In Levada-Centre. *Rossiyan potyanulo v SSSR*, 27 February 2014. Available at: www.levada.ru/27-02-2014/rossiyan-potyanulo-v-sssr (last accessed March 2015).

Gulag (2015). *Encyclopædia Britannica*. Available at: www.britannica.com/place/Gulag (last accessed August 2015).

Gulag History (no date). *Soviet Forced Labour Camps and the Struggle for Freedom*. Online Exhibit, Centre for History and New Media, George Mason University. Available at: http://gulaghistory.org/nps/about/credits.php (last accessed August 2015).

Guy, D. (2013). Cartoon capers, five minutes for Israel. Blog entry. *Israel Advocates Site,* 20 August 2013. Available at: http://5mfi.com/cartoon-capers/ (last accessed July 2015).

Hansen, D., Rotman, D., Bonsignore, E., Milic-Frayling, N., Rodrigues, E., Smith, M. & Shneiderman, B. (2009). *Do You Know the Way to SNA?: A Process Model for Analyzing and Visualizing Social Media Data*. Tech Report, July 2009. University of Maryland.

Hansen, D., Shneiderman, B. & Smith, M. A. (2010). *Analyzing Social Media Networks with NodeXL: Insights from a Connected World*. San Francisco: Morgan Kaufmann.

Harding, L. (2014). Kiev's protesters: Ukraine uprising was no neo-Nazi power-grab. *The Guardian*, 13 March 2014. Available at: www.theguardian.com/world/2014/mar/13/ukraine-uprising-fascist-coup-grassroots-movement (last accessed August 2016).

Heintz, J. (2013). Ukraine's Euromaidan: What's in a name? *Associated Press*, 2 December 2013. Available at: http://news.yahoo.com/ukraines-euromaidan-whats-name-090717845.html (last accessed February 2015).

Helleman, W. (ed.) (2004). *The Russian Idea: In Search of a New Identity*. Bloomington: Slavica Pub.

Hillis, F. (2013). *Children of Rus': Right-Bank Ukraine and the Invention of a Russian Nation*. Ithaca, NY: Cornell University Press.

Human Rights Watch (2012). *Russia: Reject Restrictions on Peaceful Assembly*, 8 June 2012. Available at: www.hrw.org/news/2012/06/08/russia-reject-restrictions-peaceful-assembly (accessed April 2016).

Human Rights Watch (2014). *Russia: 8 Protesters Found Guilty in a Flawed Case*, 20 June 2014. Available at: www.hrw.org/news/2014/06/20/russia-8-protesters-found-guilty-flawed-case (accessed July 2014).

Huntington, S. (1968). *Political Order in Changing Societies*. New Haven and London: Yale University Press.

Il'in, M. (2004). Words and meanings: On the rule of destiny: The Russian idea. In Helleman, W. (ed.) *The Russian Idea: In Search of a New Identity*. Bloomington: Slavica Pub, 33–56.

InternetLiveStats (2018). *A Real Time Update on the Internet Statistics*. Available at: www.internetlivestats.com/.

Jackson, R. (2005). Security, democracy, and the rhetoric of counter-terrorism. *Democracy and Security, 1*(2), 147–171.

Jansen, S. C. & Sabo, D. (1994). The sport/war metaphor: Hegemonic masculinity, the Persian Gulf War, and the new world order. *Sociology of Sport Journal, 11*, 1–1.

Kachkaeva, A. (2015). "Voina iz okopov peremestilas na divany": Anna Kachkaeva o novoy rossiyskoy propagande, Interview by Anna Stroganova. *RFI*, 11 February 2015. Available at: http://ru.rfi.fr/rossiya/20150204-anna-kachkaeva/ (last accessed March 2015).

Kachkaeva, A. & Kiriya, I. (eds.) (2007). *Rossijskoe televidenie: Mezhdu sprosom i predlozheniem.* Moscow: Elitkomstar.

Kantor, V. (2004). Is the Russian mentality changing? In Helleman, W. (ed.) *The Russian Idea: In Search of a New Identity.* Bloomington: Slavica Pub.

Kappeler, A. (2003). *Great Russians and Little Russians: Russian-Ukrainian Relations and Perceptions in Historical Perspective* (Vol. 39). Seattle: Henry M. Jackson School of International Studies, University of Washington.

Kassianova, A. (2001). Russia: still open to the West? Evolution of the state identity in the foreign policy and security discourse. *Europe-Asia Studies, 53*(6), 821–839.

Kates, G. (2014). 'Traitors' slur goes mainstream in Russia. *Radio Free Europe/ Radio Liberty,* 26 March 2014. Available at: www.rferl.org/content/russia-nationalism-traitors-crimea-media/25310606.html (accessed January 2015).

Kelly, L. (2014). Russia can turn US to radioactive ash – Kremlin-backed journalist. *Reuters.com,* 16 March 2014. Available at: www.reuters.com/article/2014/03/16/ukraine-crisis-russia-kiselyov-idUSL6N0MD0P920140316 (last accessed March 2015).

Kelly, J., Barash, V., Alexanyan, K., Etling, B., Faris, R., Gasser, U. & Palfrey, J. G. (2012). *Mapping Russian Twitter.* Berkman Center Research Publication.

Kendall, B. (2014a). Hybrid warfare: The new conflict between East and West. *BBC,* 6 November 2014. Available at: www.bbc.co.uk/news/world-europe-29903395 (last accessed April 2014).

Kendall, B. (2014b). Russian propaganda machine 'worse than Soviet Union'. *BBC,* 6 June 2014. Available at: www.bbc.co.uk/news/magazine-27713847 (last accessed April 2015).

Khudikova, L. (2014). Historical agreement is signed. Crimea has returned home. *Vesti.ru,* 18 March 2014. Available at: www.vesti.ru/doc.html?id=1388518 (last accessed March 2015).

Kiriya, I. (2012). Piracy cultures| the culture of subversion and Russian media landscape. *International Journal of Communication, 6*(21), 446–466. Available at: http://ijoc.org/index.php/ijoc/article/view/1196/713 (accessed June 2014).

Kiriya, I. & Degtereva, E. (2010). Russian TV market: Between state supervision, commercial logic and simulacrum of public service. *Central European Journal of Communication, 1,* 37–51.

Klimov, I. (2007). Social'nye vyzovy 'privatizirovannogo' televidenija. In Kachkaeva, A. & Kiriya, I. (eds.) *Rossijskoe Televidenie: Mezhdu Sprosom i Predlozheniem.* Moscow: Elitkomstar.

Klishin, I. (2014). Svobodu Slova Kazhdoye Pokoleniye Tsenit Po-svoyemu. *Vedomosti,* 14 August 14 2013. Available at: www.vedomosti.ru/opinion/news/15191431/uslovno-dosrochnaya-svoboda-slova (accessed July 2014).

Kobzev, A. (2015). Seichas my dlya Kitaya – starshaya sestra, Interview with Andrey Kortunov. *Lenta.ru*, 20 February 2015. Available at: http://lenta.ru/articles/2015/02/19/riac/ (last accessed March 2015).

Koltsova, O. (2006). *News Media and Power in Russia*. London: Routledge.

Koshkin, P. (2014). The political cartoon as a tool in modern information wars. *Russia Direct*, 21 January 2014. Available at: www.russia-direct.org/analysis/political-cartoon-tool-modern-information-wars (last accessed August 2015).

Kovalenko, E., Lapunin, O. & Cherednichenko, E. (2006). *Analiticheskaya spravka o rezultatah sotsiologicheskogo oprosa "Organizovannaya prestupnost glazami sovremennoy molodyozhi: sotsialno-kriminologicheskiy I eticheskiy aspekty"*. Analytical report. Saratov: Saratov Centre of Organised Crime and Corruption Studies. Available at: http://sartraccc.ru/print.php?print_file=Explore/analit_maf.htm (last accessed February 2015).

Kremlin (2014a). *Pryamaya Liniya s Vladimirom Putinym*. Complete Transcript, 17 April 2014. Available at: www.kremlin.ru/events/president/news/20796 (last accessed August 2015).

Kremlin (2014b). *Podpisan Zakon, Napravlennyi na Usileniye Mer Protivodeystviya Extremismu*. 30 June 2014. Available at: www.president.kremlin.ru/acts/46118 (accessed July 2014).

Krijnen, T. & Van Bauwel, S. (2015). *Gender and Media: Representing, Producing, Consuming*. London: Routledge.

Krongauz, M. (2014). Slova nenavisti zamenyayut argumenty, Interview by Nataliya Granina. *Lenta.ru*, 29 November 2014. Available at: http://lenta.ru/articles/2014/11/28/language (last accessed April 2015).

KrymInform (2015). *Dlya prokurora Kryma Poklonskoy Krymskaya vesna nachalas 8 marta*, 6 March 2015. Available at: www.c-inform.info/news/id/19817 (last accessed August 2016).

Kullberg, J. S. & Zimmerman, W. (1999). Liberal elites, socialist masses, and problems of Russian democracy. *World Politics, 51*(03), 323–358.

Kuzio, T. (2015). Competing nationalisms, Euromaidan, and the Russian-Ukrainian conflict. *Studies in Ethnicity and Nationalism, 15*(1), 157–169.

Kwak, H., Lee, C., Park, H. & Moon, S. (2010, April). What is Twitter, a social network or a news media? In *Proceedings of the 19th International Conference on World Wide Web*. New York: ACM, 591–600.

Laruelle, M. (2014). The "Russian Idea" on the small screen: Staging national identity on Russia's TV. *Demokratizatsiya. The Journal of Post-Soviet Democratization, 22*(2), 313–333.

Levada-Centre (2011). *Opros Na Prospekte Sakharova 24 Dekabrya*, 26 December 2011. Available at: www.levada.ru/print/26-12-2011/opros-na-prospekte-sakharova (accessed March 2012).

Levada-Centre (2013). *Otnosheniye k Stalinu v Rossii i stranakh Zakavkazya*. Report, 5 March 2013. Available at: www.levada.ru/sites/default/files/stalin.pdf (last accessed March 2015).

Levada-Centre (2014). *Rossiyan potyanulo v SSSR*, 27 February 2014. Available at: www.levada.ru/27-02-2014/rossiyan-potyanulo-v-sssr (last accessed March 2015).

Lincoln, Y. S. & Guba, E. G. (2000). The only generalization is: There is no generalization. In Gomm, R., Hammersley, M. & Foster, P. (eds.) *Case Study Method*. London: Sage, 27–44.

Lipman, M. (2010). *Civil Society and the Non-Participation Act*. Presentation. 42nd National Convention of the American Associations for Advancement of Slavic Studies, Los Angeles, CA, 17 November 2010.

Lipman, M. (2014). The Hundred-Ruble Crusade. *The New Yorker*, 9 July 2014. Available at: www.newyorker.com/news/news-desk/the-hundred-ruble-crusade (last accessed September 2015).

Lipman, M. & McFaul, M. (2010). The media and political developments. *After Putin's Russia: Past Imperfect, Future Uncertain*, 4, 109–132.

Lipset, S. (1960). *Political Man. The Social Basics of Politics*. Garden City: Doubleday & Company.

Lurkmore (2014). *Putin – Krab*. Available at: https://lurkmore.to/%CF%F3% F2%E8%ED_%97_%EA%F0%E0%E1 (last accessed February 2015).

Malgin, A. (2014). Vnimatelno chitayem zakon o blogerakh, prinyatyi vchera Dumoi. *Echo of Moscow*, 23 April 2014. Available at: www.echo.msk.ru/ blog/avmalgin/1306048-echo (accessed July 2014).

Matthews, B. & Ross, L. (2010). *Research Methods*. Boston: Pearson Higher Ed.

McKee, A. (2003). *Textual Analysis: A Beginner's Guide*. London: Sage.

Medhurst, M. (2012). Introduction. In Medhurst, M., Ivie, R., Wander, P. & Scott, R. (eds.) *Cold War Rhetoric: Strategy, Metaphor, and Ideology*. East Lansing: MSU Press, xiii–xvii.

Meduza (2015). *Vezhlivye Lyudi. Kto oni?* Available at: https://meduza.io/ special/polite (last accessed July 2015).

Milanovic, B. (1998). *Income, Inequality, and Poverty during the Transformation from Planned to Market Economy*. Washington, DC: The World Bank, 186–90.

Milner, R. M. (2013). Media lingua franca: Fixity, novelty, and vernacular creativity in Internet memes. *Selected Papers of Internet Research*, 3, 1–5.

Mulvey, L. (2009). Visual pleasure and narrative cinema. In Braudy, E. & Cohen, M. (eds.) *Film Theory and Criticism: Introductory Readings*. New York: Oxford UP, 711–722.

Nechepurenko, I. (2014). How nationalism came to dominate Russia's political mainstream. *The Moscow Times*, 3 August 2014. Available at: www.themoscowtimes.com/news/article/how-nationalism-came-to-dominate-russia-s-political-mainstream/504495.html (last accessed January 2015).

Negroponte, N. (1995). *Being Digital*. New York: Alfred A. Knorpf.

Neuman, W. L. (2014). *Social Research Methods: Quantitative and Qualitative Approaches*. Boston: Allyn and Bacon.

Newsru (2014). *Putin Podpisal Zakony o Zimnem Vremeni, "Prezidentskoi Kvote", Reklame na TV I Dannykh Internet-Polzovatelei*, 22 July 2014. Available at: www.newsru.com/russia/22jul2014/putin_3.html (accessed July 2014).

Nissenbaum, H. (2011). A contextual approach to privacy online. *Daedalus*, 140(4), 32–48.

Norris, P. (2007). Political activism: New challenges, new opportunities. In Boix, C. & Stokes, S. (eds.) *The Oxford Handbook of Comparative Politics*. Oxford: Oxford University Press, 628–652.

Noth, W. (2007). Self-reference in the media: The semiotic framework. In Noth W. & Bishara N. (eds.) *Self-Reference in the Media*. New York: Mouton de Gruyter, 3–30.

Nyhan, B. (2006). Why the Nazi analogy is on the rise. *Time*, 31 August 2006. Available at: http://content.time.com/time/nation/article/0,8599,1515951,00. html (last accessed August 2016).

Oliker, O., Crane, K., Schwartz, L. H. & Yusupov, C. (2009). *Russian Foreign Policy: Sources and Implications*. Santa Monica: Rand Corporation.

Olympic.org (no date). Sochi 2014: The hare, polar bear and the leopard. *Official Site of the Olympic movement*. Available at: www.olympic.org/sochi-2014-mascots (last accessed August 2015).

Omidi, M. (2014). WTF? Russia bans swearing in the arts. *The Guardian*, 1 July 2014. Available at: www.theguardian.com/world/2014/jul/01/russia-bans-swearing-arts (accessed July 2014).

Oushakine, S. A. (2001). The terrifying mimicry of samizdat. *Public Culture*, *13*(2), 191–214.

Parfenov, L. (2010). Leonid Parfenov. Devyanostyie. *Leonidparfenov.ru*, 10 November 2010. Available at: http://leonidparfenov.ru/leonid-parfenov-devyanostye/ (last accessed August 2016).

Parfitt, T. (2014). Seven reasons to explain Vladimir Putin's popularity cult. *The Telegraph*, 27 November 2014. Available at: www.telegraph.co.uk/news/worldnews/vladimir-putin/11257362/Seven-reasons-to-explain-Vladimir-Putins-popularity-cult.html (last accessed March 2015).

Parfyonova, A. (2014). Izmeneniya v ekonomike priveli k pereotsenke prisoyedineniya Kryma. *Kommersant*, 11 November 2014. Available at: www.kommersant.ru/doc/2608066 (last accessed March 2015).

Petersson, B. (2009). Hot conflict and everyday banality: Enemy images, scapegoats and stereotypes. *Development*, *52*(4), 460–465.

Petrovsky-Shtern, Y. (2009). *The Anti-Imperial Choice*. New Haven: Yake University Press, 1–25.

Platoff, A. M. (2012). The "Forward Russia" flag: Examining the changing use of the bear as a symbol of Russia. *Raven: A Journal of Vexillology*, *19*, 99–126.

Politnavigator (2014). *Aeroporty Simferopolya i Sevastopolya Zakhvacheny Vooruzhyonnymi Lyudmi*, 28 February 2014. Available at: www.politnavigator. net/aehroport-simferopolya-zakhvachen-vooruzhennymi-lyudmi.html (last accessed July 2015).

Poroshina, M. (2014). Eksperty obsudili "tri volny" rossiyskogo patriotizma. *RG.ru*, 10 June 2014. Available at: www.rg.ru/2014/06/10/reg-urfo/patriotizm. html (last accessed March 2015).

Powell, B. (2014). Vladimir Putin's truth problem: Five holes in the Russian President's story, *Newsweek*, 23 July 2014. Available at: www.newsweek.com/vladimir-putins-truth-problem-five-holes-russian-presidents-story-260869 (last accessed March 2015).

Prokhorova, I. (2015). Eto I Est Re-Stalinizatsiya Soznaniya, Full transcript of the debate with Yuri Saprykin, *Meduza.io*, 24 April 2015. Available at: https://meduza.io/feature/2015/04/27/eto-i-est-restalinizatsiya-soznaniya (last accessed August 2015).

Purim, M. (2014). Crimea has returned home. *AiF.ru*, 21 March 2014. Available at: www.aif.ru/euromaidan/opinion/1129331 (last accessed March 2015).

Putin, V. (2014). Obrascheniye Prezidenta RF Vladimira Putina (polnaya versiya). *1tv.ru*, 18 March 2014. Available at: www.1tv.ru/news/social/254389 (last accessed March 2015).

Putin-itogi (2012). *Zhizn raba na galerakh (dvortsy, yakhty, avtomobili, samo-lyoty i drugiye aksessuary)*, Report. Available at: www.putin-itogi.ru/rab-na-galerah/ (last accessed February 2015).

Rantanen, T. (2002). *The Global and the National: Media and Communications in Post-Communist Russia.* Lanham: Rowman & Littlefield.

Raymond, M. (2010). How tweet it is!: Library acquires entire Twitter archive. *Library of Congress Blog.* Available at: http://blogs.loc.gov/loc/2010/04/how-tweet-it-is-library-acquires-entire-twitter-archive (last accessed September 2015).

Rees, E. A. (2004). Introduction: Leader cults, varieties and preconditions. In Apor, B., Behrends, J. C., Jones, C. & Rees, E. A. (eds.) *The Leader Cult in Communist Dictatorships.* Basingstroke: Palgrave Macmillan, 1–26.

Reuters (2014). *Timeline: Political Crisis in Ukraine and Russia's Occupation of Crimea,* 8 March 2014. Available at: www.reuters.com/article/2014/03/08/us-ukraine-crisis-timeline-idUSBREA270PO20140308 (last accessed February 2015).

Ria (2013). *Positive Attitude to Stalin Prevailing among Russians [Dlya rossiyan boleye kharakterno pozitivnoye otnosheniye k Stalinu],* 5 March 2013. Available at: http://ria.ru/society/20130305/925898796.html (last accessed March 2015).

Ria (2014). *Putin Na Vopros of Vozmozhnosti Prisoyedineniya Alyaski: Zachem Nam Ona?* 17 April 2014. Available at: http://ria.ru/politics/20140417/1004299632.html (last accessed March 2015).

Ria (2015). *"Vezhlyvyie lyudi" Kak Novyi Obraz Rossiyskoy Armiyi,* 16 May 2014. Available at: http://ria.ru/defense_safety/20140516/1007988002.html (last accessed March 2015).

Riabova, T. (2012). Medved kak simvol Rossiyi: sotsiologicheskoye izmerenie]. In Riabov, E. & De Lazari, A. (eds.) *"Russkiy Medved": Istoriya, Semiotika, Politika.* Moscow: Novoe Literaturnoe Obozrenie, 338–353.

Riabova, T. & Riabov, O. (2013). Geiropa: gendernoye izemereniye obraza Evropy v praktikakh politicheskoy mobilizatsiyi. *Zhenschina v Rossiyskom Obschestve,* 3, 31–39. Available at: http://cens.ivanovo.ac.ru/publications/Riabova_Riabov_Geiropa.pdf (last accessed January 2015).

Roberts, H. & Etling, B. (2011). Coordinated DDoS attack during Russian Duma elections. *The Harvard Law Internet and Democracy Blog,* 8 December 2011.

Robertson, G. (2012). Russian protesters: Not optimistic, but here to stay. *Russian Analytical Digest, 115,* 2–7.

Rothrock, K. (2014). The Russians have weaponized Photoshop. *Global Voices,* 1 March 2014. Available at: http://globalvoicesonline.org/2014/03/01/the-russians-have-weaponized-photoshop/ (last accessed July 2015).

RT (2010). *Russian Bear – Truth Beyond Stereotype,* 19 July 2010. Available at: http://rt.com/news/prime-time/russian-bear-truth-stereotype/ (last accessed March 2015).

RT (2014a). *Putin: Kiev's Shelling in E. Ukraine Reminiscent of Nazi Actions During WWII,* 29 August 2014. Available at: http://rt.com/news/183648-putin-russia-ukraine-nazi/ (last accessed March 2015).

RT (2014b). *Vladimir Putin's New Year Address to the Citizens of Russia,* 31 December 2014. Available at: http://russian.rt.com/inotv/2014-12-31/Novogodnee-obrashhenie-Vladimira-Putina-k (last accessed March 2015).

Rucker, P. (2014). Hillary Clinton says Putin's actions are like 'what Hitler did back in the '30s'. *The Washington Post*, 5 March 2014. Available at: www.washingtonpost. com/blogs/post-politics/wp/2014/03/05/hillary-clinton-says-putins-action-are-like-what-hitler-did-back-in-the-30s/ (last accessed March 2015).

Russian Search Marketing (2017). *Research: Reviewing Russian Social Media Interests*, 18 September. Available at: https://russiansearchmarketing.com/ research-reviewing-russian-social-media/ (last accessed August 2018).

Ryzhkov, V. (2015). Kremlin doesn't have monopoly on patriotism. *The Moscow Times*, 9 April 2015. Available at: www.themoscowtimes.com/opinion/article/ kremlin-doesnt-have-monopoly-on-patriotism/518902.html (last accessed August 2015).

Sampat, R. & Bugorkova, O. (2015). Russia's (non) war on memes? *BBC Trending*, 16 April 2015. Available at: www.bbc.co.uk/news/blogs-trending-32302645 (last accessed July 2015).

Saunders, G. (1974). *Samizdat; Voices of the Soviet Opposition*. New York: Pathfinder Press.

Scott, J. (2013). *Social Network Analysis*. Thousand Oaks: Sage.

Seddon, M. (2017). LinkedIn remains banned in Russia after refusal to comply with local laws. *The Financial Times*, 7 March. Available at: www.ft.com/ content/fe968d7c-fa4b-3120-8d9c-f6c8b294deb9 (last accessed August 2018).

Sen, A. K. (2014). Wanted: A credible response to Putin's nuclear threat. *Newsweek*, 3 April 2014. Available at: www.newsweek.com/wanted-credible-response-putins-nuclear-threat-311388 (last accessed March 2015).

Shevchenko, V. (2014). "Little green men" or "Russian invaders"? *BBC Monitoring*, 11 March 2014. Available at: www.bbc.co.uk/news/world-europe-26532154 (last accessed March 2015).

Shifman, L. (2013). Memes in a digital world: Reconciling with a conceptual troublemaker. *Journal of Computer-Mediated Communication*, *18*(3), 362–377.

Shokhina, E. (2014). Vygodnyi Krym. *Expert Online*, 11 March 2014. Available at: http://expert.ru/2014/03/11/vyigodnyij-kryim/ (last accessed March 2015).

Simons, G. (2006). The use of rhetoric and the mass media in Russia's war on terror. *Demokratizatsiya: The Journal of Post-Soviet Democratization*, *14*(4), 579–600.

Snegovaya, M. (2015). Paternalizm kak chast neproduktivnoy kultury. *Vedomosti*, 15 April 2015. Available at: www.vedomosti.ru/opinion/ articles/2015/04/16/paternalizm-kak-chast-neproduktivnoi-kulturi (last accessed April 2015).

Sobchak, K. (2012). Norkovaya revolutsiya: pochemu bogatyie vyshli na ulitsu, Talk show Narod Protiv with Natella Boltyanskaya. *Echo of Moscow,* 18 January 2012. Available at: http://echo.msk.ru/programs/opponent/849239-echo/ (last accessed August 2016).

Sobytyia (2015). *Iz Rossiyi Otpravlyayut v Krym "Turistov" s Voyennym Opytom,* 28 February 2014. Available at: www.sobytiya.info/news/14/38970 (last accessed March 2015).

Soldatov, A. & Borogan, I. (2015). What spawned Russia's 'troll army'? Experts on the red Web share their views, open line. *The Guardian*, 8 September 2015. Available at: www.theguardian.com/world/live/2015/sep/08/

russia-troll-army-red-web-any-questions?CMP=share_btn_tw (last accessed September 2015).

Sperling, V. (2012). Nashi devushki: Gender and political youth activism in Putin's and Medvedev's Russia. *Post-Soviet Affairs, 28*(2), 232–261.

Sperling, V. (2014). *Sex, Politics, and Putin: Political Legitimacy in Russia.* Oxford: Oxford University Press.

Stein, A. (2005). Make room for daddy anxious masculinity and emergent homophobias in neopatriarchal politics. *Gender & Society, 19*(5), 601–620.

Suleimanov, S. (2014a). Radioaktivnyi pepel Kiselyova. *TJournal.ru*, 17 March 2014. Available at: http://tjournal.ru/paper/nuklear-kiselev (last accessed March 2015).

Suleimanov, S. (2014b). Retro: Nu Vot I Vsyo. *TJournal*, 14 March 2014. Available at: https://tjournal.ru/p/lentaru (last accessed May 2016).

Sunstein, C. R. (2001). *Republic.com 2.0.* Princeton: Princeton University Press.

Swinford, S. (2014). David Cameron compares Russia to Nazi Germany on eve of Putin meeting. *The Telegraph*, 14 November 2014. Available at: www.telegraph. co.uk/news/politics/david-cameron/11230326/David-Cameron-compares-Russia-to-Nazi-Germany-on-eve-of-Putin-meeting.html (last accessed March 2015).

Syomin, M. (2014). A wave of protest against new Ukrainian government's policy has spread over the South East of the country. *1tv.ru*, 2 March 2014. Available at: www.1tv.ru/news/world/253252 (last accessed March 2015).

Szporluk, R. (2000). *Russia, Ukraine and the Breakup of the Soviet Union.* Stanford: Hoover Press.

Teper, Y. (2016). Official Russian identity discourse in light of the annexation of Crimea: national or imperial? *Post-Soviet Affairs, 32*(4), 378–396.

Tetrault-Farber, G. (2014). After Crimea, Russians say they want Alaska back. *The Moscow Times*, 1 April 2014. Available at: www.themoscowtimes.com/ news/article/after-crimea-russians-say-they-want-alaska-back/497154.html (last accessed March 2015).

The Economist (2015). *Understanding Putin's Plans*, 31 January 2015. Available at: www.economist.com/news/europe/21641278-russian-president-stepping-up-both-war-ukraine-and-his-confrontational-rhetoric (last accessed March 2015).

The Moscow Times (2014). *Vkontakte Founder Pavel Durov Becomes Citizen of St. Kitts and Nevis*, April 28 2014. Available at: www.themoscowtimes. com/news/article/vkontakte-founder-pavel-durov-becomes-citizen-of-st-kitts-and-nevis/499038.html (accessed July 2014).

Toler, A. (2015). Inside the Kremlin troll army machine: Templates, guidelines, and paid posts. *Global Voices*, 14 March 2015. Available at: http:// globalvoicesonline.org/2015/03/14/russia-kremlin-troll-army-examples (last accessed April 2015).

Travin, D. (2015). Putin kak glamurnyi personazh. *Fontanka.ru*, 24 March 2015. Available at: www.fontanka.ru/2015/03/24/098/ (last accessed March 2015).

Traynor, I. (2006). Slobodan milosevic, obituary. *The Guardian*, 13 March 2006. Available at: www.theguardian.com/news/2006/mar/13/guardianobituaries. warcrimes (last accessed August 2015).

Tsygankov, A. P. & Tsygankov, P. A. (2010). National ideology and IR theory: Three incarnations of the 'Russian idea'. *European Journal of International Relations, 16*(4), 663.

van Wynsberghe, A. (no date). *To Use or Not to Use? When and for What Should Researchers Use Data Obtained from Social Networking Sites,* Conference presentation. Available at: www.aimeevanwynsberghe.com/uploads/1/4/6/0/14604548/presentation_april_3.pdf (last accessed September 2015).

Varlamov, I. (2014). Setevyie khomyachki. *varlamov.ru,* 7 April 2014. Available at: http://varlamov.ru/1043837.html (last accessed February 2016).

Vechernyaya Moskva (2012). *Sotsiologicheskoye opisanie khomyachka setevogo,* 8 November 2012. Available at: www.vm.ru/news/sotsiologicheskoe-opisanie-homyachka-setevogo1352396557.html (last accessed February 2016).

Volchek, D. & Sindelar, D. (2015). One professional Russian troll tells all. *Radio Free Europe/ Radio Liberty,* 25 March 2015. Available at: www.rferl.org/content/how-to-guide-russian-trolling-trolls/26919999.html (last accessed April 2015).

Volkov, D. & Goncharov, S. (2014). *Russian Media Landscape: Television, Print and the Internet,* Report, Levada-Centre, June 2014. Available at: www.levada.ru/sites/default/files/levada_report_media_0.pdf (last accessed September 2015).

Volkov, V. (2002). *Violent Entrepreneurs: The Use of Force in the Making of Russian Capitalism.* Ithaca, NY: Cornell University Press.

Volodarskiy, Y. (2014). *Lev Rubinshteyn: Krym otzhali po-patsanski, eto oni umeyut.* Interview with Lev Rubinstein. *Forbes,* 17 April 2014. Available at: http://forbes.ua/lifestyle/1369445-lev-rubinshtejn-krym-otzhali-po-pacanski-eto-oni-umeyut (last accessed March 2015).

Walker, S. (2014a). Inside Putinworld, where few risk speaking truth to power. *The Guardian,* 29 August 2014. Available at: www.theguardian.com/world/2014/aug/29/putin-world-kremlin-moscow-power-circle (last accessed August 2015).

Walker, S. (2014b). Sochi 2014 has begun and, for now, patriotism has taken over from protest. *The Guardian,* 9 February 2014. Available at: www.theguardian.com/sport/2014/feb/09/sochi-2014-patriotism-protest-russians-olympics (last accessed March 2015).

Weil, J. (2014). Putin's power: Why Russians adore their bare-chested Reagan. *Time,* 22 July 2014. Available at: http://time.com/3020513/why-russians-love-putin/ (last accessed March 2015).

Williams, A. (2013). We have been expecting you 007! Russian leader Putin goes full Bond baddie in his mini submarine. *Daily Mail,* 15 July 2013. Available at: www.dailymail.co.uk/news/article-2364513/Vladimir-Putin-pulls-Bond-villain-impression-trip-research-sub.html#ixzz3XZPBbq3T (last accessed April 2015).

Wouters, C. (2010). Sexualisation: Have sexualisation processes changed direction? *Sexualities,* 13(6), 723–741.

Yaffa, J. (2014). Putin's new war on 'traitors'. *The New Yorker,* 28 March 2014. Available at: www.newyorker.com/news/news-desk/putins-new-war-on-traitors (accessed December 2015).

Yaroshevsky, A. (no date). Of Russian origin: Mochit' v sortire, Russiapedia. *RT.com.* Available at: http://russiapedia.rt.com/of-russian-origin/mochit-v-sortire/ (last accessed August 2015).

Yuhas, A. (2014). Russian propaganda over Crimea and the Ukraine: how does it work? *The Guardian*, 17 March 2014. Available at: www.theguardian.com/world/2014/mar/17/crimea-crisis-russia-propaganda-media (last accessed December 2015).

Zaidi, H. (no date). *Examples of Advertising Techniques, Sales and Marketing for "You"*. Available at: www.sales-and-marketing-for-you.com/advertising-techniques.html (last accessed March 2015).

Zassoursky, I. (2000). Politics and media in Russia in the nineties. In *VII World Congress for Central and East European Studies*, July.

Zimmer, M. (2010). Is it ethical to harvest public Twitter accounts without consent? *MichaelZimmer.org*. Available at: http://michaelzimmer.org/2010/02/12/is-it-ethical-to-harvest-public-twitter-accountswithout-consent (last accessed September 2015).

Zimmer, M. (2015). The Twitter archive at the Library of Congress: Challenges for information practice and information policy. *First Monday*, *20*(7). Full text online at: https://journals.uic.edu/ojs/index.php/fm/article/view/5619/4653 (last accessed February 2019).

6 US Memes on Donald Trump and Hillary Clinton in 2016

Beyond nation borders: why and how digital publics employ memes to discuss the values of American politics

In 2016, the world learned the name of the new President of the US from dozens of screens. Unlike the previous years, television screen it was not. Social media, websites, forums, all the vehicles of electronic communication – practically, the same habitat that the voters have spent much time in during the campaign.

Donald Trump won the elections through weaponising memes, some researchers claimed (Taveira & Balfour, 2016). Another line of thought nurtures the idea that Russian trolls and bots were potent game-changers in the election campaign (Shane, 2017). Both these assumptions deserve more critical resistance that they have received so far. The recent study on 'filter bubbles' and 'fake news' (Guess et al., 2018) is a great cornerstone to the more rationalised, empirically backed research on the influences and non-influences in digital politics. The researchers studied browsing histories of over than 2,500 Americans and realised that 'filter bubbles' were not as prevalent as was assumed before. People tend to get their daily news from the established media sources, not random social media accounts or 'fake news' websites. The 'fake news' or the websites with false and dubious claims occupy less than 10% of the browsing interest of the US publics (Guess et al., 2018). Therefore, the question remains to what extent the exposure to digital influences can affect one's voting decision.

Memes may not have changed the course of American history. Yet, what they probably did is they highlighted and promoted the trending discourses around both candidates. Memes are a rapid virus – but a virus of a choice. People make quick decisions on whether to endorse, share or like a meme that they see online. From this perspective, memes appeal to the immediate, unreflective reactions of the Internet crowds. Following this logic, one can curiously agree with the user on the Internet forum 4chan who remarked: 'We actually elected a meme as a president' (Ohlheiser, 2016).

Trump used the social networks in 2016 in a smarter way than his Democratic opponent. Hillary Clinton, coming from the long-serving political and financial establishment, bonded with celebrities and went to the late-night television shows (Taveira & Balfour, 2016). Trump, in the meantime, broke the rules of the traditional campaigning and relied on inappropriate, often racist, sexist or somewhat rebellious tweets and public statements.

The course of the election campaign resembled a carnival (Denisova, 2016). The amount of billingsgate, mutual offences, vulgar jokes turned the politics in a playful pageant, spectacle for the millions. In the 1850s, there was this American movement of 'know-nothings'. People were disenfranchised from the hegemonic politics and claimed of *be proud of knowing nothing*, not understanding much of politics; they were keen on 'purifying' America from migrants and social vice (Anbinder, 1992; Denisova, 2016). This aggressive self-proclaimed ignorance probably came from the disillusionment and detachment from mainstream politics. The scenario sounds familiar to the US of the late 2010s, where over half the country voted for the president who rejected political correctness and intellectualism as part of his strategy.

This chapter looks into the memes that circulated on Twitter on the eve of the election day, 7–8 November 2016. The analysis is not representative of the main themes of the memes on Trump and Clinton throughout the campaign, yet it pinpoints the trending discourses that people were endorsing close to the voting point.

Memes have become the fast food of modern politics. Hillary Clinton has been blamed for adopting the inauthentic media campaigning style, such as trying to appear funny on Ellen DeGeneres show (Taveira & Balfour, 2016). Yet, the polished presence of the Democratic candidate was not convincing for many voters – as much as her campaigning posters, offline and online. Baudrillard would be proud to see how many voters were seeing through this 'simulacrum' of an approachable and caring candidate. Twitter users deployed memes to challenge Hillary Clinton's political persona (Figure 6.1).

The attempt to appeal to the Internet slang or gestures (such as using the 'dab' move in the meme above) did not look convincing. The traditional, celebrity-backed character of the campaign was not enough for the older publics, while its more modern tactics that were aimed at the younger, digitally savvy crowds were not engaging or shareable for the youths. The visuals that supported Hillary Clinton's campaign remained somewhere in the limbo between the offline classics (posters) and emerging online formats (memes and gifs) (Denisova, 2016).

The opponents of Clinton, though, demonstrated their digital savviness. One of the smart moves of the anti-Clinton users was to prank the overly conservative visual language of the campaign by faking the posters and spreading them online, pretending to act on behalf of Clinton supporters. These digitally spread images challenged Clinton's feminist

Figure 6.1 The meme depicts the dance move that Hillary Clinton performed at Ellen DeGeneres' show.

rhetoric. The posters circulated widely on Twitter on the eve of the election day. They suggested that if Clinton wins, women will be obliged for military service, along with men. The depicted young women and girls in military uniform referenced Clinton's original tag line 'I am with her', but claimed that they would need to 'fight for her' (Figures 6.2 and 6.3).

The polished, high-resolution production value of these posters make them look as if they actually originated from Clinton's office. The meme makers here fought Clinton not just with content, but with the shape of expression. They mocked her promotional materials. They even added the sarcastic note in the corner 'Paid for by Hillary for America', which was also fake. These memes also point to the puzzling public understanding of feminism in the modern America. As memes suggest,

Figure 6.2 The meme suggests that Hillary Clinton will implement obligatory military service for women, if elected as the president of the US. The memes look like the posters of her promotional campaign and call to #fightforhillary.

Figure 6.3 Another meme that resembles professional campaign materials. It presents a young woman who claims that she would be a fighter in Russia, as Hillary is a fighter in a more general sense.

feminism is something of a threat to the society. The memes here use the classic propaganda tactic of omission and suggest equal duties for men in women in the society of gender equality, without acknowledging the equal opportunities that a society like that entails. The #DraftOur-Daughters meme series did not receive many likes, yet has become a thrilling case of a deliberate meme campaign that sought to undermine the candidate's official campaigning style on several levels.

Other memes that attacked Clinton drew attention to the FBI scandal. This was a potent way of using memes to influence the awareness of the population; it also connected the topics of mainstream media with social media users. Even those who did not follow the likes of CNN or NBC would have learned about the FBI scandal via social networks and memes that mocked the issue. Similar to the Russian case, where politically active citizens often exploited memes as attention baits, English-speaking meme sharers exploited memes to direct public attention to the complex issues in the US. FBI started an inquiry in the fact that Hillary Clinton was using her private email servers for sending classified information to high governmental officials. The long and tedious investigation resulted in calling Hillary 'extremely careless', but no charges were filed against her. The further round of controversy happened right before the election day when the head of the Bureau suddenly reopened the investigation, which may have influenced the public opinion of Clinton. The results of the second round were the same as the first – no charges.

While the final verdict on Hillary's case was still pending, mainstream media spent thousands of hours on air and thousands of words in print to discuss the topic. The meme discussion on FBI scandal in social networks was different to the discussion in the media – with main difference lying in the amount of analysis and doubt. Little analysis and no doubt about Hillary's guilt were left in the memes. The memes that accused her of compromising national security gave the verdict long before the Bureau did. These memes took Hillary's guilt for granted and mixed it with other stories. This rhetorical tactic is extremely compelling – it already presents the fact of Hillary Clinton's transgression as given, and uses it as a comic vehicle. The previously mentioned meme of Hillary at Ellen DeGeneres show exhibits that FBI's case is put on the same list as 'covering rape, letting 4 Americans die in Benghazi'. It presents assumptions as truths – and invites those who agree with at least one accusation to equally believe in others. Memes have the power of serving as 'inside jokes'. People who pretend to be knowledgeable of politics may take their information from the memes like this – and then, without questioning the content, promote these ideas to the others.

Hillary Clinton's FBI scandal prompted Donald Trump to name her 'crooked Hillary'. His supporters embraced this unsophisticated nickname and used it in their Twitter campaigning. Then, in the absence of other topics to compromise Clinton's integrity, there were flows of memes that accused her of heavy drinking. These did not have any particular backing in the media and probably came straight out of Trump's campaigning office. These memes mostly relied on the awkward photos and tried to mix this accusation with other themes, such as collaboration with the Russians (Figure 6.4).

Yet, the topic of #DrunkHillary and selling uranium to the Russians did not pick up. These memes received tiny amounts of likes and shares.

Figure 6.4 The meme depicts Hillary Clinton having a drink. The tag line implies that she is cheering to securing a nuclear deal with the Russians.

This may suggest that people still rely on the information and analysis from the traditional media. Major outlets pressed the FBI story, but not much about drinking or relationship with Russia. Hence, the Twitter banter about these dried up fairly quickly.

Trump supporters, intriguingly, did not mind sharing the controversial quotes of their candidate, including sexist or racist jokes. It seemed that many Twitter users recognised Donald Trump as a rude yet amiable lad – the one who makes all the wrong jokes, but does not hide anything beyond the powdered political lingo. Unsurprisingly, the memes that praised Trump's laddish demeanour featured references to The Game of Thrones, the hugely successful fantasy saga that operates on the pillars of violence, sex and savage characters. The smashing success of the show in the present-day America gives food for thought to those who are wondering about Trump's victory. For large chunks of publics, 'political correctness' and 'establishment' became more of curse words than the curse words themselves. Often, users with female-sounding names or userpics would joyfully share a meme of Trump saying sexist things without noticing any trouble with it (Figures 6.5 and 6.6).

The critics of Trump acted in a disconnected fashion. None of their arguments or buzzwords reached the same level of visibility as 'crooked Hillary'. Plenty of memes mocked Trump's tan and hair style. This is another proof that memes are polarising and polarised. When a person makes fun of someone's hair and compares it to a runaway hamster, not much dialogue can be achieved with the supporters of this hair's owner.

Other criticisms to Trump came in the shape of pumpkin memes (referring to the tan of the candidate), corn on the cob memes (referring to the candidate's hair when disturbed by the wind) or memes about the

Figure 6.5 The meme shows various images of Donald Trump who is making various hand gestures. The meme maker presents them as sex-related and supplements with sexual descriptions. It implies that Trump encourages people to have heterosexual encounters rather than homosexual ones.

foreign provenance of campaign merchandise. The last one had the most factual evidence to back it up, compared to the rather superficial and infantile memes on appearance. Critics lambasted Trump for disrupting the trade with Mexico and other countries and returning production to the US. In the meantime, as the memes revealed, the hats of the campaign supporters were mostly made in China, Mexico and Bangladesh.

Those who exposed Trump's inconsistency and use of Mexico-made merchandise utilised the juxtaposition method, which many Russian journalists and media activists apply to distort propaganda. The memes

Democrats for Trump
@YoungDems4Trump

(Follow) ∨

#ImVotingBecause I believe that American people still have the guts to stand up to corrupt establishment.
#DemocratsForTrump 🇺🇸

🗨 73   ⇄ 1.7K   ♡ 2.7K

Figure 6.6 The meme borrows characters and actors from the popular movie saga *The Lord of the Rings*. It depicts the dwarf Gimli (played by John Rhys-Davies) and Legolas (played by Orlando Bloom) as having a conversation about US politicians. Gimli starts with supporting Bernie Sanders, as his hat implies, but then changes his mind after the conversation with Trump-supporting Legolas. Gimli changes his hat to the one saying 'Hillary for prison'.

on Trump accessories that used juxtaposition received a considerable number of likes and shares. It is a sign that fact-checking and exposure of the unbacked claims can gain visibility on Twitter.

The meme wars around Donald Trump and Hillary Clinton on the eve of the election day in November 2016 revealed a pattern: people are polarised in their opinions and share memes that endorse their pre-existing views. The use of memes in the political talk in the US fits in the global tactics of meme usage – they mostly exaggerate the trending topics from the media, they subvert and challenge traditional media and campaigning messages, and they try to insert new themes in the discussion. There is a significant amount of vulgar, lad humour that would be considered inappropriate in the offline conversations – this feature of 'macho politics' is prevalent both in Russian and US memes. It suggests that memes

exist beyond the boundaries of political correctness. They belong to the
ethos of the carnival, playful and jovial banter on the easily digestible
politics. As the fast-food communication of the social media, memes
convey the ideas from the media discourse in an unreflective and subjective manner. Rarely a meme can be neutral – it is the emotional appeal
of a meme that becomes the quick trigger to make you 'like' or 'share'
it. Last but not least, this analysis of memes on the US presidential candidates in 2016 proves that memes alone cannot change minds and win
elections. They serve as sensitive monitors of the public opinion – they
shed light on the topics that people endorse and the styles of communication that they favour (lad, vulgar, sarcastic, etc.).

Memes amplify and propagate – yet, it is still down to the awareness
of the Internet crowds to interpret and make sense of memes. Memes
may not have won the election for Donald Trump, but they may have
given the bonding spirit to those who united against the establishment.
The circulation of memes among like-minded individuals helped these
users feel that they were not alone in their beliefs. While he or she may
have never met many similar-minded users in person, the online sphere
and meme sharing generated this vibe of collective involvement and
community feeling. From this perspective, maintaining the noise in the
carnivalesque Twitter communication was the winning political strategy
of Trump's supporters.

Bibliography

Anbinder, T. (1992). *Nativism and Slavery: The Northern Know Nothings and the Politics of the 1850's.* New York: Oxford University Press on Demand.
Denisova, A. (2016). How the Internet turned US election into a medieval carnival. *The Conversation*, 10 November. Available at: https://theconversation.com/how-the-internet-turned-the-us-election-into-a-medieval-carnival-68281 (accessed August 2018).
Guess, A., Nyhan, B. & Reifler, J. (2018). *Selective exposure to misinformation: Evidence from the consumption of fake news during the 2016 US presidential campaign.* European Research Council.
Ohlheiser, A. (2016). 'We actually elected a meme as president': How 4chan celebrated Trump's victory. *The Washington Post*, 9 November. Available at: www.washingtonpost.com/news/the-intersect/wp/2016/11/09/we-actually-elected-a-meme-as-president-how-4chan-celebrated-trumps-victory/?utm_term=.0fa7939f4228 (accessed August 2018).
Shane, S. (2017). These are the ads Russia bought on Facebook in 2016. *The New York Times*, 1 November. Available at: www.nytimes.com/2017/11/01/us/politics/russia-2016-election-facebook.html (accessed August 2018).
Taveira, R. & Balfour, E. (2016). How Donald Trump won the 2016 meme wars. *The Conversation*, 30 November. Available at: https://theconversation.com/how-donald-trump-won-the-2016-meme-wars-68580 (accessed August 2018).

Conclusion

In the recent decades, memes have grown from the inside joke from the geek forums into the mainstream means of digital communication. Internet users exploit these viral messages to communicate on all subjects, from popular culture and relationships to society and politics.

Memes as the Means of Political Communication in the Challenging Media Environments

The potential of Internet memes for political communication and mobilisation is a relatively new topic in academic studies. Internet memes are the viral units of digital communication that flourish on user adjustment and replication. Yet, when used strategically, they become 'mindbombs', or symbolic texts with condensed ideas and ample connotations, that help to attract attention to the political issues and suggest alternative interpretations to the news.

Memes are strong in overcoming censorship due to the allegoric style of expression and ambiguity of the commentary that they carry. In order to read a meme, members of the audience often have to be aware of the broader political context and be familiar with this format of Internet communication. The characteristic of memes as 'in-jokes' has further advanced their exploitation for political deliberation in restricted media environments, and the examples of China and Russia prove so.

When users share memes on political subjects, they intervene in the media discourse. They can promote or confront the hegemonic interpretation of the events; they can suggest an alternative interpretation; they can present an event in a specific context that would be educational for others. The deliberation of political issues in the language of memes can take a form of a carnival – the exchange of screams and shouts, billingsgate and vulgar jokes, nonetheless contributes to the formation of the political picture. The medievalist and philosopher Bakhtin appealed to the concept of the historical carnival as the allowed resistance, and the examples of memes exchanges in censored countries are similar to this. People cannot speak openly and criticise the elites, yet they are relatively free to rely on metaphors, allegories and humour – memes.

Memes as the Fast-Food Media and Coping Strategy

Memes can serve not only as political discursive weapons, but they can also fill the void for the critical media. This is especially evident in the countries with the limitations on free press and freedom of speech. In Russia, the participants of my research did not give memes much credit as the weapons of political mobilisation, but acknowledged their significance as the supplementary devices of spreading the awareness and calls for critical thinking. This is what professional independent media had been doing for years – until they were forced to shut down or compromise their principles. The remaining critical voices can be found in blogs, microblogs and few remaining digital liberal media. Memes have become powerful teasers that attract attention and direct social media users to the investigations in resistant blogs or articles in liberal outlets.

The format of Internet memes was instrumental in creating a 'fast-food media', an understandable objection to the state rhetoric. They are simple enough to reach broad audiences, yet sufficiently sophisticated to stimulate critical thinking. Many opposition microbloggers have been deploying memes as tactical media, on a daily basis, as immediate responses to the activity of the Russian government and media. These exposures of state manipulation have constituted an alternative flow of information and analysis.

As exciting and inspiring the creation and sharing of memes can be, they are still limited in reaching large crowds. Resistant social media users in Russia can be popular (over a million followers to top accounts), but they cannot compete with the popularity and access of the mainstream media. The critical meme makers whom I have interviewed acknowledge this limitation. They keep making, sharing and remaking memes nonetheless. This persistent meme production (often on a daily basis) exhibited another function of meme sharing as the coping strategy for liberal users who felt incapable to settle with the disturbing political reality. There is yet another motivation behind meme making and distribution: the necessity to protect one's peace of mind and actively confront the aggressive hegemonic discourse. Academic research has not yet covered this trait of memes as soothing practices of digital users in the oppressed media environments. "I tweet to keep the sanity of my mind from brainwashing" – one of the interviewees confessed. This shows the potency of memes as a comforting practice for the users in restricted media ecologies.

Memes as Contestation Sites for Collective and National Identities

Memes are sharp and abstract at the same time. Sharp – as they point to the specific event, person or saying, and require the contextual knowledge of the audience to understand the joke. Abstract – as they often appeal to much larger narratives, stereotypes and ways of thinking. It is this interplay of two levels that makes memes fascinating to decode, fun to consume and revealing to research.

The existing studies on the use of Internet memes focus on the immediate reactions and context of meme sharing. I am arguing, as a result of this book, that memes touch on larger issues – they are invaluable in negotiating national, individual and group identities in an unconventional manner. Memes are the tip of the iceberg of the underlying discourses that have a large impact on the societies. Through memes, we can see what concepts, identities and claims do resistant and pro-government publics endorse in their communication; what are the stumbling points of discourse over national identities and symbols; and to what extent can memes facilitate the contestation of mainstream thinking and propaganda. People post memes quickly, hence the choices they make illustrate the subconscious as well as conscious reactions to the agenda.

For example, in the Russian case, many pro-government meme makers followed the state propaganda and fortified the interpretation of patriotism as absolute loyalty to the government, as nationalism. In another instance, the whole idea of 'power' was reduced to 'macho culture', the rule of force over the rule of diplomacy. Liberal meme makers utilised memes to contemplate these discourses and suggest alternative interpretations (patriotism as critical citizenship; compromise and respect instead of pushy macho culture, etc.). It is essential to see through memes to understand what the meme makers understand as good and evil, desired and rejected. We can read the society through memes.

The popular narratives that memes are often based on become crucially important when one wants to understand the public opinion and generate a change in the country. For instance, the analysis of Crimean memes brought forward the popular Russian narrative on the unique path of the country in the global economy, politics and culture. This isolationist narrative has long formed a crucial part of Russia's national identity, but was not as visible in the 2000s; it made a swift comeback in the 2010s.

The return of this rhetoric is not challenged in the traditional media – but it is persistently discussed in the memes. The liberal meme makers confronted many of these popular myths and allegories by either substantiating them with facts and logical interpretation, or ridiculing by obscenities and laughter. These memes may ask the audience to see things differently and assess the present and the past of the country through a critical lens.

The pro-government utilisation of memes shows how users can adapt the traditional media indoctrination to the digital platforms. They do not differ dramatically from the anti-government users in the ways they exploit memes: all meme sharers appropriate varying techniques and very diverse styles of humour. The main difference between pro-government and anti-government meme sharing is the type of relationship with the dominant media agenda. People produce memes either "actively" or "reactively" in relation to the mainstream news. Liberal users mostly **responded** to the agenda suggested by the hegemonic discourse, while pro-Kremlin users could **piggyback** on the already popular notions and freely offer personalised alterations in the digital realm. In Russia, resistant users were often compelled to create the oppositional agenda from scratch, as they suffered from the absence of popular independent media in the public space.

Carnivalesque Polyphony: Why Memes Connect Ideas, but Not People

Memes are more likely to connect ideas than people. The meme makers in my research do not see how memes can coordinate people for mobilisation or maintain a meaningful discussion. Like-minded individuals may identify each other's ideological position by the memes they share. Yet the act of sharing memes does not link people, as memes are anonymous.

In this instance, memes correspond with Bakhtin's concept of 'polyphony' of voices that marks any carnival. Political resistance by means of Internet memes may seem an array of disconnected voices; however, all of them promote the diversity of ideas and opinions. When prominent meme makers share memes on social networks, they invite and empower other, less active users to come and join the entertaining but critical deliberation of politics. Many meme makers from the Crimean study declared that watching other people satirically express themselves in the digital realm and openly criticise hegemonic politics was liberating and encouraging: they acknowledged that they were not alone in their discontent with the elites. Russian political resistance via artful memes of the Crimean case further proves that 'carnivalesque' dissent facilitates the articulation of 'forbidden' ideas, makes ordinary voices heard, and permits laughter at the elites.

Power holders seem to tolerate these last sanctuaries of alternative political communication in order to gather information on the opposition publics and allow them to let off steam. Unable and probably unwilling to completely silence the protest discourse, Russian elites resemble the medieval authorities that granted to the public the bounded squares for informal mockery, open criticism and billingsgate. On the one hand, the self-awareness of being 'lonely warriors' rather than a consistent community of protesters is a common trait for many alternative meme makers of the Russian Twitter. On the other hand, this managed opposition keeps the protest 'flame' burning on low heat, until political opportunities emerge.

Concluding Remarks: Why Memes Globally Are Interdependent on Media Agenda

This research has analysed the role of Internet memes in the contemporary Russian and US discourses and unveiled their potential for the deliberation of politics. Memes have grown into a persuasive, significant and ideology-free vehicle of communication that influences our societies. We know memes as the common language and folklore of the Internet crowds that enable people to express themselves on all possible topics. The politically active English- and Russian-speaking users often utilise memes as discursive weapons and mindbombs that they share in social networks to drag attention to news and opinions; they benefit from the reputation of memes as Internet darlings and familiar slang of digitally savvy users. This approach to exploiting memes as political mindbombs contributes new dimension to the research on social media activism. It reveals that the circulation of the Internet memes can promote alternative political discussions, shed new light on hegemonic ideas and representations, and therefore increase the visibility and connectivity of the political dissent among digital crowds.

What both the studies on the Russian Crimean case and the US 2016 Elections case have revealed is that memes are interdependent on the media agenda. Those themes that were not present in the media and were freshly baked by the Twitter warriors did not receive much traffic and visibility. The same tendency was spotted in the Russian case: it was close to impossible for the resistant users to promote the topics that were not in the media discourse or have not been endorsed by opinion leaders. Active – instead of 'reactive' – memes had little chances to reach larger publics. This leads to the conclusion that memes alone cannot change minds and politics, but they (1) shed immediate light on the trending opinions and stumbling points and (2) serve as fast-food media that condense the important topics and deliver them in an easily digestible form to the publics.

Memes are a novel phenomenon of the political communication and activism of the digital age. They have a vast potential to induce political change, tell us more about our societies and counterbalance the hegemonic media agenda. Remarkably, this communication conduit is not limited to the East or West, and overcomes language boundaries. It is highly visible in the deliberation of politics in democratic and authoritarian political regimes, Western and non-Western media environments alike. Memes are an intriguing part of our global and local digital life.

Index